MUSIC IN CANADA
1600~1800

Willy Amtmann

MUSIC IN CANADA 1600~1800

HABITEX BOOKS

- Cover Design by MICHEL BERARD

This book has been published with the help of a grant from the Humanities Research Council of Canada, using funds provided by the Canada Council.

Distributors:

Collier-Macmillan Canada Ltd.
539 Collier-Macmillan Drive
Cambridge, Ontario N1R 5W9
Tel. (416) 449-7115 / (519) 621-2440

Bernard Amtmann Inc.
1529, Sherbrooke West
Montreal, Que.

ISBN-0-88912-020-X

 2

Bibliothèque nationale du Québec
Dépôt légal — 1er trimestre 1975

To Martha

Preface

The story of early Canada is told in the chronicles of the explorers and in the narratives of the early travellers; it is presented in the historical writings of Lescarbot and Sagard and related in the reports of priests and missionaries; it is documented in the vast amount of royal edicts, governmental ordinances and official correspondence that are preserved in Canadian and French archives. Growing interest in the historical background prompted closer investigation into the early events and episodes while the political and social history received sympathetic interpretation from the pen of loyal historians and erudite clerics.

The historical panorama would not be complete without a survey of the cultural aspects and numerous books are devoted to the chronicle of painting and sculpture, literature and the theatre, architecture, handicraft, the making of furniture and of agricultural utensils. As for the musical history, however, it was not until recently that references to music and musical events appeared in articles or chapters, reiterating mainly certain musical items that were based on traditional but unsubstantiated testimony until such alleged evidence had become historically established facts.

The scholarly and informative work by Kallmann presented for the first time Canada's musical history in an exemplary, thorough and objective manner, but even in that valuable source book it is difficult to find more than a few indications to music in early Canada. A discouraging scarcity of documentary evidence frustrated the efforts to reconstruct early musical life in the French colony and research into the nature and extent of musical manifestations has yielded but few results. On the other hand, it would be fallacious to conclude that New France was entirely deprived of a musical life, albeit on a small scale. While it would be unrealistic to hope for future discoveries of such magnitude as to substantially alter the present picture, the existing documentation does allow for a fair amount of assumption without placing exaggerated emphasis on musically irrelevant episodes in the desire to satisfy patriotic sentiment, or inventing semi-fictitious stories for the glorification of a romantic past. Whatever had been recorded in the annals of early Canada represents episodes of honest, simple, but historically unimportant musical activities. The few musical items preserved in the early chronicles are scarcely indicative of the *grand siècle* and its great musical tradition. In contrast to the other arts in New France, secular musical art was relegated to a meagre existence mainly to serve as handmaiden to light and shallow entertainment or as the pleasant recreational diversion in the form of folksong.

The purpose of this work is to extract from our annals some of the forgotten musical items and to examine them in the light of their artistic interest and historical significance. No claims to completeness can be made, but it is hoped that a critical evaluation of certain conditions and obstacles that governed musical progress in early Canada will illuminate to some extent the neglected pages of the Canadian story.

It remains the pleasant duty to express sincerest thanks to John Churchill, of Carleton University, for the encouragement and splendid advice of which he gave freely, and for the patience with which he read the manuscript, and to R.P. Adrien Pouliot, s.j., for his assistance in the writing of the chapter on *La Ste. Famille* and other ecclesiastical matters. Special gratitude is due to my brother, Bernard, whose book collection of Canadiana sparked curiosity and whose enthusiasm for historical research inspired the desire to trace the springs of musical art in early Quebec. And lastly I acknowledge the debt I owe to my wife who encouraged, helped, and waited.

Ottawa, August 1974   W.A.

CONTENTS

I

Introduction

HISTORICAL BACKGROUND

« Pour n'y avoir des violons et autres récréations en la Nouvelle-France, il n'y a encore lieu de se plaindre: car il est fort aisé d'y en mener. 1 »

In the summer of 1607, a small vessel plied her way homeward-bound towards the coast of France. Among her passengers was Marc Lescarbot, a young French lawyer and poet, who returned from New France where he had gone to escape a corrupt world and a decadent civilization and, as he had said, to seek freedom in a society of free men of equality. In the company of free men he had spent a year at Port Royal 2, satisfying his curiosity and his quest. Neither the primitive and rude condition of pioneer life in the far-away wilderness nor the absence of the cultural amenities 3 to which he had been accustomed had dimmed his enthusiasm. With unbounded idealism he had envisioned a brilliant future for the new land; he took issue with those of faint heart or those who ridiculed the new country and derisively pointed to the lack of *plaisirs*, for he believed that all the shortcomings could easily be repaired by bringing prosperity, education and culture to the shores of the new French World.

Yet a hundred and fifty years later a great and famous philosopher scornfully dismissed Canada. He had found it absurd that men should cut their throats for some miserable *arpents de neige;* he had implored the King's minister to deliver France from the untenable and embarrassing burden of the colony; he had hailed the British victory at Quebec as the triumph

of liberty over clerical despotism, and he had declared that "...
like the public, I love peace more than Canada and I believe
that France will be happier without Quebec. 4"Where Lescarbot
had stood at the cradle of New France, Voltaire had witnessed
the curtain fall on the French tragicomedy in the New World;
and in the brief span of time that separated the unknown French
lawyer and poet from the great and influential philosopher un-
folds the short but colourful history of New France and with it
the story of art and music in early Canada.

    The historical background is known: French claims to
discoveries date back as early as 1488, French cod fisheries existed in Newfoundland presumably already before Cabot's voyage
in 1497, and French mariners and explorers are believed to have
reached the shores of the unknown Continent in the early years
of the 16th century. Already in 1506, Captain Denis of Honfleur
is supposed to have explored the Gulf of Saint Lawrence, followed by Captain Aubert of Dieppe who in 1508 brought back the
first American Indian ever to set foot in France 5. Verrazano's
explorations in 1524 enabled Francis I to lay claim to the coast
from Newfoundland to Northern Virginia but it was not until
1534 that Jacques Cartier, having planted a cross and the *fleur de
lis* at the gateway to the Northern Continent, took possession of
the new land in the name of his God and his King. It was, however, an acquisition in name only: France had left her calling-
card at the door of the immense new territory but did not pursue
the matter any further and for another few decades Canada returned to primordial and undisturbed sleep. It was not until the
beginning of the 17th century that courageous explorers and enterprising merchants returned to the shores of the unchartered
wilderness: Pierre du Gua de Monts established Port Royal and
.Samuel de Champlain soon followed and built Quebec at the
foot of the famous cliff; there was also Marc Lescarbot who had
brought to the beginnings of French colonization a glimmer of
the artistry of France. For a short moment, it seemed as if the

new land would flourish in the spirit of French culture and civilization.

It is of great interest to see the fundamental differences which are apparent in the histories of the various American colonies from the Gulf of Mexico to Hudson Bay. In each of them the political, economical, sociological and cultural development varied according to the concept which had initiated colonial enterprise, shaped its destiny and determined its ultimate success or failure. Political power, religious passion or mercantile ambition were the basic motives that drove men into the great Unknown. The spirit of human endeavour sparked the search for new horizons and lured adventurous explorers beyond the sea to discover the new Continent and to find the elusive route to the Far East. In their steps followed the valiant soldiers of crown and cross who penetrated the vast wilderness, the former to conquer the land in the name of their king, the latter to claim the soul of the native people for the greater glory of God. From the strife-torn nations of Europe came some in search for religious liberty, others to escape feudal servitude or political persecution. Looking hopefully ahead to the new land's uncertain future, all these men were willing to face the cruel and dangerous present and to leave behind a disavowed past. Still others went across the ocean in pursuit of commercial exploit, driven by the desire for the fabulous riches of the new Continent. Environment and purpose thus moulded the political, economical and physical aspects of the new life while tradition and custom preserved the cultural and spiritual link with the past. The political and economic development depended on the support from the mother-country as well as on the determination and tenacity, on the courage and resourcefulness of the pioneer.

But intellectual and artistic guidance was also needed to preserve the heritage and to lay the foundation for a future tradition. The degree of collective cultural and artistic growth depended on the difficult balance between materialistic pursuit and cultural sustenance just as it depended on the individual's knowledge, devotion, initiative and indefatigable spirit.

In the domain which France had conquered for crown, commerce and catholicism, cultural development received all too little encouragement, even though the era of New France coincided with the *grand siècle* of Louis XIV, the glorious cultural and artistic epoch that was France of the 17th and 18th centuries. New France was not destined to partake in that royal culture. Ruled by transient Frenchmen for the benefit of France, cultural or artistic development of any sort remained stagnant in a country that was little more to them than a trading-post. Colonization was not compatible with exploitation, the all-important fur-trade would have suffered through immigration; the mercantile rulers never intended to populate the country and the trading companies successfully opposed the settlement of pioneers for many years. Even as late as 1650 the population totalled a mere five hundred Europeans including clergy, officials and soldiers. Not without reason did Marie de l'Incarnation, the renowned Superior of the Ursulines, deplore the attitude of the rulers and the lack of support from the mother-country without which "... neither we nor all of Canada can survive another two years ... if this aid is lacking, we must die or return to France. 6" The crown, however, was far more occupied with politics and royal splendour and only reluctantly granted her dominion the bare minimum of men, money and material. New France remained the half-forgotten and half-despised outpost of the French empire and of French civilization. While this is not the place to assess the political failure of France, the neglect of New France certainly added to her decline from a great colonial power that had held land from Labrador to Louisiana. The loss in 1763 was a complete one: New France passed into British hands, Louisiana became Spanish property and all that remained of the great French colonial dream in the New World were the little islands of St. Pierre and Miquelon in the gulf of the St. Lawrence.

But New France still had a powerful protector. From the early days the Church had accompanied the explorers and the cross which Cartier in 1534 had planted on the shores of the new Continent became the symbol of perseverance and the emblem of the future. « One great fact stands out conspicuous in Canadian history, — the Church of Rome. More even than the royal power she shaped the character and the destinies of the colony. ₇ » In dauntless courage and tenacity of purpose, priest and missionary served with zeal and sacrifice the cause of Christianity in the barbarous wilderness. The courageous attempts of the Recollects, the heroism and martyrdom of the Jesuit missionaries, the chronicle of the selfless devotion and charity of Ursulines and Hospitallers, all bear testimony to Catholic determination and dedication to a country that had otherwise been regarded with contempt and derision ₈. Indeed, the priests regarded New France as their domain for she was destined to become a bastion of ultramontane Catholicism, reminiscent of the primitive church and flavoured with a strong touch of puritanical Jansenism engendered by the triumphant force of Catholic revival in France. This spirit of religious revival and renewed energy gave support to the new colony, it permeated Quebec and brought pious missionaries and devoted priests to the distant shores to face the immense loneliness of the land and the tough fibre of its people.

As in other colonial enterprises such as New Spain or New England, the religious substance moulded the political and spiritual destiny of the French domain and guided and guarded its cultural manifestations. In the symbolism of liturgy and ritual, in religious paintings and sculptures of saints and angels, in the portraits of nuns and bishops, of martyred missionaries, in the ex-votos, the finely wrought silver chalice and the richly ornamented vestment, in all is exemplified the artistic expression of the colony. The liturgy had found in the small and crudely built chapels on the St. Lawrence a new abode from where it was to spread to wherever Catholicism extended its charitable arm. Music was part of the liturgy and the faithful companion in the daily life of the priest from the midnight psalms to the evening prayers of the next day; it was his solace in times of danger and need and his accessory in the task of conversion. So did Frère Sagard describe the role of music: « One must always keep smiling, show a modest, contented face, and now and then sing a hymn, both for one's own consolation and to please and edify the savages who take a singular pleasure in hearing us sing the praises of our God. ₉ » So did every priest carry in his breviary the venerated tradition of liturgical music. All had a certain amount of musical education, all were trained in the singing of hymns and chants and there were of course those who may have possessed more than the customary basic knowledge of music. Some could play an instrument and others knew how to compose; with musical sound the former would attract the Indians to the ceremonies while the latter would adapt the canticles to the native language. The priests became the first music teachers, teaching the rudiments of plain-chant and the singing of sacred songs to Indian and Frenchman alike. Thus, in an almost mediaeval spirit, art and music were in the service of religion and in the care of the priests. Indeed, regardless of the field of art into which the priests would venture — whether they designed and built their churches and chapels, decorated and adorned their houses of worship, played, sang, composed sacred music, painted religious images, recorded the history of the colony — whatever their artistic and cultural activities, the chronicle of New France would be deprived of almost all of its artistic manifestations had it not been for the Church who, faithful to her renowned tradition as the patron of the arts, came to the rescue of the culturally neglected realm of French civilization.

Religious fervor tolerated only those artistic activities that were expedient to its needs and in agreement with its dogmatic tenets. It was a tradition which confined its artistic expression to *ars sacra,* to religious images and sculptures and to the devotional music of the liturgy. It was the ascetic tradition which proscribed the sensuous and emotional in music, whether it incited to wordly pleasures or affected the ritual. Mgr. de Laval, Canada's first bishop, obediently followed the teachings of St. Augustine when he censured the Ursulines of Quebec for their dramatic, emotional manner of singing which, as he feared, might distract the celebrant. His advice had also been strictly followed by the vigilant priest of Quebec who penetrated the homes and hearts of the people to inculcate the concept of moral law as legislated by a theocratic society. Indeed, the Jesuits watched and guided all and everything from the political actions of the governor to the attendance at mass and confession of the common labourer, from the extravagant and sinful dresses of women to the dances before and after sunset. It was Mgr. de Laval who had firmly impressed on the King that vigilance and authority were needed to "enforce order, suppress sin, and crush heresy !" This state of affairs did not go entirely unchallenged by the laity, particularly the visitors from France. The outspoken Baron de Lahontan had only bitter comment for the clergy whom he found ridiculous in their actions because they excommunicated maskers and, as he writes, watched over the conduct of girls and women with more care than fathers and husbands 10. The state of temporal and spiritual vassalage in which the colonists lived is also indicated in the writings of the Recollect priest and historian, Le Clercq, who related that the French population in a desperate attempt had sent deputies to France in order to beg relief "and to let it be known the hell in which the consciences of the colony were kept by the union of the temporal and spiritual authority in the same hands. 11"

Mgr. Saint-Vallier found it necessary at times to advise the *curés* of Quebec not to absolve those who "... have paintings or lascivious representations; those who compose bad books, verses and *chansons*; those women who through their scandalous bareness of shoulders and neck lead others to sin. [12]" Even the Vice-regal couple could not escape admonition with regard to dinners and festivities, balls and dances, theatricals and other immoral amusement: "It is of greatest importance for the glory of God and the salvation of others that Monsieur and Madame remain firm, not only to avoid the houses where *balls* and *dances* are held, but also forbid Mademoiselle their daughter, to enter into such diversion." Nonetheless, Mgr. Saint-Vallier is capable of modifying his episcopal advice for he his aware that: "... since the age and vivacity of Mademoiselle their daughter has need for some diversion and recreation one may condescend to allow her some honest and moderate dances but with persons of her own sex only and in the presence of Madame her Mother for fear that one should take liberties with the words of the chansons that are dishonest and indecent ... and never in the presence of men and boys, such mixing of the sexes being, to state it frankly, the cause of inconveniences and disorders at the balls and dances. [13]"

What was considered necessary for the Governor was even more imperative for the lower classes. In his circular letter to the priests of Acadia, Mgr. de Pontbriand advises the clergy not to condone dancing on Sundays or Feasts after sundown and never if lascivious chansons are sung. And he warns the Father Confessor never to tolerate kissing, as this will certainly furnish occasion for mortal sin. However, the bishop is pleased to point to the laudable custom at Port Royal where even at wedding festivities boys and girls never dance together but only with members of their own sex, a custom which, in his words, revives the early centuries of the church ! [14]

Yet it cannot be denied that the severe concept of morality may indeed have been a necessity as well as a blessing in a frontier setting that was constantly threatened with danger of lawlessness, depravity and demoralisation. Paul Le Jeune, the first Superior of the Jesuits at Quebec, reported that the population was composed of "choice and well-selected souls and others base and degraded [15]" and he noticed that the trouble-makers were those who came in the boats, "... they wish to make merry and are given to excesses. [16] " Undoubtedly, in the best of Gallic spirit these transient merry-makers sang the ribald chansons of the time and perhaps danced the popular dances of France to the sound of the *vielle-à-roue* (hurdy-gurdy) or *musette.*

Song and dance were, however, not restricted to the "base and degraded" merry-makers. Gradually, a different type of social life developed around the small but important *élite* of Quebec, in the Château of the Governor or the modest salons of the high-ranking government officials or in the homes of the more prominent citizens. Lahontan's reference to "maskers" may well be seen as evidence of the cherished entertainment of masked balls and dances which quite understandably provoked the scorn of the clergy. We lack information with regard to the music played at those dances and festivities and other mundane entertainment. However, it is logical to assume that music and dance were analogous in type and style to their French origins, though probably different in the crude and unpolished manner of performance. To be sure, it would be entirely wrong to assume that the priests who condemned the sinful dances would have objected to expressions of serious art music had such artistic manifestations of a more refined nature occurred, but unlike his English counterpart the French immigrant did not enrich the New World with the noble and lofty musical culture of the 17th century. The practice of secular art music seems to have been extremely rare while popular music was of concern to the church only where the abuses of such sinful digressions, as theatricals, balls, dances, etc., threatened the very foundation of the theocratic society.

Ironically, it is through these episcopal interventions that we know of popular entertainment; the *Mandements des Evêques* provide a thoroughly reliable source of information, though unfortunately the substantial number of warnings, denunciations, reprobations, condemnations and even the threat of excommunications merely emphasize clerical vigilance without elucidating in detail the musical activities which contributed to the bishop's concern. The *Jesuit Relations*, the most extensive documentation of the early years, remain reticent about mundane pleasures and the stream of letters from the pen of Marie de l'Incarnation indicates no active musical life. Chroniclers, travellers and other contributors to the history of New France were conspicuously hesitant about cultural matters. The many historical works relating to the colony devote hardly a few lines to the musical or artistic manifestations of the Europeans and although New France was related by birthright to the glorious century of French art and music, it was easier to find its artistic expressions repeated in a thousand residences all over Europe than in the home of the representative of the French King in the French colony or in the *manoirs* of Quebec's *élite*. While even the smallest principality of Europe indulged in imitation of the Baroque grandeur of Versailles or relished the charmingly illusory, lascivious and decadent world of the French Rococo, Mason Wade's remark that New France had an unequal share in the glory of France's greatest age applies not only to the inferiority of Quebec's Château Saint-Louis or Montreal's Château de Ramezay but is equally well apparent in the poverty of musical life and achievement [17].

This interesting phenomenon is indicative partly of the cultural isolation from the mother-country which had existed in New France long before the new British rulers had imposed the material severance from the maternal source and partly of the concept that had pervaded French music for more than two centuries. Obviously, it was not possible to present in Quebec the favourite entertainment of the *grand siècle*, neither the magnificently staged opera nor the spectacular ballet. Yet even the characteristic instruments of the period seem to have been rare on our musical scene. The lute has been in great favour during the 17th century, it was the instrument not only suited to the aristocratic aloofness of the upper social strata but it was also the instrument of the people; the *clavecin*, characteristic of the *grand siècle*, which more than anything else evokes the spirit of the court of Versailles also remained highly popular throughout the 17th and 18th centuries. It seems unlikely that musical life at Quebec should have been totally deprived of the graceful *clavecin* music of the Chambonnières or the Couperins, or that none of the charming lute-literature should have sounded in the *salons* of the colony, yet neither instruments nor music are mentioned in our annals. Based on our sources, it seems that, in contrast to the English colonies, instrumental music was hardly cultivated in New France.

It is important to remember, however, that the French have a very great love for the *chanson*, and they often prefer intelligibility of the poetic text to the abstract expressions of instrumental music. Whereas English music has always, but especially since the Golden Age of Elizabeth I tended towards the practice of instrumental music, the instrumental idiom did not attain some degree of popularity in France until the 19th century. "Not that it was not practiced, but it failed to please the French, who up to this day insist upon *du chant*, and always desire music whose sounds please the ear while its words engage the mind. [18]" This fundamental characteristic of French rationalism, discernible in every manifestation of French art, was clearly apparent in the elegant and lascivious *chansons,* sung to the tinkling accompaniment of *clavecin* or lute, in the popular *chanson à danser,* in the charming love songs and boisterous drinking songs and also in the unaccompanied, simple and beautiful folksong, the only flower of French musical culture that had been transplanted into Canada by the pioneers, both the early settlers, and the later immigrants from the various regions of France. These were the people who lived around the *seigneuries* or in the villages and small towns, they led a simple, unsophisticated life, simple in everyday matters, in education and cultural activities. Their need for diversion was satisfied with dancing to the sound of the hurdy-gurdy or the *musette*, and with the singing of the old folksong — provided that neither dance nor song offended the spiritual leaders. Although the paucity of art music has frequently been excused by reference to the "unfriendly environment" or apologetically explained as characteristic of the "frontier setting of the pioneer life", it is also due to the disdainful attitude with which a haughty European society and an ignorant Canadian *élite* regarded the task and problems of cultural development.

MUSIC IN THE NEW WORLD

It is advisable to compare the musical scene in Quebec with the by far more propitious state of musical affairs in the Spanish and English colonies on the North American continent. Such comparison is possible and permissible if only to illuminate the disparate development of various transplanted cultures under conditions which were often similar.

Indeed, it is in the comparison with parallel activities in related areas on the contemporary scene on the American continent that the causes of the inferior musical life are best revealed and the effects clearly discernible. Kallmann believes that "... the historian would miss the point of his task if he examined early Canadian concert life simply to show how primitive it was in comparison with music in London or Paris or how wonderful it was because it took place in a frontier setting. [19]" Yet comparison, not criticism, is the yardstick of historical evaluation; it places in true perspective the conditions to be investigated. No purpose is being served by conveniently explaining the musical poverty of New France with the hard and demanding pioneer life or to stress the poor immigrant's lack of musical education, to point to priority in political necessities or a precarious economic condition, to emphasize the effects of clerical objection or to even blame the adverse climatic circumstances for omissions and disparities. Similar conditions prevailed to a greater or lesser extent in other colonial enterprises. In some areas of the New World religious antagonism to music surpassed the severe clerical vigilance of New France. Pioneer conditions were essentially alike in the Southern regions, in the East, in the central colonies and in the North. Neither intellectual nor artistic aspirations on an elevated level had been expected of the simple and illiterate pioneer, the hired labourer or the tradesman who eked out their meagre existence, whether in the primitive quarters of Quebec or Montreal, on the poor farms of New France or in the small towns of New England, Pennsylvania or the Southern States. The climatic conditions in New France remained unchanged when the colony became Canada under British rule, and indeed the validity of the argument is nowhere more strikingly demonstrated than in the development that followed in the wake of the British conquest. In spite of the harsh climatic conditions the sudden and amazing intrusion of a rich musical life contrasts strongly with the inferior conditions of music in the former French possession.

A glance at conditions to the South shows an interesting contrast. Musical art in the American colonies had since their inception been far in advance of the conditions in New France. Loosely attached to England the British settlement of Jamestown (1607) developed into a plantation colony, ruled by a haughty, aristocratic and rich society. Artistic life blossomed in the more congenial surroundings. By 1722, the South could boast of a permanent playhouse and record the first performance of a ballad opera. There were concerts, European artists performed in Charleston, professional musicians were active, and while the high society enjoyed the pleasures of the lighter entertainment, it also sponsored the performance of serious art music.

Not far from the British settlement in the South was the French domain of Louisiana; by 1723, the population numbered only some 500 persons, yet notwithstanding its small size, secular music seems to have had its place in New Orleans. In her letters of 1728 to her father, Sister Hachard de Saint Stanislaus speaks of secular musical activities in the city, and also refers to the use of instruments at liturgical ceremonies and to the singing of motets in four parts during mass [20]. In comparison with New France there appears a significant difference in musical manifestations in the two French territories, which corroborates the unequal support musical art had received from the same maternal source. It also confirms the fact that musical development in the various regions of the Continent differed greatly according to environment, concepts and motives of colonization, the temperament and tradition of the settlers, and the initiative and guidance of the leaders.

The founders of New England cherished different concepts from those of their Southern neighbours. The group of people who landed at Plymouth Rock in 1620 were "... neither peasants nor soldiers, but a substantial Puritan yeomanry, led by Puritan gentlemen and divines in thorough sympathy with them; they were far less fugitives from oppression than voluntary exiles seeking the realization of an idea. [21]" They had brought with them the austere Puritan spirit, but they also brought their music; their whole life was permeated with religion and the desire to serve God with iron discipline of mind and morals. They had come to the New World to find liberty of conscience and to create a new England based on a democratic theocracy in a permanent agricultural colony. The motivating force that had welded the Puritans into unity of aim and determination was not discernible in the diversified and opposing ambitions that had brought merchants and missionaries, soldiers and settlers to the French dominion, which may be one of the chief reasons why "England succeeded where France failed. 22" And perhaps England succeeded also in the field of musical art because the newcomers, particularly those that emigrated to the Southern regions, had brought with them the musical tradition of the Elizabethan era. Even the Puritans could not combat such tradition, they did not entirely prohibit music or musical instruments although it is true that they believed music to be often sinful and a danger to society. Violent controversies raged in Boston concerning the use, function and manner of performance of religious music. Organs were not allowed in churches until the early 18th century, and instruments had been considered "... wicked, blasphemous and popish." Dancing was a devilish invention, and even the old and harmless merriment of Maypole dancing was looked upon with apprehension, for "... t'was not the time for New England to dance. 23"

However, in his treatise of 1647, entitled *Singing Psalms a Gospel Ordinance*, the Reverend John Cotton stated quite clearly that the "private use of any Instrument of Musick" was not forbidden. Indeed, the documented list of instruments that had served the music-loving amateurs of Massachussetts is quite remarkable both for its quantity as well as the type of musical instruments referred to. In striking contrast to the few instruments recorded in 17th century Quebec, viols were quite common in New England; so were flutes and other wind-instruments. Judge Samuel Sewall, of Salem Witchcraft Trial fame, noted in his diary of December 1699 that he had inquired at the repair shop of a Mr. Hiller in Boston about the progress of work on his wife's virginal. And soon after, in 1716, one Edward Enstone, organist at King's Chapel, advertised in the Boston News-Letter the arrival of an impressive collection of instruments, such as "... Flageolets, Flutes, Haut-boys, Bass-Viols, Violins, Bows, Strings, Reeds for Haut-Boys, Books of Instruction for all these Instruments ...", and he informs the public that "... any person may have all instruments of Musick mended, or Virginalls and Spinnets Strung and Tuned at a reasonable Rate, and likewise may be taught to Play on any of these instruments above mentioned ... 24" How pitifully inadequate must Canada's musical life have appeared to Frederic Henry Glackemeyer, Quebec's first professional musician, music merchant and teacher, who as late as 1783 complained about the poor progress of his pupils which he attributed to "... a miserable old spinet − there being only one Piano in Quebec. 25"

The disparity in the development and progress of music on the American Continent assumes even greater proportions when we consider the striking contributions of the newcomers who established the central colonies between New England and the South. Swedes, Germans and Moravians brought with them their fine musical tradition, their instruments, and their great love and devotion to the art. As early as 1700, the chronicle of their musical life abounds in accounts of fascinating activities in sacred as well as secular music. There were composers and musicians, there was music performed on viols, oboes, trumpets and kettledrums, on harpsichords and organs. Here too had been a continuous struggle with the religious concepts of the Quakers of Pennsylvania, who like the Puritans were fervently opposed to music of any sort. Nonetheless, the desire and firm intention of these ethnic groups to preserve the rich cultural and musical tradition of their respective homelands triumphed over religious opposition. Music flourished in the central colonies because the people had been determined to transplant their music, successfully adapting their culture to the new environment with a contribution which enriched the musical scene and influenced musical life in America for years to come. The little town of Bethlehem in Pennsylvania was settled by the Moravians in 1741, but already three years later the Germans and Moravians had formed the *Collegium Musicum* to encourage the study and performance of chamber music, symphonies and choral works (the first performance of Handel's *Messiah* and Haydn's *Creation* are to the credit of the *Collegium*), while in 1762 the city fathers of Charleston in South Carolina founded what is generally believed to be the first musical society in America, the St. Cecilia Society, for the "encouragement of the arts of Music and for the sponsorship of Musical Concerts." From accounts in Josiah Quincy's *Journal of a Voyage to South Carolina* we learn that the society not only engaged professional musicians but also paid good-sized fees: " The music was good — the two bass viols and French horns were grand. One Abercrombie, a Frenchman just arrived, played the first violin, and a solo incomparably better than any one I ever heard. He cannot speak a word of English, and has a salary of five hundred guineas a year from the St. Cecilia Society. 26" Philadelphia, which already around 1700 had been a flourishing music center, became in 1737 the birthplace of Francis Hopkinson, the first American composer of merit; and even Boston and the New England States soon recovered the ground lost in the early years due to Puritan rejection of music.

If the splendid musical achievements in the North American colonies are already in some contrast to the plight of music in New France, even more amazing are musical events that took place in Mexico some years before Cartier had landed in Canada. Pedro de Gante, a friar of the Franciscan order, had been among the first missionaries who accompanied the adventurous *conquistadores* to the New World. Soon after his arrival in 1523 he founded a school for the native population, and having realized the Indian's propensity for music, added singing as well as playing and construction of musical instruments to the subjects of basic education. His school became the center of cultural activities and the training ground for skilled craftsmen to build chapels and convents, for teachers and sacristans to propagate the faith, for instrument makers to construct organs and to build other instruments ; and it became the school of music for singers and musicians required for the celebration of the sacred services. Beautifully illuminated musical manuscripts are preserved from the first half of the 16th century, the works of the highly adept Indians who under the tutelage of the devoted and capable Fray Pedro had acquired the art of composition and musical notation. As early as 1527, his pupils achieved the surprising feat of organ-building, and soon after in the churches that had been built by native craftsmen, indigenous organists played on small instruments that had been constructed by native organ builders. A music printing press was set up in Mexico City in 1539, and a few years later appeared the first book printed in America to contain music for the ritual of the mass. In 1536, one hundred years before Father Le Jeune began to instruct the Canadian Indians in Quebec, the College of Santa Cruz de Tlatelolco for Indians opened with 60 students who were taught reading, writing, Latin grammar, rhetoric, philosophy and music. There are records of 25 music schools in the missions of New Spain during the 17th century. Contemporary sources confirm that the Indians manufactured flutes, oboes, viols, cornets, and also organs which they played in monasteries and convents. "The other instruments which serve for solace or delight on secular occasions are all made here by the Indians who also play them : rebecs, guitars, trebles, viols, harps, monochords ... a few years after the Indians had learnt the chant, they also began to compose. Their *villancicos,* their polyphonic music in four parts, certain masses and other liturgical works, all composed with adroitness — as adjudged by Spanish masters ... [27] "

Pedro de Gante [28] was a Franciscan from Louvain; he was born around 1486 at Ayghem near Ghent, and had been a relation to Charles V ; his accomplishment is partly an example of Spanish civilization, but far more an admirable illustration of human initiative unparalleled, as we believe, in the history of Catholic missions in America. Another very successful Franciscan monk was Arnoldo Basac who was French born and belonged to the Province of Aquitania. He went to Mexico in 1530 and became one of the first music teachers at the college for Indians at Tlatelolco.

This fascinating chapter in the history of American music is still largely unexplored; already the as yet fragmentary and incomplete evidence has brought New Spain into the forefront of colonial musical achievement. Against it, all later musical endeavours in the French and English colonies pale into insignificance. What distinguished the colonial ventures was not merely the regional difference, the political system or economic condition, it was also the cultural environment that had to be created anew in each case, the artistic tradition that had to be imported from the respective homelands and while the essence of the cultural heritage remained, its form changed with each succeeding generation.

Musical life in the various regions reflected the degree to which the population fostered a changing tradition in a new environment. But there was no Pedro de Gante, no Monsieur Abercrombie nor a *Collegium Musicum* in New France; in Quebec, it was the French tradition of the *chanson*, the folksong and the dance, the *joie de vivre* so characteristic of the Gallic temperament. Instead of references to the music of the great masters we read of balls and dances; instead of concert performances we learn of festivities which followed each other in constant succession. Mme. Begon writes, "... would you believe, dear son, that even the devout Mme. Verchères danced all night? Our priests will have much to preach about; to give a ball on the day of Notre-Dame in Advent! But even better: there is to be a ball at Mme. Lavaltrie tomorrow, and after tomorrow at Mme. Bragelogne. Alas, this is the despair of M. le Curé. [29]" Monsieur le Curé was indeed in despair. The wrath of the clergy fell on the

young men of good family who had disgraced the paternal a-
bode and had been sent to the colony under *lettre de cachet*. Mason Wade describes their activities: "They were loath to work
with their hands and so lived by their wits. Many of them acted
as itinerant schoolmasters. They amused themselves gallantly
with the habitants' wives and daughters and introduced scandalous songs; their loose behaviour did nothing to increase the
prestige of education with the simple country folk. Nonetheless,
they enriched French-Canadian folklore with many a gay song
whose origin goes back to the Middle Ages. [30]" How the young
Canadian students of European descent must have enjoyed the
glamorous, witty and well-educated French schoolmaster who
was neither qualified nor capable to teach music other than the
scandalous and gay songs [31].

Music education consisted mainly — if not entirely — of
some instruction in the rudiments of plainsong and the singing
of hymns. Comparisons illuminate the point: while the music
school established by Fray Pedro de Gante in the first half
of the 16th century at the convent of St. Franciscus at Tex-
coco, Mexico, remains the shining example in the musical
history of the American colonies, unmatched by any later
endeavour anywhere, there was also extensive instructional
activity as early as 1700 in Philadelphia where the German Pietists under the leadership of Johann Kelpius
played and taught music on various instruments, including
organ and harpsichord. (Kelpius himself ordered from Germany already in 1708 two clavichords "with additional
strings.") Except for the memorable efforts by Mother St. Joseph
of the Ursulines, instrumental training in Quebec seems to have
been almost completely lacking. It seems that French music
teachers and musicians preferred the thriving and populated
English colonies to the less favourable atmosphere of New
France. Immigration to New France had always been insufficient, the need for manpower had never been adequately

filled, a historical fact which has long been considered the fundamental error of French colonial policy in general. Regardless of enticing rewards and governmental encouragement to early marriage and in spite of the subsequently large increase by natural means, the country remained underpopulated, weak in manpower and slow in economic development. Confined by the geographical isolation, left to their own inadequate resources, the people were unable to develop their own tradition and came dangerously close to losing their heritage. Deprived of the stimulating influence of French music and of the contact with the constantly renewing cycle of art, their musical expressions could not proceed beyond the folksong of bygone days.

FROM FRENCH TO FRENCH-CANADIAN

It is perhaps due to this geographical isolation, the seemingly unbridgable physical separation and spiritual distance from the mother-country that the French of New France became even before the British conquest the French-Canadians of Canada. The French of France themselves were quick to realize the growing diversity between Frenchman and Canadian, between the old France and her neglected offspring. Some of the visitors suggested a few useless remedies for the physical and cultural ills that plagued the young country; others were satisfied to describe the strange and exotic life with a sort of haughty and disdainful curiosity. All had noticed the difference particularly in cultural matters, in education, in customs and habits and also in the character trends of the people, but none looked more closely at the underlying cause. The visitors could indeed not fail to notice the poverty into which the colony had fallen; they also saw the brave efforts of the near destitute society to maintain some semblance of a gracious and civilized mode of living; but they all agreed that the frontier setting at the edge of the wilderness was not a place for the literary and artistic salons of 18th-century

France. Only a few writers remarked briefly on musical matters, but such observations concerned almost entirely the singing of folksongs or referred to the popular entertainment of dances and festivals.

On a brighter note the noted Jesuit chronicler, Father Charlevoix, found in Quebec "... a select little society which wants nothing but to make life agreeable ... one finds circles as brilliant as in other countries ... everybody does his part to make the time pass pleasantly ... science and the fine arts have their turn, and conversation does not fail ... our language is nowhere more purely spoken. [32]" But other writers draw a picture of a society that revelled in balls, dances, in orgies and drinking parties, sumptuous meals and card games, particularly towards the end of the French regime.

The ruling class of New France has been accused of being one of the causes of the French loss of Canada. It was this group of citizens, the descendants of Charlevoix's "select little society" who saw the transition from French to British rule, that had formed the privileged class and from whom some cultural accomplishment might have been expected. Instead of returning to France, as had been offered to them after the treaty of Paris in 1763, they had decided to remain. Among those who stayed were 130 *seigneurs*, 100 gentlemen and burghers, 125 important merchants, 25 lawyers (including former members of the Superior Council), 30 doctors and surgeons, a large number of notaries and other prominent citizens; which is indicative of the good relations "established between the conquerors and the conquered soon after the Battle of the Plains in 1759. [33]" But it is also clearly indicative of a society of educated citizens that had existed before the transition, yet had not left any evidence of cultural exercises. It is indicative of a society that had done nothing to foster the arts, and nothing to encourage serious music. Some Canadian historians have tried to excuse the intellectual and artistic inertia of Quebec's society by stressing the social climate which in times of approaching disaster had not been conducive to cultural manifestations. Some observers have defended the inferior conditions with references to assumedly similar conditions in other colonies, or even in the provinces and towns of France. We have already pointed to the dubious nature of such assertions. It is indeed not the similarity with conditions elsewhere but the difference in approach and attainment which is the striking factor. Not only in the disdainful neglect from the mother-country but to a greater extent in the disinterest and inertia from within the society itself are found the roots of the colony's cultural poverty. If this society has been accused of a share in the ultimate political downfall of New France, it has likewise been guilty in the cultural field, for more than anyone else, this society of educated citizens, of seigneurs and officials and even of the educated clergy, could have become the patron if not participant in a new art in a new France instead of leaving it to the conquerors to bring music and theatre to the new Canada.

A new era announced itself in the pages of the newly established newspapers, it reverberated in the streets and squares from the sounds of the regimental bands, it became evident in the significant signs of cultural progress such as the appearance of the merchant of musical paraphernelia. This was the beginning of a musical era and long before the 18th century had come to a close there were public concerts which introduced to the music lovers of Quebec the immortal masterworks of Handel, Haydn and Mozart, together with the forgotten compositions of the Kozeluchs, the Davosts and others of minor stature. Quebec's French citizens, while understandably apprehensive of the political yoke imposed upon them by their new masters, could now subscribe to the "Gentlemen's Subscription Concerts", they could purchase a "genteel organ with five stops", or acquire strings for "Harpsichord, Pianoforte, Guitar and Violin" — if they owned one of these instruments. They were free to attend concerts by the "Band of the 10th Regiment", or to enjoy the theatrical performances of Molière's works in French as performed by the "Gentlemen of the Garrison".

The Treaty of Paris in 1763 ended the Seven-Years War and with it sealed the political fate of the French colony. The French greeted the loss of their former dominion with an audible sigh of relief — Voltaire and the Encyclopedists had long advocated the surrender of New France, failing to recognize the growing importance of colonial expansion. The annalist of the Ursulines had good reason to complain:

> Almost all of the eminent men in France at that time seem to have underestimated the importance of the events which took place in America, and Canada was not only neglected but even regarded as an obstacle in the Alliance with Austria ... very soon our poor people experienced with bitterness the sad truth that King Louis did not care anymore for Canada ... It is far easier to perceive than to describe the feelings of the Canadians ... they had very well felt the steadily growing indifference of the (French) government during the last years, but to *know* that France had abandoned them ! [34]

Indeed, France had abandoned the neglected fledgling across the sea. Lescarbot's society of free men remained an unfulfilled dream, the "violins and other recreations" had never been brought to the new land. Yet in the voluntary isolation into which the Canadian of French descent retreated, his spiritual, social and cultural attachment to the mother-country assumed new proportions. He began to treasure the memory of his ancestry, he cherished the meagre heritage of the past, his songs again echoed the sentiments of *la doulce France,* while his paintings and poetry, his artisanat and architecture, expressed the new French-Canadian environment. Whereas France soon forgot this inglorious episode of her long and glorious history, *je me souviens* became the symbolic reminder of a glorified past and a determined resolve for the future.

II

Music in New France

PRELUDE WITH CARTIER

The prelude to our musical history is recorded in the narratives of Jacques Cartier's voyage to Canada. Music is already mentioned in the account of his first expedition in 1534. Brief references describe the exuberant reaction of the Indians who, at the sight of the Europeans, gave vent to their excitement in song and dance [1]. On his second expedition, a year later, Cartier sailed up the St. Lawrence and on October 3rd, 1535 entered with appropriate pomp and flourish the fortifications of Hochelaga. A tremendous welcome awaited the explorer and his crew; a tumultuous crowd greeted the arrival of the white men with singing and dancing [2]. Cartier read a portion of the Gospel of St. John, and "for two hours with loud voice word for word the Passion of our Saviour. [3]" Then followed the distribution of presents to the delight of the natives after which "the Captain ordered the trumpets and other musical instruments to be sounded.[4]" Elated with joy, rapt in astonishment, the Indian received the gifts of civilisation — a thrilling moment in the recorded history of Canada; and with the sounds of trumpets at the first ceremonial meetings of the two cultures begins the story of art and music in New France.

Cartier remained in Canada until May, 1536; in the fortification which his craftsmen and mariners had built on the banks of the St. Charles at Stadacona, he and his men endured the rigours of their first Canadian winter. Although he did not leave us evidence of any musical activities, it is quite reasonable to presume the singing of folksongs as a welcome relief from the dismal conditions in the new environment. If secular music is not recorded, devotional services are frequently mentioned. Two priests, Dom Guille Le Breton and Dom Antoine, accompanied Cartier on his second voyage; their presence justifies the assumption that the divine service had been celebrated in the prescribed manner, including the singing of chants and hymns. We do not know, however, whether the priests were still alive in the spring of 1536 or participated in the first religious procession on Canadian soil. During the winter a malignant scurvy took a considerable toll from among the Europeans. To invoke divine aid, Cartier ordered a procession of all who could "still walk or crawl"; the image of the holy Virgin was placed against a tree and the poor Frenchmen, in great need of spiritual comfort, weakened by illness and despair, "prayed and sang the litanies and the Seven Psalms of David. [5]"

As was to be expected, the brave captain from St. Malo had not been concerned with musical events. One or two episodes constitute all the activities of which we have recorded evidence. Yet it is permissible to reconstruct within the framework of our early history a musical life that must have existed at the early as well as subsequent attempts at colonisation. All of these endeavours were accompanied by religious manifestations, be it the ritual of the mass or the singing of hymns and there could also have been occasion for some simple, unpretentious entertainment in rare moments of relative contentment. In expeditions, such as the one of 1541, under the command of the Calvinist François de la Roque, Sieur de Roberval, a large number of hopeful colonists of diverse background, education and social standing braved the cruel wilderness of the New World. Clearly, among the noblemen, soldiers, craftsmen, labourers and adventurers, women and children, there were those who not only could sing the hymns and psalms of the liturgy but were capable of enlivening the otherwise dreary scene with song and dance. The chronicle of this important venture is related in various documents 6. Cartier, whom Roberval had appointed Chief-Pilot and Captain-General, put to sea in May 1541 with five ships and a large crew, estimated by some sources as high as 150 men. At Cap Rouge, he and his crew again endured a long and cold winter, wrought with misery, illness, starvation and death. In the spring of 1542, disgusted and discouraged with country, climate and colonization, Cartier abandoned the unfriendly New World.

The story is told of how on his way home to France he met Roberval whom unexpected delays retained in France and who with additional ships and settlers had arrived in June 1542 at St. John's in Newfoundland, but anxious to close the chapter of his third voyage to Canada, Cartier defied Roberval's orders to return to the abandoned settlement at Cap Rouge and escaped with his vessel and some men under the cover of darkness. Roberval continued his voyage westward, determined to establish a colony. The prospects for a successful founding of the settlement were promising but Roberval's attempt turned to disaster and the collapse of the colony was not long in coming. Its failure added to the general disappointment at the French court in any Canadian adventure. Even Cartier found himself discredited. It was soon discovered that the "precious stones" and "gold" which he had gathered at Cap Rouge as proof of the immense wealth of Canada turned to be neither precious nor gold — which caused the French to coin the proverb, "as false as Canadian diamonds". Yet it is perhaps ironical that, while the adventurous enterprise hardly affected French governmental initiative towards the new colony, Roberval's expedition seems to have stimulated artistic sentiment in 16th-century France. Roberval and his courageous attempt became the object of literary expression in the works of French poets and writers. Rabelais called him Robert Valbringue; André Thevet in his *Cosmographie Universelle* left most valuable information about the colony and its leader; there were the court poets, Clément Marot and Michel d'Amboise, who dedicated their works to him. Another trace of the impact on French intellectualism is the anonymous Calvinist-inspired poem *Robervalensis Epitaphium* which commemorates Roberval's voyage to Canada and his violent death in 1560. And lastly, even the romantic love affair of Roberval's niece, Marguerite de la Roque, banished by her austere Calvinist uncle on a lonely and haunted island in the St. Lawrence (*Ile des Démons*), is recounted in the *Heptameron* by Marguerite de Valois, sister of François I.

In the summer of 1543, the King sent Cartier once more to Canada to rescue Roberval and the few survivors from the ordeal of Cap Rouge. With the return of Roberval the prelude to the French drama in the New World had come to a close and for more than half a century, Canada was all but forgotten.

PORT ROYAL — MARC LESCARBOT

In spite of all obstacles and frustrating experiences of the past, the desire to unveil the secrets of the New World continued to kindle the ambition of the explorers and the avidity of the merchants. New commissions were granted by the King, titles and privileges changed hands and in 1603, Pierre du Gua de Monts, Calvinist and Governor of Pons in Saintonge, was appointed lieutenant-general "of the coasts, lands, confines of Acadia, Canada and other places in New France". He had received the royal privileges and patents to establish a colony of Catholics and Huguenots, to settle colonists and to convert the Indians; and he had been given the all-important monopoly to the fur trade.

The vessels that sailed from Le Havre in the spring of 1604 had been laden with supplies. On board were Catholics and

Huguenots, skilled artisans and architects, carpenters, masons, soldiers, vagabonds, several noblemen as well as two Catholic priests and a Calvinist minister. And on board was Jean de Biencourt de Poutrincourt together with Samuel de Champlain whom de Monts had invited to join in the adventurous enterprise as cartographer and geographer. Having reached the coast of Nova Scotia, de Monts navigated the Bay of Fundy and anchored at last on the north-western shore near the border between Maine and New Brunswick. Champlain discovered a stony and barren island, surrounded by rocks and shoals — ideal for defence, but otherwise without merit.

It was here that the French built the first settlement. But the island of St. Croix proved uninhabitable. Exposed to inclement weather, weakened by illness and near-starvation, the men endured an exceptionally severe winter with all the unpleasant symptoms of former colonial attempts. When spring came, de Monts decided to abandon the desolate island; he crossed the Bay of Fundy to its south-eastern shore and with the few survivors — the number had dwindled to a mere handful — established the settlement of Port Royal. Thus we have arrived at the first episode of considerable interest in our musical chronicle. The story of Port Royal bears testimony to a remarkable early example of French culture in the New World, it is the story of some artistic activities and the story of Marc Lescarbot, whose intellectual curiosity and social consciousness, initiative and artistry brought to this brief episode the spirit of French civilisation. And music was part of the story, part of the artistic manifestations. It was heard in the first theatrical representation, it contributed to harmony and enjoyment among the settlers and, although as yet neither extensive nor of notable quality, it heralded a significant beginning.

The place was ideal, the surrounding beautiful, the fertile soil promised abundance, the woods were full of game and the streams and rivers well-stocked with fish. And the land was waiting for its people. The Baron de Poutrincourt sailed back to France in the autumn of 1605, taking with him a cargo of furs and hoping to return with colonists and craftsmen. It was not an easy mission; much persuasion was needed to attract immigrants to the prospect of life in an unknown wilderness far away from home and only the promise of good monetary reward could induce transient labourers. Nonetheless, Poutrincourt left La Rochelle on May 13th, 1606, with a number of hardy and hired souls together with Louis Hébert, the first apothecary, and Marc Lescarbot, the first historian and poet of New France.

The events of the long and wearisome sea voyage were recorded by Lescarbot. He remembered the stormy ocean when during the meals "our dishes flew from one end of the table to the other" and he also remembered the calm moments which retarded the voyage and "during which we washed ourselves in the sea, and danced on the deck, climbed up the main top and sang together in harmony. [7]" No doubt he found already during the long ocean-crossing an opportunity to display his initiative and to entertain his companions with his artistic talent.

It was on July 27th, 1606, that the *Jonas* at last anchored in the harbour of Port Royal. The sounds of trumpets and the roar of cannons greeted the men who had come to establish the colony, to build the nation. Lescarbot marvelled at the beauty of the countryside, the sloping hills and lovely meadows which he envisaged as the happy refuge of free men. His enchantment was shared by Poutrincourt who had received the rights and privileges to Port Royal and who fully intended to settle with his family in the future colony.

Soon after the arrival of the *Jonas*, Poutrincourt and Champlain embarked on an exploratory expedition to the south, leaving Marc Lescarbot in charge of Port Royal, "to keep an eye on the house and to maintain harmony among its inmates. [8]" So Lescarbot took care of the house and garden and of the spiritual needs of his companions to whom, in the absence of priests, he read from the scriptures 9. With keen interest he studied plant life and explored the surrounding territories; he was particularly impressed by Indian life and customs and recorded the peculiarities and characteristics of the tribes at Port Royal as faithfully as he related the activities of the Europeans.

Canada's first poet and historian, first musician and playwright, gathered material for his historical writings; he composed poems, odes and sonnets; he recorded Indian songs and wrote or arranged the incidental music to his most remarkable creation, *Le Théâtre de Neptune,* probably the first secular theatrical representation anywhere in the Americas 10. Intended to be the unpretentious and spontaneous artistic offering of the cultured amateur, the amusing example of Lescarbot's poetic talent is of considerable historical, literary and musical interest.

Le Théâtre de Neptune and its presentation "upon the waters of Port Royal" on the 14th of November, 1606, was to celebrate the return of Poutrincourt and Champlain from their expedition. Lescarbot had thought it appropriate to enliven the event with some entertainment faintly resembling the *ballet de cour* of the 16th century with its elements of chorus, poetry and music. Considering the circumstances, the *mise-en-scène* must have been an amazing feat of resourcefulness, combining the talents of carpenters, painters and costume-makers.

The script calls for the action of the play to begin as the barque carrying Poutrincourt and his companions approaches the wharf. Attired in appropriate garb, trident in hand and accompanied by six tritons, Neptune welcomes in well-rhymed verses the returning Sieur. The God of the Sea pledges by his sacred insignia to assist the noble Sieur in his efforts to establish the Kingdom of France in these distant regions. His lengthy oration is followed by the sound of the trumpets which, as the script explains, "encourages the Tritons to do likewise."

Poutrincourt expresses his appreciation for such tremendous welcome to Neptune and to the other Thespians, after which all participants are invited into the fort "to break the bread and drink the wine" — which is the cue for Neptune's group to sing *"in four-part harmony"* a short verse, invoking Neptune to grant everyone a safe return to France:

> Vray Neptune donne nous
> Contre tes flots asseurance,
> Et fay que nous puissions tous
> Un jour nous revoir en France [11].

Regrettably, we have no information with regard to the music. We do not know whether Lescarbot himself composed the short vocal piece or perhaps adapted an existing folksong, as had been suggested by Marius Barbeau [12]. Neither the *Histoire de la Nouvelle France,* nor the collection of poems, including the *Théâtre de Neptune,* published under the title *Les Muses de la Nouvelle France,* contain musical notation.

The education of the cultured *gentilhomme* of the period included a thorough knowledge and understanding of the arts, in particular literature and music, both of which were considered essential to his intellectual and social attainments. The astonishing number of amateur musicians and active composers in the second half of the 16th century had been due to a musical education which was exemplary and cannot even be approximated in modern times [13]. It may well be assumed that Lescarbot's education included music; he was influenced by the humanistic concept of the *Pléiade* and the *Académie,* by Ronsard and Baif and their interpretation of poetry and music as an undivided art; he had been inspired by the artistic ideas of his time and was without doubt well aware of the contemporary musical practice of the *vers mesuré* [14]. His knowledge of music is attested by his ability to record Indian songs. It is therefore reasonable to suggest that he may have been capable of composing the short piece of music in four parts with which he concluded the *Théâtre de Neptune.*

Thus the play ends with singing and with trumpet fanfares and the whole colony joins in the welcome and merry-making which ensues. Lescarbot apologized for his unpolished rhymes which "had been prepared in haste". Nonetheless, he decided to include them in *Les Muses,* partly because they served the *Histoire,* but also to demonstrate the joyful life of the colonists. Indeed, the joyful life at Port Royal, so pleasantly enriched by cultural activities, was in striking contrast to earlier attempts at colonization. The establishment of an agricultural community had been the first step towards thorough and lasting settlement and Port Royal attested to the importance of the cultivation, not only of the land, but also of the mind for, as Lescarbot said, "in vain can one live in a land where there is nothing to live for ... there are enough prisons everywhere without having to look for one so far away. [15]

In the colourful Canadian autumn of 1606 the prospects appeared bright; assured of royal support, sustained by the generous de Monts and liberally supplied with the vital provisions by interested merchants in France, the colony seemed well on the road to success. For the first time a settlement existed without the despair and desolation, without the famine and sickness which had so tragically ended earlier ventures. With body and mind well cared for, even the threat of winter held no terror for the colonists. Solid buildings gave shelter, well-organized labour prevented idleness and moments of leisure had been enriched with agreeable entertainment. Food and drink was plentiful and everything contributed to the good cheer and joyous mood. The desire and determination to prepare for a prosperous future united Catholic and Huguenot in a spirit of equality and mutual respect that may well have set an example for the ultramontane Canada or the Puritan New England. Even the hired labour, the transient craftsman who had come to build the homestead for

others, enjoyed a happier life in freedom and a greater appreciation for his work than in feudal France and for the first time in
the colonial history of New France, secular artistic and recreational activities — limited though they had been — crowned the
auspicious endeavour. One must at this point note the secular
nature of this contribution for, unhampered by clerical vigilance,
Port Royal enjoyed wordly entertainment which in later years
would almost certainly have been frowned upon in Quebec.
And there was no lack of such entertainment. "It would be too
long to describe in detail what happened here during the winter", says our poet-historian 16, and while much to our regret, he
does not elaborate on the artistic fare offered at that time, he describes with relish the gastronomic delights offered by *l'Ordre du
Bon Temps* 17, the first gourmet club in the New World. And he
does not fail to express his pleasure at the mild days of January
1607, when with great enjoyment "on a Sunday, the 14th day of
the Month, in the afternoon, we sported ourselves singing music
upon the river l'Equille. 18"

While Lescarbot relates the events of daily life among
the Europeans, he does not neglect the native population. In a
spirit of tolerance, understanding and broad vision he describes
Indian customs and habits; indeed, his intelligent and impartial
observations are not only a natural source of information but
also helped greatly to expose the bizarre and fictitious disguise
in which the Indians had been represented since Cartier had
brought two natives to France in 1534.

Of particular interest and considerable value to our chronicle is Lescarbot's amazing attempt at recording in letter notation of some Indian songs. The strange experience of native music and dance attracted his attention and stirred his imagination,
and with the scholarly curiosity of the time he investigated and
recorded the display of a primitive and unfamiliar civilisation.
Untroubled by qualms of religious conscience, he studied the

meaning of the ritual dances and incantations, those of ceremonial significance and others intended to eulogize warfare and heroes. He compares the orgiastic and licentious excesses — which were to repulse the missionaries of later days — to the sacrificial rites of ancient peoples and draws a parallel between the sensuality in the dancing of the Europeans and the absence of voluptuousness in the bodily movement of the Indian. Not content with a literary interpretation, he illustrates his account of Indian music with an example of native songs. While in the light of modern research this primitive attempt cannot claim scientific importance, nonetheless it represents without doubt the earliest recorded examples of North American Indian music.

The occasion to record the melodies presented itself to Lescarbot when, as he relates, "one day going to walk in our meadows along the river, I drew near Membertou's cabin and did write in my table-book part of that which I understood. [19]" He transcribed the songs in letter-notation instead of the tone-symbols of his time. Presumably he had not been prepared for the opportunity and was not equipped with the accessories needed for a more involved and complex musical notation, while on the other hand the system of solmization was a device universally adopted for theoretical and demonstrative purposes.

He noted certain characteristics common to Indian music which have since been corroborated by modern investigation. He remarked on the narrow tonal range, the frequent repetition of section and the reiteration of syllables and sounds, but did not indicate the rhythmic element nor mention the purpose and function which connects songs to specific ceremonies. A textual peculiarity astonished him; he thought he heard the familiar *alleluya* interspersed in the otherwise incomprehensive mumble of words: "I attentively harkened upon this word *alleluya* repeated sundry times and could never hear any other thing. Which makes me think that these songs are to the praises of the devil, even though this word means to them that which it means in

Hebrew, which is: Praise ye the Lord. [20]." Our chronicler apparently did not consider having been deceived by a certain phonetic sound formation derived from the trilling of the tongue against the palate, a vocal technique common in primitive cultures [21].

In his writings Lescarbot frequently resorts to comparison with analogies of ancient times to support his theories and observations. He invites the reader to compare the songs of the Souriquois (Micmacs) of Port Royal with two examples of Indian music from Brazil drawn from Jean de Léry's narrative of a voyage to South America [22]. The same narrative contained information concerning instruments such as trumpets made of large cane or hollow branches or flageolets and flutes made of human bones and Lescarbot compares these instruments with those which he had noted among the Indians of Acadia who had greeted the arrival of the white men: "As soon as the Sieur de Poutrincourt had landed, there were among the multitude of savages a goodly number of fifers who played long flageolets made of reed-cane and painted on top, though not with such harmony which our shepherds can make; and to show us the excellence of their art they whistled with their noses while cutting capers according to their customs. [23]"

END OF AN EPISODE

Remarkable as had been Lescarbot's contribution to the cultural history of New France, neither his thoughts nor his work influenced its cultural development. The example of his artistic initiative remained unique and indeed unparalleled throughout the history of New France and the story of Port Royal became merely another brief episode in the annals of early Canada. Political events brought to an abrupt end the efforts of the idealistic French scholar and with it his hopes to find "liberty and equality in real brotherhood of men". The promising enterprise of Port Royal was not destined to develop in a climate of progress and energy ; dark clouds had appeared on the eastern horizon. Before Poutrincourt's dream of an agricultural community in the fertile surroundings could become reality, the seeds of intrigue smothered the bright hope that had inspired the imagination of Champlain and the visionary spirit of Lescarbot. De Monts became victim of sinister schemes instigated at the French court by mercantile jealousy and religious antagonism and, with the royal patents and privileges as arbitrarily withdrawn as they had been granted, the founders of the colony saw themselves deprived of the legal and material support without which the settlement could not survive. There was no other choice but to abandon Port Royal. The incomprehensible pattern of French colonial policy had repeated itself: strangely incapable of realizing the immense possibilities of the New World, unable or unwilling to develop her overseas possessions, France abandoned Acadia even before English piracy put the torch to the dilapidated remains of the colony.

Disappointed and with sad heart, Lescarbot left Port Royal in the summer of 1607, exactly one year after his arrival. He returned to France, to his legal profession and to his literary work. In 1609 appeared the first edition of the *Histoire de la Nouvelle France* which contains the first collective documentation of the early expeditions to the French territories overseas from the explorations of Verrazano to the ill-fated Huguenot missions to Brazil and Florida and from the narratives of Cartier to the annals of Champlain [24].

Les Muses de la Nouvelle France contains the poems, odes and sonnets in praise of his friends de Monts, Poutrincourt, Champlain and others. Lescarbot extols the beauty of Acadia as well as the valour and grandeur of the great Membertou, the chief of the Souriquois tribe with whom the Europeans had lived in friendship and harmony [25]. His fondness for farewell-odes — he had written *L'Adieu à la France* at his departure from La Rochelle in the spring of 1606, and *Adieu aux Français* ("retournans de la Nouvelle France en la France Gaulloise") in the autumn of the same year — now finds a last theme, a lengthy farewell-ode to New France into which he pours his admiration for the new land, combined with regret, resignation and also reproach and criticism at the political machinations that had brought about the end of Port Royal:

> A-DIEV A LA NOVVELLE FRANCE — Du 30. Iuillet 1607 —
> Favt-il abandonner les beautez de ce lieu
> Et dire au PORT-ROYAL vn eternel Adieu?
> Serons-nous donc toujours accusez d'inconstance
> En l'établissement d'vne Nouvelle-France? [26]

Thus the first true agricultural colony of France in the New World was abandoned; the buildings, the cornfields and gardens, "and all the dawning prosperity of Port Royal" were left to the agony of slow decay. "It had been an inspiring essay", says Parkman, "the leaders of the enterprise had acted less as merchants than as citizens; and the fur-trading monopoly, odious in itself, had been used as instrument of a large and generous design ... In one respect the enterprise of de Monts was truer in principle than the Roman Catholic colonization of Canada, on the one hand, or the Puritan colonization of Massachusetts on the other, for it did not attempt to enforce religious exclusion. [27]"

Whatever the opposition from clerical and commercial quarters, whatever the difficulties and misfortunes, Poutrincourt did not abandon his dream to establish a happy and prosperous colony of France in Acadia. After much delay and vexations, the adventurous Baron de St. Just saw his persistent efforts crowned with success.

By 1610 he received royal confirmation of his grant to Port Royal and immediately embarked on a new venture, resolved to continue where he had been forced to yield three years earlier. He had a powerful and influential ally: The Society of

Jesus ardently desired to establish itself in Acadia to bring Christianity to the Indians and to prevent a renewal of Calvinism in those regions. Poutrincourt, however, did not cherish such pious ambitions nor was he particularly fond of the Jesuits. Though a good Catholic, he was far more concerned with rebuilding the colony than with religious fervor because, as his good friend Lescarbot explained, "one must first build the Republic without which there can be no Church. And for that reason the first assistance should go to that Republic and not to those who have the pretext of piety; when the Republic has been established, it is to her to invest those who attend the spiritual. [28]"

And successfully Poutrincourt evaded complicating issues and indignant Jesuits and sailed in haste for New France; instead of the two Jesuit priests, Biard and Massé, who were supposed to go to Acadia, he took with him a priest, Jessé Fléché, whose subsequent and somewhat hasty conversation of some twenty Indians, including their chief Membertou, was intended to please the noble patrons and the court and at the same time to disprove the need for Jesuit activity at Port Royal. The Jesuits disavowed as irregular and superficial this *"chef-d'oeuvre* of Christian piety", as Lescarbot had called the sprinkling of holy water; but he also relates that the new converts listened devoutedly to the divine service which "was ordinarily sung *to music composed* by the said Sieur Poutrincourt. [29]" This reference to Poutrincourt's musical ability is ambiguous; the content of the divine service is not stated, nor has the nature of Poutrincourt's *composition* been disclosed. The accuracy of interpretation hinges on the solution of a linguistic problem, that is, the proper definition of the verb *compose*. The many different meanings inherent in the verb make it difficult to establish whether Lescarbot referred to the creation of music or to the setting of existing music for a special service. It is, however, unlikely that Poutrincourt *composed* items of sacred music while, on the other hand, the musical aspect of the service may have been *composed of* several traditional hymns and prayers that had been selected or arranged by him. Nonetheless, it is entirely justified to credit Poutrincourt with a good knowledge of music, based on the musical education which the social standing of the noble Sieur demanded and it is quite possible to accept the statement that during his sojourn in Acadia, Poutrincourt endeavoured "with his musical ability, scholarship and sensitive taste to foster in the little colony for which he was responsible, a love for the finer things in life. 30

To sum up so far, nothing is known of the part which other inhabitants of Port Royal may have played in the artistic manifestations at the colony, yet among the fifteen members of the Order of Good Cheer were men of high standing and education who probably took part in the performance of the *Théâtre de Neptune* or contributed to the singing "in four-part harmony", be it at the conclusion of the play, at the joyful singing "on the river l'Equille", at the divine service, or at any other occasion that called for vocal participation. All of them helped to make Port Royal the most inspiring episode in the otherwise uneventful prelude to the cultural and musical history of Canada. It was because of these men that Port Royal became a unique example of initiative, resourcefulness and vision. To these men music and art were not strange and incomprehensible matters and the prodigious display of their artistic talents — insignificant as that display might appear in the wider context of our history — clearly demonstrated the necessity at that time of support from the cultural resources of the mother-country. But such support unfortunately never came. The episode of Port Royal was soon forgotten, its lesson went unheeded. Instead, a new influx of clergy introduced a different, more sophisticated but on the whole less artistic era. Jesuit erudition began to impress its mark on New France through spiritual edification and clerical education, and cultural development was henceforth in the care of the Church. The chronicler must now follow the activities of the clergy if he is to record — in the wording of the *Jesuit Relations* — "ce qui s'est passé en la Nouvelle France".

The Jesuit era began in the early summer of 1611, when after a voyage that had lasted for four months, a small vessel, appropriately called the *Grace of God,* anchored in the harbour of Port Royal. Two Jesuit priests, Pierre Biard and Enemond Massé, stepped ashore anxious to begin their missionary work, the salvation of Infidel and Huguenot, and to lay the foundation of a Catholic empire in the Northern hemisphere of the New World. Father Biard found little grounds for rejoicing but met only with animosity from the leaders of the small community who had viewed his coming with misgivings and even his strenuous attempt at conversion was of no avail. He made great efforts to learn the native language but found the Indians "lazy, gluttonous, irreligious, treacherous, cruel and licentious".

To the chronicle of music Biard contributed an amusing description of an incident which occured during an exploratory journey to "the country of the Armichiquois, some eighty leagues from Port Royal". Safely separated by an expanse of water from the arrows of the hostile Indians, the small band of French explorers and soldiers came upon a native encampment where "all night there was continual haranguing, singing and dancing, for such is the kind of life all these people lead when they are together — I had our people sing some sacred hymns, as the Salve, the Ave Maris Stella, and others ... and when they came to the end of these, as the French are natural mimics, they began to imitate the singing and dancing of the Armichiquois, and did so well that the Indians stopped to listen; at which our people stopped too; and the Indians began again. You would have laughed to hear them, for they were like two choirs answering each other in concert, and you would hardly have known the real Armichiquois from their imitators. [31]

The various historical sources differ in their interpretation of the events which took place in 1613. The prominent feature was certainly the illegal attack on Port Royal by Captain Argall when England and France were not at war. As for music, there was none. The customary din of trumpets and drums that signalled the beginning of Argall's attack also sounded the end to the brief episode of musical life at Port Royal.

III

Mission and Music

Of the three factors in the establishment of New France, none had a stronger influence on cultural development than the Catholic church. Crown and commerce were only perfunctorily concerned with the life of the colonists, the former as feeble protector, the latter as powerful exploiter in the service of mercantilism. Neither was interested in the propagation of culture and education or indeed capable of building a politically and economically strong and lasting colony. Thus it was left to the missionary church to protect the religious and secular affairs of the settlers while at the same time attempting to transplant roots and spirit of French civilization into this distant and neglected cultural domain.

But salvation and conversion, not secular culture, were the primary objectives of the church and artistry was to express itself only as a means to the spiritual end. In the realm of music it was mainly the repertory of the Gregorian chant, varied occasionally with one of the *Cinq Messes Royalles* of Henri Dumont in the new modern style of *Plainchant Musical Français* or the more traditional sacred music of Artus Auxcousteaux, Marc-Antoine Charpentier, or Michel de Lalande. A few items of liturgical music, such as motets and a *prose* may have originated in New France but claims to that effect have not been substantiated. It is also important to note that church music did not influence secular musical life in the colony and although the church was the first and, throughout the French era, the only source of musical instruction both for the young Europeans and for the Indian converts, such instruction was confined to the rudiments of "plainchant together with the fear of God" — clearly not the most expedient means to encourage musical art or to train musicians.

In marked contrast to the limited scope of musical activities clerical interest encouraged the plastic arts, and already in the first half of the 17th century the church imported men who began to create significant works of art, modest and perhaps uninspiring sometimes, but important enough to become the foundation of a tradition of skilled craftsmanship which distinguished Quebec well into our time. For example, paintings depicting the story of religion decorated the walls of church and chapel and expressed more eloquently than words the pleasures of Paradise and the horrors of Hell; sculptures and statues of saints and angels watched over the faithful, and exquisite silverwork, fine embroidery and gilded leatherwork served the requirements of the ritual.

With the founding of the School of Arts and Crafts at Saint-Joachim in the latter part of the 17th century, this artistic endeavour received its strongest impulse. Such an institution had already as early as 1665 been the concern of Mgr. de Laval and the newly-arrived Intendant Jean Talon, and while the former was mainly concerned with the education of future priests, the latter — in the tradition of his Minister Colbert, the great organizer of French industry and art — thought in terms of self-efficiency and economic independence. Established primarily for the education of the sons of humbler colonists, the *Ecole des Arts et Métiers* was a sort of agricultural-technical school with a monastic atmosphere where, in addition to theology and mathematics, were taught painting and sculpture alongside with carpentry and weaving, shoemaking and agriculture — in short, everything except music ! Thus not only was there hardly any encouragement from the mother-country but within the country itself little was done for the art of music. In the brilliant mosaic of clerical initiative and cultural attainment the development of musical art alone remains a somewhat colourless, sadly neglected and insignificant segment. And this is the picture which will confront us as we continue the musical chronicle of Quebec.

CHAMPLAIN AND THE RECOLLECTS.

The story of clerical supremacy begins in Quebec, and the story of Quebec begins with the Sieur de Monts who, after having bequeathed to Poutrincourt the shattered hopes of Acadia and the ruined remnants of Port Royal had returned to Paris. But passion for discovery and the noble ambition of establishing colonies — interests which he shared with Champlain — had become an irresistible force. Thus he again solicited and obtained the monopoly to the fur trade, equipped two vessels and gave the command of one of them to Champlain. The latter sailed from Honfleur in 1608 with men, munitions and material to build the new settlement on the banks of the St. Lawrence and at the foot of the well-known cliff, near the place where some seventy-five years earlier Cartier had built the first stronghold of France, Champlain planted in August 1608, the emblem of his God and King.

The first winter descended upon the new Quebec and took the small settlement into its icy grip. In the *habitation* which Champlain designed and of which he has left us a curious and charming sketch, he and his crew of twenty-eight men spent the long hours in enforced idleness. It would have been interesting to know their activities during that first winter but Champlain, who was most likely the only man among the crew who could write, did not record the daily life 1. The rigorous climate and the poor living conditions extricated the usual toll of misery and illness; only eight men of the crew survived the inevitable scurvy to see the coming of spring in 1609. Musical activities, not surprisingly, are not recorded and, in the apparent absence of ecclesiastics, even the devotional ceremonies would be without liturgical music. The trumpet sounding from the watchtower at night made the only music.

Champlain was not only a man of high cultural and intellectual attainment, he was also a devout and practical Christian, a firm believer in the spiritual, economic and political advantages to be gained from the Christianization of the Indians. On one of his frequent returns to France, in 1615, he visited a Recollect monastery near Brouage, the ancient port and fortress, where he had occasion to address the friars of that ascetic and austere branch of the Franciscan order. It is perhaps irrelevant to search for the motives which prompted him to invite the poor and mendicant Recollects to take charge of the spiritual and moral direction of the colony rather than the rich, powerful and erudite Jesuits; similarly it would not be appropriate to discuss the artistic merits and cultural achievements of the various orders; but it is interesting to recall the splendid example furnished by the astonishing artistic attainments of the Franciscans in Mexico and it is not mere coincidence that from the ranks of the Recollects came in later years some of the most capable priest-artists to New France.

Four priests were assigned to the new mission; "they packed their church ornaments" relates Champlain, "and we our luggage", and the grey cloth and peaked hood of the Recollects was first seen in Canada in the early summer of 1615. Already one month after their arrival, Father d'Olbeau celebrated in the newly built chapel "la première messe qui soit jamais dite en Canada". Nothing was missing to render the event solemn and dignified; the *Te Deum* was sung to the acclamations of great joy from the assembled populace and to the salvoes fired by the small artillery of the fortification[2]. Thus the revered item of the liturgy inaugurated musical activities in Quebec just as it had enhanced the first and impressive ceremonial encounter between French and Indians at Hochelaga some eighty years earlier and as it was to express thanksgiving in years to come.

With a liturgical hymn began the musical history of Quebec and liturgical music permeated the entire period of the French regime. Whatever the secular entertainment of the pioneer may have been, no record of such activities exists; no chronicler has described in detail the first wedding ceremony when Estienne Ionquest and Anne Hébert, the daughter of Louis Hébert, Canada's first apothecary and colonist, took the sacred vows and Father Le Caron chanted the liturgical songs and prayers. Presumably the ceremonial act was followed by as much traditional rejoicing as the circumstances allowed. Perhaps the *branle* of the Normandy, the groom's home-province, was danced to the accompaniment of clapping hands and stomping feet; perhaps the sound of a *vielle-à-roue* provided the drone bass of the simple harmony to the gay chansons and popular songs that enlivened the joyous event [3].

Our sources — clerical in the main — reveal clearly the disapproval of the ecclesiastic for the lascivious and vulgar songs. The Recollect friar, Gabriel Sagard — the first historian of his order in New France — had noted that the natives "showed singular pleasure in listening to the sacred hymns and prayers", but on the other hand, "expressed repugnance at the profane and dissolute songs of the French", and he added the pious wish and fervent hope that "Jesus may condemn the evil Christian singers of dissolute and mundane chansons [4]." Thus it seems that the good Frenchman became the evil Christian singer as soon as he sang the witty and frivolous chansons he had brought along in his cultural baggage. Yet Sagard's fervent supplication, although disarmingly naive, is not without some significance, and while his entreaty testifies largely to his religious sentiment, it is also unwittingly an important allusion to the Indian's concept of music and to his recognition of a familiar idiom in the music of the liturgy. The affinity in character between Indian incantations and the devotional chants of the Church is quite apparent in the syllabic style, in the free rhythm as well as melodic motion, in the inflection, intonation and in the similarity of function. Hence the music of the ritual was closer to the Indian's understanding than the more expressive sensuous melodic, harmonic and rhythmic structure of the French secular chanson. The priests soon recognized the Indian's natural ability for music and music became a most valuable ally in missionary work and in education. Moreover, while music helped to convey the mysteries of the faith, the natives, particularly the younger element, enjoyed the singing lessons so that already a few years after the arrival of the Recollects, the Superior could report that at the celebration of Quebec's ten-year jubilee some of the Savages "who were somewhat advanced in religious instruction, recited the prayers, singing with us as well as they could 5."

Ten years after its founding, Quebec was still a small trading post with a mission-station attached to it. The population, including a few women and children, did not even reach one hundred people. The few genuine settlers, poor peasants from Normandy, were the true pioneers of France in the New World. The majority of the population consisted of transients; the fur-traders were in pursuit of profitable exploitation, the men in their employ were concerned with the monetary reward and their eventual return to France; there were a few officials and soldiers, reluctantly attending to their duties; there were a few tradesmen and artisans, and during the shipping season a number of sailors and mariners. The trade monopoly was in the hands of merchants from St. Malo and Rouen; some were Catholics, others Huguenots and religious dissension joined commercial rivalry. The small establishment was in fact in a very unsettled state. Champlain, nominally in charge, saw his authority undermined by the traders and merchants who were not only jealous of his powers but openly opposed to his aims and endeavours. Gabriel Sagard registered bitter indignation at the custom of Huguenot merchants or ship captains who forced their Catholic labourers to join in the heretic prayers on board their vessels anchored at Quebec and to sing the "chants de Marot [6]." The Huguenots had been forbidden to exercise their religion within the limits of New France, but they paid little attention to the royal edict and roared "their heretical psalmody with vigor from the ships on the river [7]." As matters grew from bad to worse, the Viceroy Montmorency, duly informed by the indignant priests of such outrage, issued orders which prohibited "all praying and psalm-singing on the St. Lawrence [8]." At this the Huguenot sailors revolted, and whether their anger was aroused by the attack on their religious sentiment or by the attempt to curtail their predilection for vociferous singing or because they were prevented from displaying their defiance of the papists, the Viceroy was forced to a compromise which stipulated that the enraged sailors would not "sing the hymns, but would assemble for prayers [9]." Thus at the expense of music a truce was assured and the Calvinist hymns and psalms which at the same moment resounded at the prayer meetings of New England's Puritans, perhaps not with equal vigor and temperament but with greater strength of conviction, were never to be heard again at Quebec.

JESUITS IN QUEBEC

It may seem pretentious to suggest that the episode of Calvinist hymns provoked important developments in New France, but it is conceivable that the heretical enthusiasm of the Huguenot sailors influenced decisions which were of far-reaching impact on the colony. There were the Recollects, weak in number and resources, but attempting courageously not only to bring conversion and salvation to the infidels (there were five Recollect missions from Acadia to Lake Huron) but also to extend spiritual welfare to the lawless, drinking, roving and gaming Europeans. The task apparently exceeded their powers for in the end they yielded their priority in the missionary field and requested the assistance of the powerful and energetic Society of Jesus and for the second time in the history of the young colony, in 1626, fourteen years after the unsuccessful interlude of Biard and Massé at Port Royal, the black robes of the Jesuits arrived in French North America. The significance of this important event is clearly mirrored in the musico-historical consequences. The arrival of the Jesuits marks a turning point in the cultural development and their profoundly religious and passionate fervor will soon influence the artistic and musical life in Quebec [10].

The task of the Jesuits had been made easier by the decision of Richelieu to bar any antagonistic religious element from the colony. The great mastermind of absolutism had taken the mismanaged affairs into his powerful hands and the Huguenot merchants saw their privileges annulled. The Company of the One Hundred Associates was formed with the Cardinal at its head and nobles, ecclesiastics, officers and merchants as members. The aim and pledge of the Company was not only to draw the profit from the expanded trade but also to settle the land with emigrants, provided that every settler was a Frenchman and a Catholic — or perhaps in reverse order [11]. New France was henceforth protected by royal decree from the heretical but nonetheless stimulating inspiration of Huguenot music and musical thought.

The decree, however, did not protect it against armed assault. Some of the French Huguenots who had been expelled earlier returned as avengers on board of vessels which in the early summer of 1628 sailed up the St. Lawrence and before Richelieu and his Company could initiate their ambitious plans, Champlain had no alternative but to surrender a starved, weakened and beleaguered Quebec to the combined forces of English and Huguenots under David and Lewis Kirke. Quebec was devastated and, with the exception of the courageous Madame Hébert and her small family, abandoned by the French. Jesuits and Recollects returned to France and the Kirke brothers sailed with their bounty and some prisoners — including Champlain — back to England. The strange consequences of this interlude in Canadian history are well known. Charles I of England did not consider keeping the conquered colony and, more concerned with the need for money than with the possession of a wilderness thousands of miles away, restored Quebec and Port Royal to the French Crown in settlement of Queen Henrietta's only partly paid dowry. Exactly three years after the surrender of Quebec, New France was again French territory. The Jesuits welcomed the signing of the peace treaty of St. Germain-en-Lay in 1632 and the return of the colony to French rule. They found themselves re-instated as the sole masters in the field of religious activities. The Recollects, whose only claim rested on the foundation of the mission of New France, were excluded from the scene of their early and successful missionary labour and they were not to return to Canada until many years later.

Once more the return of the Jesuits opens a new chapter in the musical history of Canada; the meagre chronicle of music becomes a narrative of Jesuit contribution to religious musical life in the colony, to their educational efforts and their vigilance of secular musical activities. It has already been remarked that in the selection of missionaries and priests for service in New France consideration and preference was given to musical qualification, particularly after it had become clear how well the Indians responded to sacred music. Music was part of a remarkable general education in the monastic colleges of France and most of the priests who arrived at Quebec had undergone a musical training which aided them in the pursuance of their task. It has also been remarked how the clergy assumed the initiative in every form of art as soon as they were convinced of its efficacy. Conversion and education were of primary concern and went hand in hand; one without the other would not be of lasting value 12.

Paul Le Jeune arrived in the colony in 1632, to become the first Superior of the Canadian mission. He perceived that the natives were lacking not in intelligence but in education and instruction, factors essential to conversion. He began to teach Indian children the liturgical chants: "I carefully pronounced the *Pater* or the *Credo* which I had arranged in verse for them to sing; they followed me word by word, learning very nicely by heart; and when they had learnt some verslet or strophe we sang it at which they had great pleasure 13." For better understanding he had translated the spiritual canticles into the native language: "We end with the *Pater Noster* which I had composed, quasi in rhyme in their language, and which I made them sing; it is a pleasure to hear them sing in the forest that which they have learnt 14." Evidently the children enjoyed these musical activities, especially when at times the singing exercises were conducted in public or when, as on one occasion, they performed on board a vessel anchored in Quebec harbour. "I had taken only six or seven with me", relates Le Jeune, "and I made them sing their *Pater Noster* in native language on the vessel — of which our Frenchmen took great pleasure 15." Still greater was the delight of the children in whose honour the captain, after having distributed the cherished delicacies of cheese and candies, had the cannon fired. Le Jeune is quite certain that the little Indians would like to gain their livelihood by singing if one would pay for their songs in such delightful way 16. In the small seminary which he had established, the young natives received lessons in singing the liturgy together with the young sons of the French colonists. The result pleased Le Jeune: "It is a sweet consolation to hear them sing in our chapel the symbols of the Apostles in their own language. Now, in order to animate them even more, our Frenchmen sing one strophe in our language, then the seminarists another in Huron, and then all together sing a third verse, each one in his own language and in nice harmony 17." The good father is delighted with every ship that brings immigrants from France. Although the new arrivals are mainly composed of "choice and well-selected souls" there are also, it seems, those who are indeed "base and degraded". Yet a change takes place in them which is nothing short of miraculous: "I do not believe there is to be found anything in the bosom of Nature which produces types of wheat after having received only thistle seeds. Yet this miracle happens quite often in New France 18." The chapels are by far too small to hold the crowd and he confesses humbly that his heart "was deeply moved the first time I attended the Divine Service, and seeing our French all rejoicing to hear the singing, loud and publicly, of the praises of the great God in the midst of a barbaric people 19." Our chronicler mentions the reaction to liturgical singing of two of these "barbaric people" who, for curiosity's sake, attended the service and who had wondered whether "He who had made All, will give us what we asked ... and since we were too slow for their liking, they said: Certainly, He does not want to give it to them — see how they are all shouting as loud as they can — (we were singing Vespers at the time) 20." Le Jeune has also left us an interesting reference to the *Vielle-à-roue,* or Hurdy-Gurdy; he related that at a gathering of Indians and Europeans, the natives begged "that as a token of the rejoicing and the mutual love for each other, some of our young should dance to the sound of a *vielle* which was held by a young Frenchman 21."

Paul Le Jeune was born at Châlons-sur-Marne in 1591; of Huguenot parentage, he turned to Catholicism and entered the Jesuit noviciate in 1613. In the course of his studies he acquired the knowledge of the essentials of music; he knew the practical application of the rules and laws that govern plainchant and, according to his own words, was quite aware of the elements of harmony and composition. With the devoted enthusiasm of the missionary he employed religious music in his efforts to bring Catholicism to a pagan Continent and with the unflagging spirit of the educator he endeavoured to sow the seeds of French civilization where, as he hoped, the fertile soil would produce a gratifying harvest. It was he who at the early stage initiated the trend in education that was to be maintained throughout the history of the colony, namely to bring to French and Indian alike the knowledge of "the plainchant and the fear of God". Within this limited scope of music education the priests succeeded in later years in making choirboys out of young Indians and Frenchmen. They also provided instruction in the rudiments of music for the older seminarists and probably initiated some training in the playing of the organ.

Among the priest-teachers of the early days were some remarkable men. Jean de Quen taught at the seminary from 1635 to 1637, was a missionary at Sillery and Tadoussac, and the first white man to enter the region of Lake St. John. From 1652 to the time of his death in 1659, he remained at Quebec, officiating as Superior of the Jesuits and, at the same time, as Rector of the College and member of the Souvereign Council of Canada. If his musical achievements are not spectacular, he enriched, nevertheless, the musical scene of early Quebec through his efforts as teacher and through his vocal ability. As far as the latter was concerned, we rely on Father Lalemant, who reported in March 1646, that on Good Friday "we held the service whereby the Passion was sung in three (voices) to wit: Monsieur de St. Sauveur, evangelist, Monsieur Prior, who sang the choir (Synagogue), and myself. I thought then that Father de Quen would have done better than M. de St. Sauveur in that part [22]."

Even more emphatic is the Superior's critical remark on the following day when the service was held "with the same ministrants ... and it seemed to me again that for the *Exultet* Father de Quen would have sung better [23]." And Father Lalemant should have known, for he himself seems to have been an accomplished singer and well-trained musician. Such and other references of similar nature endorse de Quen's musical talent and ability, both of which he also successfully applied to his missionary work. He was particularly interested in the use of original Indian songs with spiritual text translated into Indian language, thus advocating the application of the vernacular in word and sound.

Monsieur de St. Sauveur, although not having received the fullest musical approval of the Superior, was one of the notable priest-pioneers of music in New France. Born in 1598 in the Normandy, he had decided to come to Canada in 1634 as the first secular priest, with the intent and desire to serve the religious needs of the increasing number of compatriots from his native region who had emigrated to New France. Among these was his friend and patron Jean Bourdon, the first civil engineer and surveyor in the colony. It was presumably Bourdon who persuaded Monsieur de St. Sauveur — the Abbé Jean le Sueur — to follow him to the new land, to stay at his *Seigneurie* near Quebec and and to instruct his children. Until Le Sueur's arrival only members of monastic orders — the Recollects and the Jesuits — had come to the colony. Le Sueur soon became the accepted curé of the French population and so great was his popularity and esteem among clerics and laymen alike that his position was never contested, even though the jurisdiction of his office depended on the privilege obligingly accorded to him by the Superior of the Jesuits and later by the Bishop himself. He did not teach at the College or Seminary; instead he became the first private tutor in Canada. Of particular interest to this study, however, are his musical talents. With his apparently fine voice and good knowledge of musical rudiments, he contributed to the religious ceremonies at Quebec and it is interesting to note that his participation at the ritual enabled the earliest performance of liturgical music in three to four parts. From the meagre information at our disposal it is difficult to assess Le Sueur's ability as a singer. Father Lalemant may have criticized his performance in the Passion without necessarily criticizing the quality of his voice. The three parts of the Plainsong Passion — for this was the type performed at Quebec — use recitation tones on three different pitch levels and speeds, which do not require special vocal skill such as it is necessary in the later polyphonic Baroque Passions. Nevertheless, our severe critic exonerated the abbé when he recorded that "Monsieur de Saint-Sauveur sang very well during the procession" and also in his reference to the Easter Passion in April 1647 when he found that Monsieur did better with the *Exultet* than in 1646. Moreover, the performance of that particular Easter Passion differed from that of previous years as Father Lalemant reported that he sang the Passion alone since he could not sing the three parts. We do not know the reason for this change, obviously connected to a shortage of singers but a small notice in the annals may perhaps furnish a significant clue; it had been customary to have the Passion performed by three priests, each singing in a distinct manner one of the parts of Christ, Narrator and Crowd. In the earlier performance the part of the *turba* (Synagoga) was sung by René Chartier, the Prior of Notre Dame de la Monaie, France, who had come to Canada in 1643 and who served as chaplain of the Ursulines until 1647. Monsieur le Prieur appears to have been a competent singer and is frequently mentioned in the annals in connection with liturgical music. He also applied himself with pious devotion to the salvation of the Indians but it seems that his spiritual zeal did not leave him indifferent to temporal gain. In the "Journal" of June 1647, we read that 260 pounds of beaver skin had been taken from his room after he had boasted "not to give the skins to the magazin (of the Company) but for a good price". Presumably the mercantile initiative had become a source of embarrassment for the church authorities or perhaps the Superior did not consider commercial interests compatible with ecclesiastical dignity or liturgical music. At any rate, Monsieur le Prieur did not sing at Easter and left for France a short while after.

THE URSULINES

Entrusted with modest beginnings of education in New France, the persevering Jesuits erected in 1635, just one year before the founding of Harvard College, a small building within the confines of Quebec which was to house the seminary for Huron boys and the college for young Frenchmen. The young females of both races were still without the benefit of education, but not for long. The fervour of the Jesuits had already inspired the enthusiasm and pious sentiment of their female patrons in France and from the mother-country were soon to arrive the devoted nuns to begin the arduous toil for the propagation of faith and civilization. The ship that embarked in May 1639 at Dieppe carried a handful of zealous women to the shores of New France. There was Madame de la Peltrie, the foundress of the Ursulines of Quebec, together with their illustrious first Superior, Marie de l'Incarnation; there were two other Ursulines from the convent of Tours, Cécile de Ste. Croix and Marie de St. Bernard. In their company were also three Hospitaller nuns sent to Quebec by their noble benefactress, the Duchess d'Aiguillon, to found the *Hôtel-Dieu* in the colony; and there were the Jesuits Chaumonot and Poncet, together with Father Vimont, the successor to Le Jeune. To the sounds of fifes and drums and to the roar of the cannons, "the saintly group took possession of the post which God had assigned to it on the banks of the St. Lawrence [24]."

Of all the many worthy nuns who came to New France to serve their cause with humility and devotion, only Marie de St. Bernard — Marie de St. Joseph by her religious name — is known to have contributed to our musical history. Born in 1616 as the daughter of a nobleman, she entered the convent at Tours at an early age, intending to break all ties with the outside world and to embrace the life of religion. The monastic annals overflow with praises of her saintly existence and indicate in passing the young novice's obvious musical talent. She received a musi-

cal education including lessons in playing the viol at the Ursulines at Tours and brought both her breviary and her viol to the
New World where, no doubt, her instrument added its mellow
and delicate timbre to the voices that sang the liturgical hymns
at the religious services. But it also served other purposes. From
a letter by Cécile de Ste. Croix, written soon after her arrival in
Quebec, we learn that the viol was an object of irresistible attraction for the Indians: "It is a pleasure to see the Savages, men
and women, gathered around the viol when it is played — they
are enchanted. One of them said that we should teach their
daughters to play the instrument, but we use it only to attract the
Indians to the prayers 25." However, it was not long till Mother
St. Joseph became the first teacher of vocal and instrumental
music: "Mother St. Joseph is the mistress of our young seminarists whom she loves as a mother loves her children. After cat-
echism she teaches them to sing and to play the spiritual hymns
on the viol, and sometimes she makes them dance *à la mode* of
the Indians 26." The viol presumably disappeared in the fire of
1650 which destroyed the Ursuline convent together with all the
belongings of the nuns.

As a teacher, Mother St. Joseph seems to have been very
successful. One of her pupils, a young Huron girl, delighted her
audiences with the display of her talents. Mother Marie de l'Incarnation was obviously very pleased with the progress of this
first child-artist in New France: "The name Agnes suits her very
well, since it is a lamb of sweetness and simplicity ... She has
made great progress amongst us in the knowledge of the mysteries of the faith as in good manners and morals, in handicraft
and reading, as in playing the viol 27." The young viol-virtuoso
astounded not only the nuns but she also contributed her art for
the entertainment of her amazed compatriots who, as Mother
Marie relates had at times been treated not only to wondrous
music but also to "most magnificent meals", consisting of black
prunes, bread, cornmeal and lots of lard "because that is what

they like best". The meals that had been served the Indians differed hardly from the daily food of the nuns themselves but, far from complaining, the Mother Superior is rather pleased to explain that in spite of culinary restrictions she "had never before felt so strong. If in France one would eat nothing but Lard and salted Fish, as we are doing here, one would soon be sick and have no voice at all; but we are all very well and we sing far better than in France [28]."

The Mother Superior did not often have cause for satisfaction; with insufficient means and hardly any support the Ursulines had begun their educational mission. The task was not easy, nor had it been made easy for them but their zeal and devotion had triumphed over hardship and tribulation. In one of her letters Marie de l'Incarnation wrote that in spite of all ordeals and against all persuasive attempts to have them return to the more congenial surroundings of France, "we are still here; God wants us in Canada to help young maiden, whether French or Savage; indeed, the former would be worse than the latter were it not for the Ursulines to educate and to civilize them [29]." With modesty she declines any credit and attributes to the Holy Spirit the pleasing result and the amazing disposition of the Indian girls for singing, something she had never been able to observe in young French maidens. The nuns were delighted with the progress of the young native females who, as the annals recount, "quietly slipped sometimes into the choirstalls, and placing themselves here and there, holding a book in their hands, they behaved like us during the holy offices; they sang *Ave Maris Stella* and the *Gloria Patri,* making the same inclinations which they saw us make; and as they did not know but that hymn by heart, they sang it twenty and thirty times untiringly, imagining that they are praying most pleasingly to God, such innocence is ravishing [30]." However, over the years the Indians became less and less interested in education; their fascination with European music had lost its initial appeal; they preferred the liberty of the wild forest to the blessings of French civilization and the sounds of the drum to the timbre of the viol. Thirty years of experience had taught Mother Marie de l'Incarnation the uselessness of the attempts to civilize the indigenous race; there had been exceptions, such as Agnes, the viol-player who in later years went to teach other Indians the spiritual canticles but, as the Mother Superior admitted in 1668 "scarcely is there one in hundred whom we have frenchified (francisé) 31." At the time when Mother Ste. Hélène of the *Hôtel-Dieu* referred to the Indian as the "mean fellow" on whom the mysteries of the faith made no impression whatsoever, the Ursulines had already deleted from their act of profession the vows that had bound them to the education of young Indian girls.

In the summer of 1640 a Jesuit priest, Father René Ménard, arrived at Quebec. He had been assigned to accompany four nuns (two Ursulines and two Hospitallers) on their journey to Canada and to look after their spiritual needs. One of the Ursulines, Mother Anne de Ste. Claire, relates that Father Ménard's fervent prayers to St. Joseph as well as the regular celebration of the mass "even at the roughest and most troublesome times" prevented shipwreck and other perils. "The good Father said every week a votive mass in his (St. Joseph) honour; he had composed some motets which we sung after Elevation 32." Mother Ste. Claire's letter seems unmistakable evidence of a musically important item; yet, as so often in our chronicle, we face the frustating experience of insufficient information. Little is known of the composer and nothing of his musical work; neither his motets nor other compositions are mentioned anywhere in later references.

Antiphonaries, missals, and other books pertaining to the ritual had been brought to New France in fairly large numbers, as is evident from the many copies still extant in Quebec. Motets, however, and in particular those composed for special occasions, were rare; only a few may still be found singly or in collections in the archives of convents and monasteries. One of these collections is the interesting fascicle of manuscripts preserved at the convent of the Ursulines at Quebec. This ancient *Recueil,* small in format and insignificant in appearance, contains motets and other liturgical music for special occasions, including songs for solo voice and compositions in two to four parts. None of the manuscripts bears indications that could reveal its origin. This is, of course, not unusual since only compositions by well-known composers frequently mention the name as well as the title of the work; such is the case with a motet by Marc-Antoine Charpentier, preserved in manuscript-copy at the *Hôtel-Dieu* at Quebec, or one of Henri Dumont's *Messes Royalles* which, also in manuscript form, is included in an old antiphonary kept in the archives of the *Hôtel-Dieu.* The anonymity may possibly be construed as modesty on the part of an amateur composer or member of a religious order or just simply an unintentional omission, but in either case we are unfortunately deprived of much valuable information.

It is quite possible that the collection had been brought to New France by one of the Ursulines but it seems more probable that the manuscripts originated in Quebec, representing in fact copies of an earlier collection. The uneven writing of text and music differs from the graceful style of French manuscripts and betrays the hand of the amateur. The extant collection may have been compiled after 1650, the year in which the Ursuline convent and all its content, including possible manuscripts of Ménard's motets, had perished in the disastrous fire. The compiler or copyist of the *recueil* is unknown, but it was obviously one of the musically literate nuns whose knowledge of the art enabled her to reconstruct the motets from memory and the most likely pretender to this claim is Mother St. Joseph. In spite of the precarious condition of her health, she continued to be active in the affairs of the community and without doubt occupied herself with the reconstruction of the lost musical material, including motets and other spiritual songs. Her death in April 1652, may have prevented her from completing this task as it is significant that the handwriting of the manuscript collection changes suddenly in the final pages.

Although it cannot be substantiated with documentary evidence, it is suggested that some of Father Ménard's motets are included in the recueil. The motet *O St. Joseph* (folio 115) may well be one of those which, according to Mother Ste. Claire, he had composed as an offering to the Saint during the hazardous voyage. It is also quite logical to assume that after arrival in New France he continued to compose motets and other liturgical music which added to the repertory of the Ursulines and other religious communities in Quebec. Father Vimont, the Superior of the Jesuits, was enchanted with the voices of Indian children singing "a motet together with the nuns (Ursulines) during Elevation and also during Vespers", and he was also highly pleased with the singing of *motets* at Midnight Mass in 1642, all of which could well have been composed by Father René Ménard.

Very little is known of René Ménard's life and nothing has been found relative to his musical activities. Born in Paris in 1605, he joined the Jesuit order in 1624 and arrived in Canada in July 1640. He was missionary at the Hurons and later at the Algonquins. For some years he held the duties as Superior at Trois-Rivières and afterwards spent two years with the Iroquois until he finally disappeared in the forest in the Wisconsin district. He had probably been a fine example of the material of which the ardent and devoted Jesuit missionaries were made — well-trained in his vocation, well versed in the practical knowledge of music and able to exploit the emotional impact of music in the task of conversion. The historian would have enthusiastically seized the opportunity to accord Ménard the place of honour in our chronicle as possibly the first composer of liturgical music on Canadian soil and perhaps in North America, but neither in France's elegant, comfortable and well-organized ecclesiastical circles nor in the poor and modest abode that was the home of the Superior of the Jesuits in Quebec was any attention paid to musical achievement, possibly because musical training had been an all-too common requirement, or perhaps the Superior did not find references to a clerical composer of motets interesting enough to warrant inclusion in his annual report.

Thus, Father Vimont, who had replaced Paul Le Jeune in 1639 and who had welcomed René Ménard as he had stepped ashore in 1640, did neglect to leave us any indication to Ménard's musical talent. The new Superior had, as almost every one of his *confrères,* received his education at the Jesuit *Collège de La Flèche* where music education ranked high in the curriculum of future priests. In addition he spent four years at the *Collège de Clermont* in Paris, an institution renowned for many proud reasons, not the least being the remarkable large scope of musical activities, including secular music. The leading Jesuit Fathers had realized that without music their students would find themselves badly exposed in the world and would lack in good manners — hence secular music entered the venerable halls of the College. Nobody considered music frivolous or sacrilegious and it seems that in later years, at the height of the classical period, the opera had "une succursale chez les bons Pères [33]" — which accentuates the difference in attitudes between Gallican France and ultramontane Quebec.

Father Vimont's knowledge of music must have given him an appreciation of Father Ménard's work just as he appreciated life in the colony. Devoted to God and nature, he enjoyed the pure and uncorrupted spirit in the pious community. "We have no enemies" he wrote, "other than ourselves, the rest does not matter; lawsuits, ambitions, greed, filth and the desire to avenge — all of which are the demons of Europe — do not appear here, our forests are not the place to kindle their fire [34]." Even the weather pleased the enthusiastic priest as he compares

the climate of France ("Vostre froid humide & attachant est im-
portun") to the piquant and rugged Canadian winter which he
finds more serene and "à mon aduis aggréable quoy que
rude 35."

In 1640 he attended the theatrical performance of a morality play. Thirty years earlier, Lescarbot had presented at Port
Royal his *Théâtre de Neptune* and, whereas that first theatrical
representation in New France had in its allegorical and mytholo-
gical character been imbued with the spirit of humanism, the
Quebec production of 1640 was clearly inspired by the spirit of
evangelism. At the occasion of the anniversary of the Dauphin —
the future Louis XIV — the devout governor Montmagny had a
tragicomedy performed in which the soul of an unbeliever is
pursued by two demons who converse in the Algonquin language. Appropriate fireworks, depicting the horrors of hell, accompanied the action. Neither title nor author of the play is
known, but the principal actor seems to have been the governor's secretary, Martial Piraubé. Father Vimont wrote, "I would
never have believed that so handsome apparel and so good actors could be found in Quebec", and he is quite certain that a
great fear of hell will befall the Indians, so that as a result of this
splendid cultural effort "these poor people will come day by day
to give themselves to Jesus Christ 36."

The Superior did not elaborate further his impressions of
the play; he did not tell us whether spine-shaking blasts from
trumpets or other ear-splitting musical sound accompanied the
awe-inspiring presentation of a fiery and thunderous hell. Primitive and naive as the Quebec production may have been, it was
a characteristic example of the contribution which the Jesuits
had made in the early phases of the Baroque towards the fine
arts, architecture, music and drama. The dramatic emotional
impact of the mystery play served a complex and multiple purpose but foremost aimed at the emotional seduction of the
individual within the context of a missionary persuasion. In its

usual presentation, the three important units — dramatic action, stage setting and stirring music — reinforced the design and purpose and it is therefore justified to presume that Jesuit ingenuity encouraged the presence of some type of musical participation at that poignant and rare example of Baroque church art at Quebec.

Two years after the first theatrical performance in Quebec, the Superior attended another inauguration of far greater importance, the foundation of Montreal. The historical aspects, the religious motives and mystical revelations that surrounded the establishment of the new settlement are well described in the annals of early Canada. It may suffice to note that in May 1642, to the solemn intonation of the *Veni Creator* and the *Te Deum* Paul de Chomedy, Sieur de Maisonneuve, took formal possession of Montreal Island in the presence of forty soldiers, artisans and labourers as well as four courageous women. Whether it was unconcern for historical documentation or just simply lack of a chronicler sufficiently interested in musical or cultural matters, signs indicating any musical activity for the next few years are almost entirely missing from our historical accounts; presumably the artistic life in what was to become Canada's largest city was at that time uneventful. To be sure, there were the sacred chants of the Mass, there were the liturgical hymns, but our annals only rarely mention such matters as secular music or song and dance. Nonetheless, there had also been, as early as August 1642, the first great festival. The arrival of ships bearing settlers, provisions and munitions was celebrated with great pomp, including the "thunder of the cannons which caused the whole Island to re-echo"; and it may safely be assumed that there had been song and dance to the accompaniment of the customary instruments of the time.

While thus the early musical history of Montreal is somewhat obscure, there appear in later years recorded in our annals a few episodes of musical significance, concerned as usual with church music. A remarkable example of true interest in the furtherance of the cause of music is seen in the activities of the Abbé François Vachon de Belmont. Born at Grenoble, France, in 1645, Belmont came to Canada in 1680, became priest a few years later, and was assigned to the mission *de la Montagne,* in Montreal. He apparently possessed a large fortune, a great part of which he contributed to the completion of the parish church. After 1700 he replaced Dollier de Casson as Superior of the Séminaire de Saint-Sulpice, a position which he held until his death in 1732. Of particular interest is his correspondence with Monsieur Tronson, the Provincial of the Sulpicians in Paris [37]. Belmont not only translated the latin text of the ritual into the native language but he also accompanied the chants on his lute. Yet it seems that the conscience of the righteous priest was greatly disturbed by moral qualms about the propriety of such an act, the more as the sound of the lute seems to re-awaken "sinful" sentiments of bygone and younger days. In reply to his doubts and anguish Monsieur Tronson, however, is certain that no difficulties will arise out of his playing the lute "... which providence made you find in Montreal", as long as he will not use the lute as "... an instrument to excite passions but to invite and to lead to devotion [38]." Elsewhere the Provincial assures Belmont that his "temptation will cause no harm if he plays the lute in church [39]." And thus Belmont, who was also the author of various books, including a history of Montreal, continued to teach the chants to the natives in their language and to accompany their singing on the lute while waiting for an organ which he had ordered from Paris.

IV

The Chronicles of Music

JESUIT RELATIONS AND *LE JOURNAL*

To reconstruct a picture faintly resembling musical life in Quebec and Montreal is in the absence of documented facts an almost impossible task and any attempt to penetrate the obscurity must rely on assumption, supposition and conjecture. Yet much of the history of New France is recorded in the *Jesuit Relations* [1], the widely accepted, indispensable written source, praised by historians from Charlevoix to Parkman as highly authentic and trustworthy documents. Thus, beginning with Le Jeune, the Jesuit superiors became the chroniclers and the *Jesuit Relations* the chronicle of New France. Primarily the annual reports from the Superior of the mission to the Provincial in France, the *Relations* recorded the important events in the colony, described the country, its flora and fauna, related the story of the Indian and of his conversion and extolled the life and work of the Jesuits. These absorbing documents were intended for a class of readers devoted to the success of the apostolic mission; they included the events and features capable of animating the intensity of religious zeal and the devotion to piety.

What had begun as a simple diary of Father Le Jeune describing his voyage and arrival in New France became one of the most important documents of our early history, although they are neither a comprehensive nor indeed the only existing

record of our past. In referring to the French population and
their daily occupation, Father Le Jeune admitted that he did not
intend to describe in detail "all that takes place in this country
but only that which concerns the welfare of the faith and of Religion ."

It is also well to remember that these fascinating narratives of early Canadian life were edited with the intention of at-
tracting money and recruits for the mission and it is therefore
understandable that in a process of judicious editing a great deal
of information of importance to the chronicle of music regarding
the social life and its entertainment might well have been considered unimportant and even injurious to the intended purpose
and desired effect and, even if mentioned by the superior, may
have been deleted by the editor. In fairness to the editors, however, it should also be considered that high cost of printing may
have prompted deletion of such items which in their opinion
were of local interest only and not contributing to the intended
purpose.

Among the omitted items of minor importance were not
only the daily events in the lives of the French people but also
some accounts of the charitable work and educational efforts of
the Ursulines. The good Sisters were not all pleased with the
treatment their reports received in the workroom of Cramoisy,
the well-known librarian and printer of Paris, or perhaps in the
chamber of the Provincial of the Jesuits. "The Mothers wrote
every year their memories, of which one might still find some
precious remnants in some of the Relations", comments the annalist of the Ursulines, "but after Monsieur Cramoisy had received these writings he omitted very often the most beautiful
pages 3." Mother Marie de l'Incarnation regretted that the educational work of the Ursulines was not given sufficient publicity,
an oversight which had not escaped the attention of her noble
patrons in Paris. However, in a curious letter to Father Vimont,
she begs the Superior not to mention any more the Ursulines:

"Suffice it that God knows with what love we serve our neo-phyte. It is enough that He alone knows what happens in this small house of ours without it being brought before the eyes of men 4."

The reference to the annual memoirs of which only "precious remnants" exists creates the suspicion that information of interest to the cultural chronicle of New France may have been withheld from publication. Could it not be that the "most beautiful pages" might indeed have contained details of musical or artistic activities not only in Quebec but also within the convent? The case of Mother St. Joseph is a good example; surely her musical activities and particularly her educational efforts must have been more substantial than the single reference in the annals might lead us to believe. Granted that personal modesty and the strict rules of the religious community did not permit to elaborate on her musical ability, nevertheless there must have been many occasions at which the viol-playing nun may have contributed her musical talent, occasions that called for ex-pressions of devotional and at times perhaps also semi-secular music.

The Superior of the Jesuits began in the autumn of 1645 to record the small incidents of daily life in Quebec as well as the minor affairs of the religious community in the *Journal des PP. Jésuites,* the title under which the printed version has become known 5. As the title indicates, it was the private diary of the Jesuits, not meant for the public and indeed not published until 1871. The valuable information recorded in its pages by the Superiors has greatly furthered historical research and the considerable amount of intimate details "had been useful not only to the members of the Jesuit Order but also to all those who, centuries later, wanted to study the beginning of our history 6." The published volume contains the events of the early years and extends — with one regrettable hiatus of nearly three years (February 1654 to October 1656) — over a period of twenty five years, from 1645 to 1670. It is known, however, that the Superiors continued to record the important or domestic happenings at Quebec from 1670 to 1755, yet no trace of these later historical accounts has been found. The chronicle of music would undoubtedly have been enriched by the references to music and musical life which the Superiors infrequently included in their diary.

Thus the *Journal* offers, as its editors remarked, as much useful information for the student of Canadian history as it had provided valuable advice for the Jesuits themselves. Much space is devoted to music at religious ceremonies; non-secular musical activities are described in a fairly detailed and informative manner. Liturgical songs are listed together and in their proper sequence at the service; irregularities are noted and criticism alternates with praise. The content of the references varies in extent and quality according to the degree of musical knowledge, background and interest which the individual Superior brought to his task or the importance which he attached to music, its place in the ritual and the manner of its performance. As a rule, the Superior was more concerned with the selection of the music rather than the mode of performance and although he carefully enumerated the titles of the liturgical songs he was neither eloquent nor reliable in his treatment of the purely musical aspects. Thus while he recorded *what* was sung, he did not elaborate on *how* or *by whom* the music was performed. His knowledge of the musical terminology of his time was adequate and he was aware of the customary tradition in liturgical music as well as of the stylistic peculiarities of the period, but some of the expressions and explanations leave a wide margin for interpretation.

However, it was not neglect on the part of the clerical annalist nor his fragmentary manner of recording which often defies attempts at interpretation. A great deal of the difficulty is caused by the ambiguity of 17th-century musical nomenclature, by a highly confusing terminology lacking the clear distinction between vocal and instrumental style, or between polyphonic and monophonic texture and by linguistic peculiarities arising out of the multiple meaning of certain words. The complexity of the problem soon becomes apparent in the maze of conflicting statements and assumptions presented to the reader of contemporary records.

Nevertheless, without the *Journal* our musical chronicle would have remained barren and meaningless. In spite of short-comings and regrettable omissions, no matter how sparse the information and how limited its scope, the *Journal* represents the first documentary source of importance for the musical history of New France, albeit that almost all of the cited references are related to *ars sacra,* to liturgical music. If secular art music is not mentioned in the *Journal* it is probably to some extent a testimony to the scarcity of serious music in Quebec. It seems inconceivable that the learned Superiors, the elite of Jesuit erudition, would have by-passed significant manifestations of cultural development. There are a few entries concerning mundane entertainment but at none of these occasions does the annalist reveal the function, scope and nature of the music accompanying the described event.

Father Jérôme Lalemant was on his way to Quebec from the Huron county where he had been active since 1638. Passing through Trois-Rivières on September 16, 1645, he learnt of his appointment as Superior of the Jesuits, an office which he held from 1645 to 1650 and again from 1659 to 1665. Born in Paris in 1593, he studied at the renowned *Collège de Clermont,* became teacher of philosophy and sciences, then minister and finally spiritual adviser at the same institution, was then appointed rector at the *Collège de La Flèche* and is considered and esteemed as one of the outstanding clerical figures in the religious and political history of New France. After his arrival at Quebec he recorded his impressions of the state of affairs in the colony (*Es-*

tat dv Pays) — and thus began the *Journal,* the Diary of the Jesuits.

In the first entry of musical interest Father Lalemant informs us that on November 27, 1645, at a wedding two violins appeared for the first time [7]. It had been the wedding of Elisabeth Couillard, grand-daughter of Louis Hébert, to Jean Guyon du Buisson who, as pupil of Martin Boutet, became the first Canadian-trained surveyor. Monsieur Boutet played one of the two violins, but nothing is known of the second player.

Some ambiguity exists with regard to musical terminology and not a small measure of it is due to the fact that the Superior's account of the event allows for varying interpretation. It is, of course, within the realm of possibility that Father Lalemant may indeed have recorded the first appearance of violins in the colony, and it seems also possible to construe his reference as indication of instrumental accompaniment at the religious service. Yet the 17th century was the classical period of the viols, particularly in England but also in France where as late as the turn of the century French musicians added a small viol, the *pardessus de viole,* to the existing types of treble (*dessus de viole*), tenor (*taille de viole*), and bass (*basse de viole*), and although the violins were making inroads into the instrumental territory of the viols, it was not until the 18th century that the modern violin became the undisputed leader in the field of string instruments. The traditionally conservative rural areas such as those from where our early settlers came were slow in accepting the new instruments and its new style of playing, its new technical requirements of bowing and four-stringed fingering. While we do not know the exact meaning of Father Lalemant's brief reference it is probably that the two instruments mentioned were of the older and common viol type and not the modern violins. The suggestion that M. Boutet played the viol rather than the violin is supported by further evidence of viols at Quebec, such as at the

Midnight Mass of 1648 and the "concert of the four viols" of a later date.

However, one month after the first wedding celebration Martin Boutet played again his violin at the Christmas celebration of 1645. The ceremony at Midnight Mass is recorded in detail in the *Journal*. The hymn *Venez mon Dieu* and the carol *Chantons Noel* were sung, Monsieur de la Ferté performed the bass part and St. Martin (Martin Boutet) played the *violin*; there was also a German flute which "... was not in tune when it came to church 8."

The entry in the Journal of December 25, 1645, describing this service is another example of linguistic peculiarities and ambiguous musical terminology 9. The Superior had noted that Monsieur de la Ferté *faisait la basse,* a vague description which renders difficult an analysis of the musical activity involved. It has already been noted that 17th-century terminology does not always clearly distinguish between vocal and instrumental music and we cannot be certain whether M. de la Ferté played an instrument or sang. The possibility that he sang the bass part is supported by a similar instance concerning M. le Prieur, René Chartier, whose singing of a part in the Passion had been described by the word *faisoit.* Moreover, had M. de la Ferté *played* a stringed instrument, such as the bass viol or the theorbe, the Superior might well have described his contribution with the same term he applied in the case of Martin Boutet, namely *ioüoit.*

On the other hand, it seems unlikely that M. de la Ferté, the vocalist, should be honoured with a special mention in the *Journal,* unless such honour was due to his high rank in the social strata of Quebec, while the other singers at the Midnight Mass should remain anonymous. There seems little justification to amplify the subordinate role of the bass part at the expense of the other voices. It is therefore possible to consider *faisoit la basse* as a colloquial phrase, indicating the *playing* of a bass-in-

strument. Father Lalemant, being unconcerned with the importance of his entry to our musical studies, did not pay much attention to the exactitude of his words but his vague description
tempts us to conjure up the picture of the first instrumental trio
in New France, with St. Martin playing the viol, de la Ferté on
the bass-viol or theorbe and for the first time also a player on
the *fluste d'Alemagne.*

Father Lalemant considered his task fulfilled when he
informed us of the German flute that had been out of tune. But
why did he omit to mention the player? Perhaps the customary
social distinction played a part in the Superior's neglect. The unknown flute player may not have been on the same social level
as either M. de la Ferté or M. St. Martin, nor was he a fellow-
priest, although some missionaries are known to have played the
flute. He may have been a tradesman or labourer or more likely,
a soldier, the fifer of the small garrison stationed at Quebec 10.

The Superior's critical remark concerning the faulty intonation of the flute was probably entirely justified, if a little un-
kind in view of aggravating circumstances. Climatic conditions
must have played havoc with the instrument; the wooden flute
was not designed to withstand the sudden change in temperature
from the cold winter's night of Quebec to the warm air in the
heated warehouse of the Trading Company that had served as
temporary chapel for the Midnight Mass of 1645 11.

PIONEERS OF MUSIC

In the annals of our past may be found a certain amount
of biographical information relating to some of the men who
were connected with the small musical world of Quebec, unfortunately the available information is not about their musical activities, but concerns mainly other aspects of their lives. We have
to be content with at best a few superficial remarks as in most
instances a lack of interest in music curtails our knowledge about

the priest-musician as well as the secular amateur who contributed to the musical beginning of Canada.

Monsieur de la Ferté and Monsieur Martin Boutet are no exception to this treatment. We know when Jean Jucherau de la Ferté was born, when he arrived in Canada and we have the record of his marriage to Marie Giffard. We are told that he played a distinguished part in the trade, magistrature and society of the colony but neither the ancient annals nor recent biographies mention his musical contribution. Had it not been for the brief reference in the *Journal,* the musical talent of M. de la Ferté would have escaped the attention of the historian and would have shared the fate of musical oblivion which undoubtedly befell many pioneer musicians of New France.

Martin Boutet has been described as "fosterer of Church music, and eminent teacher of navigation [12]." It has also been stated that while "mentally a mathematician, Saint-Martin was, emotionally, a musician [13]." But Martin Boutet de Saint-Martin was more than that, being one of the few pioneers of culture, a true builder of the colony and a devoted teacher of her youth. He had come to New France with his wife and two daughters in 1645, was an experienced musician, a capable player of the viol and a competent singer. As an active member of the parish choir, he was soon entrusted with the training and direction of the choir and seems also to have been one of the principal singers. His important contribution, however, was in the field of music education. To fill the constant need for choir boys (there were eight boys in 1650), the church council accepted the obligation to look after their training and upkeep at the Jesuit college. "This year," reports the Superior, "we have begun a seminary where the children are boarded in the care of an honest man, where they learn to read and write, and are being taught the plain-chant with the fear of God — without this our French would become Savages and have less instruction than the Savages themselves [14]."

Martin Boutet, the honest man, signed a contract with the church council to educate and to instruct the children and to conduct the choir in the first choir school of Canada. For his duties he was paid a yearly salary of 120 livres. Thus he had become the first layteacher to instruct in the elements of liturgical music, a field usually left to the clergy, and a further proof of the confidence which the prudent Jesuits had placed in his musical ability and moral integrity. Moreover, he had been the first secular teacher of academic subjects to maintain a position of influence within the highly intellectual atmosphere of the Jesuit society. The priests obviously appreciated Martin Boutet and his work. He was a frequent guest at the collation given to musicians and notables and a recipient of New Year's presents, as for example on New Year's Day of 1647 when the Superior presented him with a wax-candle, a knife with a silver handle and Loyola's *Spiritual Exercises.* In later years he became *clerc* of the Church Council, looked after the renting of church pews, and seems to have continued to play his string instrument at the devotional services and possibly at the occasional secular entertainment also. And he was to be further honoured by the Jesuits. After his youngest daughter had entered the Ursuline convent in 1660, he placed himself entirely at their disposal and was employed by them at their college. He became professor of mathematics, taught surveying and navigation and was urged by Jean Talon to extend his tutorial activities to all young Frenchmen willing to be trained as pilots. This was indeed an important and vital assignment which Boutet fulfilled to the highest satisfaction.

Martin Boutet had not been a professional nor a highly trained musician, yet his knowledge of musical matters was more than adequate for the educational work he undertook at Quebec, namely teaching the rudiments of music, the principles of plainchant and possibly the playing of the viol. Moreover, as the only music teacher in Quebec at the time, it might well be assumed that his duties included the instruction of young students in organ-playing. Greatly interested in the development of his choir, he even donated the generous sum of sixty *livres* for the purchase of liturgical choir-books. Among his pupils were the four *musiciens ordinaires* or *les quatre officiers de musique,* as the *Journal* called them. Two of these music students became famous, each in his own way: Louis Jolliet was one of the earliest organists in Canada though his fame rests upon his explorations and discoveries. The other, lesser known, though of importance to our chronicle of music, is Charles-Amador Martin, whom we shall meet later in connection with the Fraternity and Congregation of the Holy Family. Regrettably, the few extant details of Boutet's contribution to music in the colony do not allow us to form a comprehensive picture of his work but they do show the pioneer spirit with which this standard bearer of French civilization enriched the cultural life in New France.

NOTES FROM THE DIARY

The Christmas festivities of 1645 were only the beginning of the development of religious music to be recorded in the *Journal.* The Superior was, of course, primarily concerned with the spiritual welfare and not with the mundane amusement of the growing community. As the colony developed, the arrival of musically trained priests and the addition of capable lay-singers contributed greatly to the expansion of sacred music in Quebec. Even the benevolent hand of Providence miraculously guided the progress of music: to the aid of the divine art came a Huguenot soldier who, "having abjured his heresy and knowing music", made possible the singing of sacred liturgy in four parts. Monsieur de Champigny, the Huguenot soldier from Fontainebleau, changed from Calvinism to Catholicism (or as we might say from heresy to harmony), and the brief reference in December 1646 ("we began on the day of St. Thomas to sing in four parts") represents the proverbial milestone in the musical chronicle of New France [15].

The event may indeed be looked upon as an important milestone; yet already a few months before that memorable date the *Journal,* in a fairly detailed description, referred to the increased number of musical participants at the procession of the Holy Sacrament. We read that the torch-bearers were followed by four anonymous lay-singers, after whom came Monsieur St. Sauveur who, as the Superior remarked, "excellently sustained the music". There were also "four French angels and two little Indians in their native costume". Two of the children were supposed to sing some parts of the litany, which seems not to have been successful since "M. le Prieur had to come to their rescue". Nonetheless, the Superior was pleased with the proceedings: "all went well" also in the convents, except that the nuns sang instead of the children. The four lay-singers sang the litany in unison; their vocal skill was sufficient for the prescribed chants of the procession even though their knowledge of music and notation may not always have been adequate for the musical requirements of the ritual nor the intricacies of polyphonic music. It needed more competent singers, such as Monsieur de Champigny, whose knowledge of music and good tenor voice enriched not only the liturgical services but also brought a small touch of European musical culture to the weak state of music in Quebec.

In spite of the welcome notice in the *Journal,* our curiosity is far from satisfied and it remains impossible to penetrate further into that significant episode in our musical history. We do not know the compositions that had been performed on St. Thomas' Day in 1646, neither the composer nor the performers. It might well have been certain sections of the Ordinary set in polyphonic texture, or possibly some hymns or motets in four-part harmony for the celebration of the Holy Offices. The Superior failed to leave us a more detailed record and he also forgot to mention the singers who, together with M. de Champigny, formed the first vocal quartet of liturgical music.

One of them may have been Father Vimont who was still at Quebec in 1646. His musical and ecclesiastical background parallels that of his successor as Superior, Father Lalemant. Both of these priests were no doubt well acquainted with musical matters and liturgical singing — their training at the Jesuit *Collège de Clermont* corroborates this assumption and Father Lalemant's musical knowledge, vocal ability and critical faculty had already been noted on earlier occasions. Other members of the first vocal ensemble in Quebec included unquestionably Monsieur St. Sauveur to whom frequent reference is made in the *Journal*, as well as Martin Boutet, the "secular singer" (*vn chantre seculier*) who later became the principal singer of the congregation. The list of church-singers should include M. le Prieur, René Chartier, whose mercantile interest and enterprise had not yet precipitated his return to France and it is also feasible that M. de la Ferté's bass voice may have joined in the singing of sacred polyphonic music at the end of 1646.

A few months later, in June 1647, the Superior proudly reported the beginning of the liturgical services in the prescribed order of the service and the singing of High Mass on all Sundays and Feast-days. "We felt strong enough to do so", he wrote in his diary and he considered it necessary to explain that only parts of the Mass had been sung until then, namely the *Veni Creator,* the *Gloria,* the *Credo* and *Salutaris Hostia,* which, not being the regular procedure, must have been somewhat shocking to those who arrived from the mother-country expecting to find at least somewhere in New France "vne messe de Paroisse [16]." Hence, it had taken forty years after the founding of Quebec for religious services to be performed in the normal manner of the Ordinary of the Mass, as in the parish churches of France.

The efforts of the musicians who had made this development possible were well received and greatly appreciated. It became customary to reward their musical service with a good meal and a glass of good French wine ! Such splendid hospitality was offered to the musicians at the residence of the Jesuits and at times also at other religious communities 17. On New Year's Day the singers were honoured with more magnificent gifts; Monsieur St. Sauveur was given a spiritual book and a small pocket-knife. Monsieur le Prieur earned a wax-candle, as did Monsieur Nicolet, a secular priest and singer, while a collection of splendid gifts, mentioned earlier, was handed to our fine musician-singer, Monsieur Martin Boutet.

The Superior was pleased with the progress of the choir and he invited the Governor to a concert of devotional music. As usual, we do not know the programme or the artistic merits of this first concert of spiritual music which took place at Vespers on St. Michael's Day in May 1648 in the mission house at Sillery, but we are told of a collation that was given "to the Governor and most honorable gentlemen in the refectory, to the musicians in the small hall, to the sailors in the woodwork room, and to the other soldiers in the big hall; all went well 18." It seems likely that this earliest *"concert spirituel"* was a purely vocal and *a cappella* performance, though it is possible that some instruments, such as theorbes, viols, flutes, etc., may have accompanied the liturgical motets or even ventured into some secular music of the time. At any rate, the Superior was pleased and "all went well" — the dinner, the performance of the music, and the safe arrival and return of the Governor and his entourage of "honnestes gens". Presumably there were more soldiers than sailors (the latter dined in the small woodwork shop, while the former had been served their meal in the great hall) as more soldiers were needed on any such excursion in view of the increasing number of raids by the Iroquois who had embarked on their determined and devastating warfare against the French.

Such are the regrettable omissions of the ecclesiastical chroniclers which make it impossible to present an accurate as well as informative account of this first concert of devotional music or other aspects of musical life in the colony. The annalist recorded the arrival of the first horse but did not tell us when the first organ came nor where it had been installed; we know the date when the first local beer was brewed but know little about the musicians who regaled themselves with the local brew and afterwards "could not sing any more". We are aware of the drummer who, having been convicted of *crimini pessimo*, escaped the gallows to become the first executioner in New France; we know of his first victim, but nothing of his musical exploits [19]. A brief item in the *Journal* informs us that M. de St. Sauveur caught the first salmon of the season in May 1648 — we would have liked also to read about his musical and educational achievement.

None of the Superiors elaborated on musical events; their references had been succinct and more frequently in form of criticism rather than explanatory narratives. While some of this criticism concerned purely musical matters, most of it involved music and musicians in the errors and omissions to the prescribed procedures of the ritual. Many errors, for example, had been committed at one Easter procession; the Superior found faults with the Bishop who intoned the *Pange Lingua* while still kneeling at the lowest step to the altar instead of ascending to the highest before beginning the chant [20], and he blamed Father Dablon for having badly conducted the services on Good Friday; it seems that the good Father had not been properly prepared nor had he prepared the others. Moreover, "Father Dablon is not capable to sing alone the *Exultet* [21]." At another Easter ceremony the *Exultet* was not sung at all because Father Dablon did not have a pleasant voice [22] Yet Father Dablon, one of the outstanding priests who had come to New France and who had been particularly important in his capacity as Superior-General of the Jesuit Mission in the colony, seems to have been a fine musician and learned music-lover [23]. Nonetheless, his "unpleasant voice" was not the only objectionable item at the Easter service; the Superior attributed to the two officiating priests a serious confusion at the litanies; "one said St. Peter, the other St. Paul, and the responding brethren did not know whom to answer 24." And there had been many grave faults at the ceremony of washing the feet on Maundy Thursday — *"multa ibi peccata"*, wrote our critical chronicler as he regretted greatly the omission of the music from the ceremony because "one had not anticipated to prepare what one was to sing 25."

One of the obstacles preventing a clearer interpretation of the performance of liturgical music had been the difficulty of determining the true meaning in some of the expressions used to record musical events. The entry in the *Journal* of December 1648 is an example of the variety of more or less confusing expressions and it may be useful to try to elucidate this a little. The Superior had recorded that: "The Midnight Mass was preceded by Matins, which were being said for the first time ... The bell rang one quarter before, and we finished one quarter before Midnight. In this quarter a short sermon was given, which, happening by accident, should be made a matter of design. We sang the third songs of the Nocturnes in *faux-bourdon* and the responsaries to the last Nocturne in harmony: at the elevation, there was music with viols, and during the communion ... 26" In this and other similar instances of *faux-bourdon,* the manner of singing has not been disclosed, but, as the term had become associated simply with singing in multiple parts, it may well be assumed that, aided by the increased number of capable singers, the phrase *chanté en faux-bourdon* merely indicated the singing in four-part harmony.

By far more difficult is the interpretation of *en musique,* the approximate definition of which is often obscured by conflicting and sometimes contradictory evidence. *Faux-bourdon* existed for centuries as a distinct technical device; *en musique,* however, is neither a stylistic element nor a historical designation and, while the term does not denote a distinct and charac-

teristic feature, it seems to imply a certain manner of performance, variable in scope and found exclusively in French musical
nomenclature.

The juxtaposition with *faux-bourdon* leads to the assumption that *en musique* referred to polyphonic singing by the choir,
occasionally supported by instrumental accompaniment. The
Christmas entry in the *Journal* of 1648 may thus be interpreted
as the singing of the psalms at Nocturnes by four solo-voices in
chordal style (*faux-bourdon*), the performance of the Respon-
sorial in the traditional manner by soloist and responding choir
(*en musique*), while at Elevation and Communion some motets
had been sung to the accompaniment − or rather the duplication
of voice parts − by the viols. This interpretation is also confirmed by the distinctive phraseology of the Superior with regard
to *chanté* and *chanté en plain-chant* both indicating the monophonic texture of Gregorian melodies as opposed to the somewhat pleonastic *chanté en musique,* denoting polyphonic singing
in *a cappella* style.

It is possible to get entangled in seemingly ambiguous
references; the Superior at one time referred to High Mass that
had been *sung* to music ("on *chanta* la messe *en musique*") while
Vespers on the same day had been *said* to music ("on *dit* vespres
en musique") 27. Yet Midnight Mass had been said and sung to
music, "which was worth nothing", wrote the annalist, because
"they forgot to sing the *Te Deum* at the beginning 28." Not less
equivocal is the term *en musique* in the context of the Christmas
celebration quoted earlier, where *chanté en faux-bourdon* and
chanté en musique represent two musical aspects, with *musique
avec violes* being in contrast with both of them. References to
chanté and *chanté en musique* appear quite often in the *Journal*
and, while the former is more frequent in the early years, *en musique* is found regularly in the second half of the 17th century,
coinciding with the extended use of polyphonic singing, but also
with the appearance of instrumental accompaniment, including

the organ, all of which called for the adoption of distinctive terminology with which to avoid coincidence and confusion. In the
following entry the Superior carefully distinguishes between
monophonic *chanté* and polyphonic *en musique*: "... the choir
[*en musique*] began with the *Pange Lingua* immediately after
which the nuns [Ursulines] sang a short motet of the Holy Sacrament, then the choir [*en musique*] recommenced with the *Iste
Confessor,* immediately after which the nuns sang a motet of the
Saint, after which the choir took it up again with the *Domine
Salvum fac regem* ... 29" It is interesting to note that almost all
references to *en musique* relate to religious services in either the
Jesuit Chapel or the Parish Church. In both of these places of
worship the "officiers de musique" and choir boys, lay-singers
and "musiciens ordinaires" enriched the religious ceremonies
through their musical contribution as in addition to the celebration of the ritual in their own chapel, the Jesuits also looked after the devotional functions in the Parish Church, including the
musical requirements of the ritual. On the other hand, neither
Hospitallers nor Ursulines availed themselves often of lay-singers or instrumentalists, except on certain feast-days, perhaps because of monastic rules and a reluctance to disturb the cloistered
atmosphere or perhaps because of the scarcity of musicians.
Some musicians, however, must have performed on St. Ignace's
Day of 1647 at the Hospitallers as they were rewarded with a
collation after the service. In the following year the same ceremony took place at the Ursulines "except that because of lack of
musicians ... the nuns sang vespers alone 30."

The interpretation of *en musique* as singing in multiple
parts is confirmed by further entries in the *Journal* which clearly
imply polyphonic choral singing at certain rituals. Such may
have been the case at the Ursulines where we encountered the
earliest reference to *en musique* in March 1647 31; in a few and
casual words the Superior informs us that on St. Joseph's Day
the *Hic vir despiciens* was *chanté en musique* by the nuns, pre-

sumably accompanied by Mother St. Joseph on the viol. The reference to *musique auec viols* is the earliest evidence of instrumental participation in the liturgy and similar conclusive attestation is provided by such description in the *Journal* as "en musique & avec les instruments".

It is significant that the Superiors did record in their diary events of cultural value such as the early theatrical performances and in consequence it might be argued that musical manifestations of artistic value would have been noted by the educated priests had such activities occured in Quebec. Be that as it may, just as the beginning of polyphonic singing marked an important step forward in the development of music in New France, of similar significance was the introduction of the Corneillian classic drama to Quebec, and on the last day of the year 1646 the warehouse of the Trading Company became the stage for the first presentation in Canada of "Le Cid", only ten years after its premiere in Paris [32].

The first performance in Quebec of the great French drama antedated by many years similar theatrical representations in North America and even in many provincial towns of France, far larger than the Quebec of 1646. Another of Corneille's dramas, "Heraclius", was performed at Quebec in 1651, only four years after its presentation at the Hôtel Bourgogne in Paris and in the ensuing years more theatrical representations of the classical French repertory enriched the cultural atmosphere of the colony. Even if the quality of the acting, the *mise-en-scène* and the stage-setting might not have satisfied the connoisseurs of the French theatre, the courageous attempts demand our admiration; the spoken word, conveying the meaning, action and language of the play, brought a small reflection of French civilization to a land "which not long ago one called barbaric [33]."

We have no indication who the actors were who performed the masterworks of the French theatrical tradition. Martial Piraubé, secretary to the Governor, had already been mentioned as principal actor in the morality play that had been performed six years earlier. The performance of "Le Cid" had been encouraged by the Governor Montmagny and it is therefore quite acceptable that Martial Piraubé again took the leading rôle, together with other gentlemen of the Governor's entourage. A few years later even the seminarists of Quebec joined in the theatrical activities and spiritual plays and allegories were performed by young native talent in the college and seminary. In fact, after ecclesiastical opposition had greatly curtailed theatrical activities – particularly as a consequence of the incident of the intended performance of "Tartuffe" in the 1690's – it was left to the young and energetic spirit of the collegians to perpetuate the taste for the dramatic muse as an instrument of culture and a means to maintain the prestige and purity of the language [34].

Thus theatrical life, while not even faintly approaching the sophisticated glamour of the mother-country, surpassed its musical counterpart numerically and by the artistic quality of the plays performed. It was easier for the students of the seminary, the officers of the garrison and the officials of the governor's circle to perform the rôles of the classical plays – the recited word needing less special skill than the proficiency of the trained singer and musician. The grandiose and spectacular musical creations of the *grand siècle* did not, it seems, reach the colony; New France never heard an opera or saw a ballet by Lully or Rameau; and while French drama and French comedy became the entertainment, albeit sporadic, of the *petite noblesse* at the Château St. Louis, it was not until the last quarter of the 18th century that Quebec could enjoy symphonic music, and not until the middle of the 19th century that travelling opera companies visited Quebec and Montreal.

The quasi-monastic atmosphere of Quebec was not always favourable for the display of secular amusement and the few manifestations of popular entertainment are often mentioned with disparaging reserve and reproachful disdain. Yet the clerical annalist could not ignore the increasing demand of the people to enliven their drab existence with enjoyable *divertissement.* He recorded with reluctance the joyous celebrations at the wedding of Montpellier, the soldat and shoemaker, when five of the groom's comrade-in-arms "danced a sort of ballet", and all delighted in music and dance that followed in the wake of the ceremony [35]. He was not pleased with the lively entertainment which certainly accompanied the lighting of the bonfire on the eve of St. Joseph's Day. On one of these occasions, he admitted that he had lit the fire but merely in deference to the Governor's request, and with much of repugnance ; at another time he accepted the inevitable pagan ceremony after he had been assured that "the material will be separated from the spiritual". And on St. Joseph's Day of 1647 "no fire was lit on the eve as had been the custom: I was part of the reason", the Superior admits, "since I have no taste for a ceremony which is not accompanied by a devotion. [36]"

The Superior had even less taste for the "ballet" which had been danced on February 27, 1647 — one week before Ash Wednesday. His moral qualms, motivated by religious sentiment, had been shared by all members of the clergy; thus, as he recorded in the diary, "not one of our Father or Brothers attended, nor the Sisters of the Hospital or the Ursulines, except the little Marsolet [37]." Who was the "little Marsolet"; why did the Superior consider her important enough to be inscribed in the annals of New France? She had been *pensionnaire* (boarder) at the Ursulines, and it may be presumed that, unable to resist the lure of the all-too-rare mundane pleasure, the young girl went to see or take part in the fascinating entertainment in defiance of the nuns' interdiction. We do not know of any punitive measures against her, neither have we any references to the nature of the ballet.

But the Carnival spirit had reached Quebec and in spite of hardship, winter and inferior conditions there were the exhilarating activities which traditionally accompany the seasons of merry-making; there was dance, and therefore music played on instruments.

V

Episcopal Interlude

LAVAL AND MUSIC

By the middle of the 17th century the English settlement along the Eastern seaboard had consolidated into successfully established colonies. Already by 1640 the number of English settlers had increased to about 40,000; the political and economical conditions had grown favourable and, except for the Puritan domains of New England, art and music were encouraged. In contrast, at the half-way mark of the 17th century, New France was in a state of terror. The frenzied fury of the increasing attacks by the Iroquois had brought despair, misery and death to the afflicted colonists; the guns and tomahawks of the ferocious warriors had all but exterminated the docile Hurons and thereby thwarted the hopes of the fervent missionaries. History books recount the gruesome stories, and even the occasional reference to music may be found among the tales of horror and cruelty.

In addition to the perils that plagued the harassed French from without, there was unrest and domestic quarrels among the settlers, frequent discord between the authorities and the clergy, and jealousy between the rival traders; there was hardship and poverty and hardly any support from the mother-country. Apparently abandoned to its sad fate, the colony was not in a condition to receive or to enjoy the blessings of art and culture. Even the celestial atmosphere of clerical fraternity had become heavy with argument and accusation and with bitter disputes about ecclesiastical jurisdiction. The immediate cause of the brewing trouble had been the arrival of the Sulpicians — the pious order of Paris who had been instrumental in the founding of Montreal — and their intrusion into the political and spiritual domain of the omnipotent Society of Jesus. It is, however, not important for a musical historian to pay too much attention to the ensuing spectacle of ecclesiastical family quarrels, neither to follow the intrigues that crept along the corridors of Versailles, nor to listen to the denunciations and virulent attacks of Sulpicians against Jesuits and vice versa. The episode is of relevance only in its ultimate historical effect: the appointment of Canada's first bishop, François-Xavier de Laval-Montmorency, Abbé de Montigny, Bishop of Petrae.

It would be pretentious as well as redundant to comment on the life and work of the man whom so many have already portrayed in biographical notes and historical accounts, whose endeavours and achievements have been a source of inspiration to many and whom many more hold in almost saintly veneration. We are concerned with the chronicle of musical life in New France, a domain removed from his field of activity, though it would be wrong to ignore the religious and political influence imparted by the zealous prelate on the life of the colony or to disregard the impact of his severe and ascetic moral concept on the cultural development of New France. More than anyone else, Mgr. de Laval was the creator and organizer of the true New France, a major force in the history of French Canada, "who left a greater mark upon the colony than any Governor, except the great Frontenac ... ₁"

Mgr. de Laval was indeed an extraordinary man, imbued with indefatigable spirit and deep devotion, an ardent and indomitable fighter for his conviction, whether it concerned the glory of the church or the temporal affairs of the colony. On the foundation which the Jesuits had laid, Laval erected the strong bastion of the ultramontane church for his successors to maintain and to defend against all intrusions from King and Gallican church, a bulwark against heresy and sinful morals. His obedience to Rome overshadowed his loyalty to the King and this reversed position of the Church in New France — in contrast to the mother-country — caused constant trouble with the civil authorities and created an atmosphere of antagonism on both sides which in turn influenced the propagation of art and culture. Distrusting secular influences, the strong paternal hand of the Bishop assumed the task of leading the young colony on the path of law and order, of virtue and righteousness; and the legacy of episcopal severity protected its people for decades against temporal temptations. Working unceasingly for the benefits and welfare of the colony, the spiritual Father of New France is remembered and revered for his many accomplishments.

In his desire to preserve the dignity of the devotional service, Mgr. de Laval was concerned with music in so far as it was expedient to the requirements of the ritual, and in the seminary which he established for the training of young clerics the future priests were taught the singing of the plain-chant together with "other matters belonging to the duties of a good ecclesiastic". It is also laudable that Mgr. de Laval initiated the first school of Arts and Crafts in Canada which was to supply the colony with capable artisans and craftsmen who in turn were to furnish church and chapel with the indispensable religious ornaments; but the school unfortunately did not instruct organ-builders and instrument-makers, as had been done in Mexico some hundred and twenty-five years before. We are told that he brought from Europe highly talented and accomplished artists and expert craftsmen, the founders of a tradition in the arts and crafts which distinguished Quebec to this day; but we do not read that he invited musicians or music-teachers. Indeed, Mgr. de Laval does not figure in the annals of musical events in New France as patron of the art; it is difficult to accept that he "considered music as an essential part of the pioneers' equipment and way of living [2]" nor can by any stretch of imagination his contribution be considered significant to the beginning of musical life in Canada. The search for some convincing evidence of his "highly pronounced taste for musical art" has not been successful; his attitude towards music, discernible more in omission than encouragement, may be considered at best indifferent, and at worst unfriendly. He was first and foremost the ultramontane Catholic of the ascetic type, whose austere and puritan concept could not even countenance the emotional manner of liturgical singing of the Ursulines, and who saw in secular music as in other arts the distraction of the mind and not the elevation of the spirit.

Shortly after his arrival he began to examine the validity of the constitutions governing the religious practice of the Ursulines. These constitutions are the laws and rules of the community; they regulate the spiritual aspects of the liturgy and the celebration of the ritual; they contain certain privileges granted to the order, by which the community may receive novices and in general accomplish, as Mother Marie de l'Incarnation wrote, "all other functions of our institution in the same way as if we were in France". The constitutions had some years earlier been prepared by Father Lalemant, the Superior of the Jesuits and spiritual head of the Ursulines, but did not seem to have been acknowledged by Rome because of the fact that New France did not as yet have a bishop. Whether it was this jurisdictional irregularity, or whether the spiritual activities of the nuns did not find favour with the severe prelate, Mgr. de Laval proposed far-reaching changes. In one of her letters, Mother Marie de l'Incarnation expressed her great disappointment at these changes which, as she said, altered considerably the liturgical structure "so that the abridgement — which would have been proper for the Carmelites or the nuns of Calvary rather than for the Ursulines — effectively ruins our constitution". Mgr. de Laval ordered the Ursulines to abstain from singing High Mass which the nuns had done since 1642 when they took possession of their first convent in Quebec. "But we do not complain", writes the devout and obedient Mother Superior,

> "in order not to aggravate matters, since we deal with a prelate who, being of great piety, once convinced that it is for the glory of God, never turns back; ... it almost happened that all our singing had been curtailed — he left us only our vespers and tenebraes, which we sing as it was done at the time when I was at Tours. He wants us to sing at High Mass with a straight voice, regardless of how it is done either in Paris or at Tours, but only as he, according to the dictates of his spirit, finds it best; ... he fears that we will be given to vanity while singing, and become complacent; we do not sing anymore the mass because, as he said, it may give distraction to the celebrant, and moreover, he had never seen it done before ... I attribute all this to the zeal of the very worthy Prelat, but in matters of regulations, the experience should carry above all speculations" [3]..

Hardly any better evidence than this document is needed to demonstrate the Bishop's belief in the incontestable principle concerning the role of music as laid down by the Fathers of the Church and reiterated by the Council of Trent. At the same time the letter is the sole extant and authentic proof of Laval's active interest and intervention in a musical matter, the only episode of which we have definite evidence — which is not very much, considering the many years he spent as spiritual leader in New France. Curiously enough, the episode of the Ursulines' manner of singing, while of considerable musical interest, is far less known than the Bishop's connection with the importation of an organ and, indeed, it seems, that his reputation as "patron of music" is based on this much heralded but historically unconfirmed incident.

VOX ORGANUM

In the *Informatio de Statu Ecclesiae Novae Franciae* of August 1664, Mgr. de Laval described the new Parish Church at Quebec; he referred briefly to the musical aspects of the devotional services, to the singers and choir boys, and he mentioned the organ which, as he wrote, "mixes well with the voices". Apart from this brief indication, nothing further is known of the instrument as neither the *Journal* nor the *Relations* took particular interest in the important musical acquisition. Historians have based their assumptions concerning the arrival, location and use of the new instrument solely on the statements by Laval's enthusiastic biographer, the Abbé de la Tour, who, one hundred years later, claimed that "the organ which the Bishop brought with him from Paris" was being used at the Parish Church 4.

Mgr. de Laval had indeed been in France during the winter of 1662-1663 to settle the many important issues which occupied his mind and his time; there is, however, no documented evidence that he concerned himself with such mundane matters as the actual purchase of a church organ; at least, such evidence has not been brought forward. Nor has it been established who carried the financial burden involved in the purchase of the costly organ; was it the Quebec clergy, the congregation, or some noble and rich patron in France? Could it have been the Jesuits, or the Bishop himself? Yet, notwithstanding the lack of authentic information and in spite of the unsubstantiated connection with the purchase of the organ, historians have unquestionably accepted La Tour's account as indisputable evidence of Laval's interest in music.

At any rate, the Bishop returned to Quebec in August 1663, and the organ intended for the Parish Church is supposed to have arrived at the same time. From an entry in the church-warden's account book of November 1663 we learn that 300 nails had been purchased for the "erection of a staircase to the organ [5]", but we do not know the date of the inauguration — and the consecration — of the instrument. In the *Journal* the organ is mentioned for the first time as late as April 1664 [6]; La Tour asserted that the organ was not used until the end of 1664 [7], while Mgr. de Laval had already in August 1664 written to the Pope, praising the organ and its wondrous sound. Kallmann believes that the instrument was intended to replace the earlier organ which he mistakenly assumes to have been installed at the Parish Church. However, there was no organ in that church before 1663; moreover, the newly arrived instrument had *not been the first organ in Quebec.* In their reluctance to question La Tour's statement, later historians failed to investigate the by far more significant historical fact that at the time of Laval's arrival in New France in 1659 an organ had already been in use in the Jesuit Church. We do not know when this *first* organ arrived in Quebec; our annals do not mention the date partly because, as we have suggested, the arrival of the first horse seems to have been more important to the chronicler than the first organ, but presumably because the pages of the *Journal* from the years 1654 to 1656 are missing, and have never been located. Since the earliest reference to the Jesuit Church organ dates from 1661 [8], it is an irresistible temptation to consider the missing pages as point of departure for our assumption, and to conclude that the organ may have arrived together with the annual supplies from France during those "missing" and unexplained years.

Thus Quebec of 1660's could boast of two organs, a record which, although far from the astonishing feat of organ-building in Mexico in the early 16th century, is nonetheless a considerable historical achievement, a proud *First* on the North American continent. Admittedly, the by far richer and larger population of New England could well have afforded a number of organs, had it not been for their rejection of music of any sort on religious grounds; and it was not until 1711 that Mr. Thomas Brattle of Boston owned the first organ imported into New England 9. This first American organ has survived the passage of time and still exists in usable condition in St. John's Church, Portsmouth, New Hampshire. American historians, oblivious to the organs in New France, and obviously only concerned with music in the English colonies, were justified in pointing out that in all English settlements along the Atlantic Seaboard, from Maine to Virginia, organs "had been unknown in the colonies in the seventeenth century 10." But it applied in part and with some modifications to all regions of North America that "organs were costly, cumbersome to ship, and it may be doubted if there were any persons in the colonies prior to 1700 capable of playing one 11." As far as New France was concerned, the Jesuits may claim the honour of having brought the first organ to the colony; it is to their credit of having quietly and efficiently furthered the cause of music in the French domain.

The Jesuits, whose first church and mission house had burned to the ground in 1640, were already in 1651 again "at home" in their own church, and soon after in their own residence. The *Maison des Jésuites* included the living quarters and sundry accommodation, the seminary, the refectory and, of course, the church. The refectory is always noted in connection with the culinary hospitality which the Jesuits offered to the musicians in appreciation of their contribution to the liturgical services. Thus whenever such services had been followed by a collation in the refectory, we may be certain that the ceremonies had taken place in the Jesuit church; hence any reference to music or organ-playing unmistakably indicates the musical activities at the Jesuits' and not at the Parish Church.

As has already been mentioned, the earliest reference to the organ in the Jesuit church appeared in the *Journal* of February 1661. It is an important moment in the history of music in New France, and a remarkable event in the history of music on the North American continent. The Superior describes the musical aspects of the ceremonies, and refers to the organ, "... the organ played during the descent of the Holy Sacrament and the Benediction 12." The exact location of the instrument within the building could not be determined, but seems to have been in the *Jubé*, the place traditionally assigned to small organs. The *Jubé* is mentioned for the first time in January 1660 when, as the Superior recorded, "the *curé* with the clergy climbed to the *Jubé*, where he said the Vespers in cape, which were very well sung in harmony 13." Unfortunately, a description of structure and function of the *Jubé* in both the Parish and the Jesuit churches could not be located 14. But there can be little doubt that the performance of liturgical music with choir, organ and instruments, took place on the elevated enclosure of the *Jubé*. The notice in the *Journal* may therefore be interpreted as the singing of Vesper hymns by the choir (*en musique*) in harmonic texture and supported by the organ, all of which seems to have been succesful and enjoyable.

The organ in the Jesuit Church probably remained in its place for many years, serving not only at religious functions, but also as a means of instruction for future organists, for the "musiciens ordinaires de la maison" or the students at the Jesuit seminary. But it will remain impossible to trace its type or make; neither will it be possible to shed any light on the second organ which arrived at Quebec in 1663. The clerical chroniclers of New France paid little attention to an instrument to which they had been accustomed in the mother-country. They saw no particular reason to explore and explain such common matters as type, size or sound; they were little interested in technical aspects, and probably did not know the difference between the Positive and Pedal.

For the clerical annalist the organ had its place and function solely within the ritual; it was merely an accessory to the ceremonial, a welcome contributor to the embellishment of the devotion, but not as indispensable as the missal and breviary, the censer and chalice. Excusable as the omission might be, the sad combination of disinterest, indifference and ignorance deprived us of one of the more remarkable items in North American musical history. Nonetheless, a brief glance at contemporary conditions in Europe with regard to organ building might help to assess the type and quality of the two Quebec organs, albeit that under the circumstances the result will remain hypothetical and inadequate.

European organ manufacture had by the beginning of the 17th century embarked on the making of the new Baroque organ, particularly in North Germany, Holland and France. The new Baroque organ developed from the older type and somewhat primitive Gothic organ; although larger than its forerunner, it was still of relatively small size and contained in addition to several manuals and a pedal organ, from 12 to 35 stops of strongly individual sonorities. By the middle of the 17th century the master builders of France produced an organ with three manuals, a pedal organ of thirty keys and more than forty stops, allowing for an enormous number of combinations. These highly developed French instruments permitted the rise of the French organ school, particularly famous during the second half of the century, and soon French organists enjoyed the tremendous possibilities inherent in the new and magnificent organs. Even the performance of liturgical music was bound to be influenced by the development, introducing elements which were not always compatible with devotional concepts. By the time Mgr. de Laval arrived in Paris, it had become necessary to publish the *Cérémonial de Paris* of 1662 which was intended to put an end to the musical abuses, and to regulate the function of the organ in liturgical music.

None of the musical glory of 17th-century French organ manufacture, composition and virtuosity left an appreciable mark on the colony; neither magnificent organs nor highly accomplished organists are mentioned on the pages of the chronicle of New France. Financial considerations were important and so were the problems of transportation by land and sea. Quebec's organs were of modest dimensions in size and sound, inexpensive enough to avoid a strain on the precarious financial situation — if indeed either the Jesuits or the Parish could afford the purchase at all — and simple in construction to serve as models for the fabrication of later organs in Quebec. This point is important in our investigation: it is only reasonable to assume that the eager but inexperienced first organ builder of New France modelled his first instrument on the example of the early and less complicated organ which had arrived in 1663, rather than on the more intricate and larger system of later French Baroque instruments.

ORGANISTS AND SINGERS

Organs and organ-playing are not often mentioned in our ancient records, perhaps because the irregular and infrequent use had been due to inevitable mechanical failure caused by the hazards of climatic extremes; or because of the absence of capable organists. To the student of music in New France it must indeed seem strangely inconsistent that Quebec, while apparently having two organs, remained for years without competent organists and able teachers. Mgr. de Laval might well have extended his patronage to the purchase of an organ but he forgot to secure the services of a skilful player. On the other hand, whoever played the organs at the Parish Church or at the Jesuits needed no more skill as organist than was required to supply the doubling of voice parts in the liturgical items. The time had not yet come for the display of the great organ works of Marc-Antoine Charpentier or Michel de Lalande, and it is doubtful whether our organists possessed the technical skill necessary for the performance of such works or sufficient knowledge to cope with such 17th-century features as the figured bass, or improvisation on a *cantus firmus*.

It is necessary to remind oneself occasionally that, at the time of Mgr. de Laval's arrival, New France's entire population did not exceed 2200 souls, 500 of whom lived at Quebec. One cannot help but admire the courage of the few musical pioneers who, as we have already seen, braved the musical wilderness in those early years. The cultural soil of New France was not yet ready to receive the professional musician nor the trained church organist but even amateur musicians or organists are difficult to find in the records of our musical past. As far as organists are concerned, historians have attempted to gather pertinent information with which to arrive at some plausible conclusions. We find François d'Anger mentioned as organist in 1661, while François du Moussart is cited for the years from 1666 until 1670 and the famous explorer Louis Jolliet is known to have played the organ at Quebec from 1670 until 1700, "whenever his adventurous life permitted him to do so 15", which was not very often.

Lack of evidence prevents us from knowing the name of the first organist at Quebec, both at the Jesuit as well as Parish Church. Even François d'Anger, supposed to have been an organist as early as February 1661, may have had some predecessor, since it is more likely that he arrived at Quebec only in November 1662. "At about that time", records the Superior, "we took out of kindness as boarders F. Dangé & la Marque, as they did not know what would become of them 16."

Thus the "musician" had found a home, food and shelter at the Jesuits, offered to him by the good fathers more out of true charity, perhaps, than of the alleged "importance which they attached to musical talent 17." Where he had come from is not known, nor are we quite certain that he was indeed an organist as some historians believe. Nowhere is there a reference to that effect in the early reports; neither is the specific field of his musical activity anywhere indicated. Father Lalemant recorded on October 27, 1662 the arrival of "vne chaloupe biscayene" which brought, together with 100 soldiers, some 200 passengers

to Quebec. Was François among those newcomers? Having nowhere to go, he appealed to the Jesuits for help which, as we have
seen, was soon granted to him; moreover, his hosts and be-
nefactors recognized in him a certain amount of musical ability;
presumably François possessed a good voice and knew how to
read music. Father Lalemant related that at Midnight Mass all
went as in former years — and all was well. And after service in
the Jesuit church he went in company of Father Dablon to celebrate Matins to the Parish Church, "where the last psalms were
sung *en musique*[18]."

Hence, the psalms had been sung *en musique*, that is, in
multiple parts by the choir, and François may well have been a
member of the choir. The Superior had not recorded any organ
playing at the Jesuit church, nor referred to François as organist
and, furthermore, there was no organ yet at the Parish Church.
But the musical aspects of the Christmas service had been spoil-
ed by an embarrassing incident, as Father Lalemant explained:
"... there was trouble with the drinks for the singers ... I had ordered to give them apart from their beer also a pot of wine on
Christmas-eve, and the Churchwardens also gave them (some
drinks) without our knowledge. This caused Amador (Martin) to
catch a cold so that he could not sing during the festivities, and
also other musicians, François d'Anger, etc." [19]

This charming little episode strengthens our suspicion
that François was a singer — the term *musicien* indicates the customary usage — a jolly fellow with a colourful personality and
good voice who thoroughly enjoyed the festive spirit at Christmas of 1662. It was not the first time that the happy but embarrassing state of inebriation had been recorded in the annals of
early days. There was the unknown military drummer who, as
the *Journal* relates, serenaded Mgr. de Laval on his drum on
New Year's Day, 1662 and who, no doubt, had been under
singularly stimulating influences. An affectionate but noisy show
of appreciation reverberated in the corridors of the Jesuit house

yet our drummer was determined to pay his respect to the prelat in the manner he knew best. "We did not deem it advisable to send him away", explains the Superior diplomatically (at least not until the impetuous drummer had been rewarded with a silver *escu*) and he expresses the hope that such incidents will not reoccur when the Bishop has moved into his own quarters [20].

François d'Anger, however, did not have to be persuaded to leave; he simply went on his own accord; and whether it was the lure of the wild forest and its free and unbridled life, so greatly cherished by the highly romanticized *coureur de bois*, or whether it was just plain dislike of the orderly, pious and proper life at Quebec, François had disappeared in the spring of 1663. But his wanderlust was soon satisfied; or was it the cold of winter and the pleasant memories of an earlier Yuletide season which brought the errant musician in December 1663 back to the warm shelter and to the flesh-and-wine pots of the Jesuit seminary? The good Fathers again "undertook to feed him out of charity, and Mgr. the Bishop or the Parish to supply him with *vestitum* [21]." Fed, clothed and sheltered, François d'Anger may have remained in Quebec, living on the kindhearted generosity of the Jesuits and presumably in return contributing to the musical accompaniment for the religious services. Yet his musical abilities could not be determined; neither his instrumental nor vocal activity had been recorded in the *Journal* by the clerical annalist. Unimportant and insignificant as he had been in the context of the musical chronicle, he soon disappeared from the pages of history like so many other little heroes of our past.

Nonetheless, it is most likely that François sang in the choir which participated at the service of St. Mathias Day in February 1664. The Superior left an account of the ritual in his Journal: "... there was High Mass here with music at the 7½ (hours) ... the order of music was: first a motet in honour of the Holy Sacrament, then the short sermon, then the organ ... [22]" To suggest that François d'Anger played the organ would be pure conjecture but it has long become obvious that in the absence of known secular organists one of the musically trained priests supplied the instrumental accompaniment on the organ. It is also a logical conclusion that the modest and unknown cleric acted as the teacher of the young seminarists interested in organ-playing and in the study of musical theory. Although Father Lalemant did not reveal the identity of the organist, he added an interesting allusion to the vocal ability of the resident singers. A number of secular priests had arrived from France together with Mgr. de Laval in the late summer of 1663, and the Superior had invited them to officiate at certain portions of the ritual, after which they and some "special" singers had been invited to a meal. "It would be better", continues the Superior, "to give the ordinary musicians (singers) to eat before the High Mass, in order that they may better perform their singing [23]." The special singers had probably been recruited from the ranks of the social and musical notables of Quebec in order to reinforce the choir for the occasion and their vocal efforts seem to have been superior to the singing of the "local boys" ; at least, such seems to be implied in Lalemant's caustic remark ; and, while he avoids open criticism of the resident vocalists, he very clearly suggests that an empty stomach is not conducive to good singing and that in future a good meal beforehand will certainly further the cause of edifying vocal expression.

Among the "*musiciens ordinaires de la maison*" were the four Canadian-born seminarists: Amador Martin, Louis Jolliet, Germain Morin and Pierre Francheville, *les quatre officiers de musique*. The impressive sounding title indicates that the four musicians occupied an important place in the religious community. In the course of their theological studies they had acquired a good knowledge of liturgical music. Amador Martin studied the rudiments of plain-chant composition while Louis Jolliet practised organ playing; nothing is known of the musical talents of the other two church-singers.

Louis Jolliet became one of the most famous sons of New France. Born in 1645, he entered the Jesuit College at the age of eleven or twelve and, intending to enter priesthood, took the minor orders in 1662. It is quite possible that he played the organ at the church on St. Mathias Day in 1664 and it is also possible that he became the first organist at the Parish Church, inaugurating the new organ which had arrived at Quebec in 1663. After he had completed his philosophical studies, Jolliet went to Paris where he is supposed to have become an accomplished harpsichord player, although the true object of his voyage is not known [24]. But music was clearly not his chosen field of activity; he returned to Quebec to become a fur-trader only to turn soon after to explorer, traveller, royal hydrographer and, as Gosselin asserted, organist whenever his busy schedule permitted him to do so. Only two documents refer to his activity as organist; the one seems to have been a memorandum of funerals or of Requiem services to be held, and in which it is registered that on September 15, 1700, was held "a service for the late M. Jolliet in recognition for having played the organ at the Cathedral and the parish church for many years. Free of charge [25]." The other documents, being the "Extrait des Registres des délibérations de la Fabrique de Québec" of March 13, 1720 — twenty years after Jolliet's death — contains the notice: "The late Sr. Jolliet did not pay for the transfer [of the pew] as he should have done after the death of the late Sr Bissot [whose daughter Claire-Françoise was married to Louis Jolliet] because the said vestry had given him a postponement in consideration because he had played the organ and shown how to play it to many persons of the Seminary [26]."

Jolliet remains the only organist and musician during the 17th century of whose instrumental activity, sporadic as it might have been, we have unmistakable and documented evidence. Of particular interest is the reference to his tutorial efforts which he presumably shared with a resident priest at the seminary. But it could well have been he who taught a young drummer from the regiment Carignan-Salières, François du Moussart, whom the Jesuits had accepted as boarder in July 1665 because of his apparent musical talent and the intention to study music 27. Gosselin claims that already one year later François du Moussart had become organist at the Parish Church and that he remained in that position until 1670. However, no further details are available to aid in our investigation into the musical exploits of the young drummer who must indeed have been a very talented and eager student to achieve the considerable feat of organ-playing after a relatively short period of study.

VOICES AND VIOLS

Many months had passed since Mgr. de Laval had returned to Quebec with, as is alleged, the new and splendid organ. The stairway to the *Jubé* in the Parish Church had been built and, no doubt, the organ had been hoisted into its new place. But still there was no mention of the instrument, and no sign that it had been used at religious services. It was not until Easter of 1664 that our meticulous Superior inserted into his diary one of the rare remarks of musical interest: "At Holy Week, Tenebrae at the Parish (Church) and solemn service, where the Passion was first sung by three deacons; on Thursday here *Salve* with instruments as in the morning for the *Pange lingua* ... on the three Holy days following the *Salve* was done at the Parish with instruments *(for the first time)* in the *Jubé* close to the organ. All went well except that the voices and instruments are feeble for such a large edifice 28." Instruments had at various times been connected with devotional services. Viols had already been mentioned in the *Journal* of December 1648, but in February 1662 a historically important event, the concert of four viols, had taken place which the Superior described in the *Journal* 29.

The two events cited above are among the most important and significant items found in our historical sources, yet the references are inadequate and of relatively little help in the evaluation of the musical elements. To be sure, the entries in the *Journal* provide indisputable evidence that instruments had been used to accompany sacred vocal music during Easterweek of 1664, and presumably also at other times, but what were those instruments? Father Lalemant did not consider it necessary to specify the type nor the number of instruments involved, though there is his critical observation concerning the tone volume and the acoustics in the Parish Church. His remark could well be interpreted as an indication that a number of viols of different sizes, perhaps with an occasional flute and possibly some theorbes, had joined voices in the singing of the *salut* in the "Iubé proche des orgues".

The soft and mellow tone quality of such instruments, sufficient as it was for the Jesuit Church, and excellent as it might have been for the intimacy of a chamber, was "feeble for such a large edifice" as the Parish Church. But Father Lalemant's admission implies another factor : the newly installed organ did not add its voice to the musical embellishment at the Easter celebration. Its powerful sound would, as Mgr. de Laval could testify a short time later, have "beautifully mixed with the voices", and the Superior would not have had any reason to complain about the tonal insufficiency of the musical accompaniment. Mechanical failure, rather than the lack of an organist, might have retarded the inauguration of the new instrument, since only a few weeks earlier, on St. Mathias Day in February, someone had played the organ in the Jesuit Church.

Particularly disconcerting is the absence of detailed information with regard to the "concerts of the four viols". New France had claimed the distinction of the first theatrical performance, the first organ, as well as other *premières* on the North American continent. And now appears the first "consort-music" in the musical annals, the first concert of the viols. There is, of course, not much merit in being "first" if the continuance is lost in obscurity, but viols in New France are quite significant, not only in their importance to our musical chronicle, but particularly in comparison with instrumental music in the more privileged English colonies. Considering the lesser population, the slower development, the unstable political and economical situation, as well as the greater lack of instrumental tradition, it is indeed encouraging to find in New France these few traces of instrumental activities.

The newcomers to British colonies had emigrated from a country famous for its singing and for the tradition of instrumental music. Keyboard music and especially consort music for viols had been part of its flourishing tradition of amateur music-making, as England since the days of Henry VIII had led the way in the development of viol music and viol players 30. As has already been mentioned on earlier pages, many emigrants had brought instruments with them; the documented list contains such items as a "treble violl" or a "bass vyol", and already towards the end of the first century in New England's history there was an instrument maker in Boston. But while the Bostonian chronicler registered the treble and bass viol, nowhere is there any indication in 17th-century French-Canadian annals with regard to the type of instrument that had been brought to New France. Moreover, the sporadic appearance of viols in Quebec caused misinterpretation of a historical document by some modern historians and it is necessary to consider the matter briefly at this point.

As mentioned earlier, in August 1664 Mgr. de Laval had sent a lengthy letter to the Pope, describing the condition and the state of ecclesiastical history of the country. Of particular interest to the musical chronicler of those years is Laval's reference to the musical participation in the liturgical services held on major feast days in the new Parish Church. The Bishop touches on the musical aspects with these words: "*In majoribus festis missa,*

*vesperae, ac serotinum Salve, musice cantatur, hexachordo diver-
sum, et suo numero absolutum, et organa vocibus suaviter com-
mixta musicum mirifice hunc concentum adornant* [31]." Although
Mgr. de Laval seems to have been quite explicit and perfectly
clear, a certain amount of ambiguity has clouded the various interpretations of this important item. The translation and analysis
is particularly vulnerable in the case of the word *hexachordo*
which, according to some historians, is supposed to denote *viols*
or other instruments of the orchestra. As we have seen, viols and
other instruments are on record in the musical history of New
France and their participation at religious services had been registered with unequivocal testimony in the *Journal.* Based on
these facts, historians were convinced that they detected in the
Latin text of Mgr. de Laval's *Informatio* evidence of viols and
conclusive proof of the presence of an *orchestra* in the Parish
Church and Church of the Jesuits. They insisted on translating
hexachordo as *six-stringed* instrument, a literal translation of the
compound Greek word (*hexa* — six; *chordos* — string) and since
most viol-types carried that number of strings, the conclusion
was obvious. But the solution is really far from obvious; the
generally accepted interpretation and its reference to viols or
other instruments is not certain from a musicological point of
view so that the translation appears ambiguous in its linguistic
context and not convincing with regard to 17th-century musical
terminology.

No solution to the problem can be entirely satisfying; it
will remain for more intensive research into all corners of 17th-
century musical practice and nomenclature, as well as into the
customary usage of Graecism, to solve the problem in a more
convincing manner. There are, however, a few striking incon-
gruities discernible, caused primarily by the somewhat superficial examination of the term *hexachord* in its contemporary
definition. It should be pointed out that in almost all instances
the disputable interpretation had been advanced by writers ob-

viously unaware of the peculiar characteristics and specific meaning of musical terms. Satisfied with the literal translation (to which had been added a new and completely erroneous meaning, viz. *orchestra*) historians failed to investigate the highly important development of the hexachord and its rôle in liturgical music, from the complex mediaeval scale structure to the theoretical principles of our own tonal system.

On the other hand, not a single reference has been found in mediaeval or later musical treatises in which the literal translation of hexachord implies musical instruments instead of the tonal system, nor is there any accredited, modern dictionary or encyclopedia which would not explain the term as "a diatonic series of six notes" (Oxford) or "serie ascendante ou descendante de six sons, sur laquelle repose le système musical employé jusqu'au XVIIe siècle" (Larousse) 32.

We may well assume that Mgr. de Laval had been fully aware of the true meaning of *hexachord* in its relation to liturgical music, and that his reference concerned not a six-stringed instrument, but the system of six-tone relation. As far as the *Informatio* was concerned, Mgr. de Laval implied that the chants of the Mass and the Vespers were performed according to the prescribed rules of the ritual (*juxta Episcoporum Caeremoniale celebratur*), in particular the lengthy *Salve serotinum* which was sung "with all sections absolved", (*suo numero absolutum,*) and in the modalities of the hexachord (*hexachordo diversum*), while the organ, and not an orchestra or viols, blended pleasantly with the voices "wondrously embellishing that musical harmony 33."

VI

La Sainte Famille

With musical episodes primarily as subsidiary additions to religious events and liturgical devotions, the history of music in New France reflects the influential position of the church in Quebec. Since traditional chants of the ritual, a few motets and some sacred songs represent the musical element as recorded in our annals, it was inevitable that the first episode of more than minor interest in our musical chronicle be related to a religious ceremony.

In March 1664, Mgr. de Laval gave his episcopal permission and blessing to the establishment of *La Confrérie de la Sainte Famille,* and decreed that the second Sunday after Epiphany be observed as the day of the annual celebration. Twenty years later, in November 1684, the Bishop officially sanctioned the *Feast* in honour of *La Sainte Famille,* "... which should be a first class feast as it had already been celebrated since many years ₁." But as the extreme cold of January was not conducive to attendance at the church services, he designated the day of celebration from the second Sunday after Epiphany to the more convenient third Sunday after Easter. Until that time, that is from 1664 to 1684, the new Devotion did not have its own liturgical text and music but used the liturgy of the Feast of the Annunciation. To satisfy the demand for a liturgy proper for the Feast, Mgr. de Laval ordered four priests to work on a permanent liturgical text. And again twenty years elapsed before, in the spring of 1703, the new Feast could at last be celebrated with its own liturgy, its Mass and Office, just as Mgr. de Laval had envisaged many years earlier.

The Devotion has been the subject of much learned study by competent historians; there is no need to enlarge on its historical and religious significance unless required for the clarifications of the musical involvement; we are concerned with the music and with the historical aspects of some of the musical items in the Devotion.

One of these items — the Prose *Sacræ Familiæ* — is claimed to have been the first Canadian musical composition and possibly one of the earliest extant compositions on the North American continent north of Mexico. The claim is based on the information contained in an ancient and anonymous manuscript, generally considered to have been written about 1730, and according to which Charles-Amador Martin, the second Canadian-born priest, was the composer of the music. The manuscript itself is attributed to Mother Marie-Andrée Duplessis de Ste. Hélène (1687-1760), the annalist of the *Hôtel-Dieu* and many times Superior of the Hospitallers of Quebec.

In the *Mémoire sur la Devotion à la Ste. Famille, du tems, et de la manière dont la feste et la Confrairie ont esté establies* [2], Mother Ste. Hélène explains that she had gathered "with pleasure and with care what I have found written and what I have learned at first hand from persons who lived at the time when the Confraternity of the Holy Family was established [3]."

Marie-Andrée Duplessis was only 16 years of age when in 1703 the feast with its revised text and music was celebrated for the first time at Quebec's cathedral. A few years later, in 1709, the young woman asked for admission into the order of the Hospitallers, taking the holy vows of profession and the religious name of Ste. Hélène.

It is quite possible that the young novice had learned the story of *La Ste. Famille* from Mother Juchereau de St. Ignace, the Superior of her chosen community and with whom the young nun in later years collaborated in the writing of *Les Annales de l'Hôtel-Dieu de Québec*. It is also feasible that Amador Martin himself related to her the events that surrounded the origin of the Devotion and the composition of its music. Amador Martin, the *curé* of Ste. Foy and one of the Canons of the Cathedral, was not only one of the "persons who lived at the time" of the founding of the Devotion but, as will be seen shortly, was closely connected with its history as well as its liturgy. Whether written documents or verbal recollection, Mother Ste. Hélène unequivocally affirms that it had been "... M. Martin, who being a capable singer, composed the chants of the Mass and the Office as it is [4]."

This is the entire information at our disposal and, in fact, the only existing reference on which the prevailing opinion regarding the music for the Devotion in general, and the Prose *Sacrae Familiae* in particular, is based. Unfortunately, Mother Ste. Hélène did not consider the music important enough to elaborate on its various aspects in a more detailed manner, nor did she deem it necessary to substantiate her remark or reveal the source of her reference; moreover, our annalist had never specifically referred to the Prose as a new and original composition, or made any distinction between "composer" and "arranger". Enjoying highest respect and the reputation of being an accurate recorder of historical events, her testimony was gladly and universally accepted, often quoted, and sometimes hailed as evidence of the fine quality of artistic education in 17th-century Quebec.

It is not the aim of this argument to disparage the sincere conviction of friendly historians or the deep-seated belief in the accepted version of this musical episode; nor are we prepared to replace the prevailing opinion with an equally unsubstantiated supposition. The intention is solely to investigate the event from a musical standpoint and to submit to scrutiny certain aspects in an attempt to clarify the meaning in the venerable nun's reference.

Among the items of prime concern is an analysis of the word *compose* in the context as employed by Mother Ste. Hélène, since it is precisely the ambiguity in that term which impedes the proper interpretation. As in a similar occurence, discussed on earlier pages, we must again distinguish between *compose* in the sense of *select, arrange* or *assemble* on the one hand and the artistic process of creating on the other.

Indeed, this distinction governs the study of the music for *La Ste. Famille.* How many items of the liturgy had been selected from the vast repertory of the traditional chants and assembled or arranged for similar function in the Mass and Office of the newly established ritual, and which (if any) items had been especially created, that is composed or set to music? Only if this issue has been clarified and the two aspects involved duly separated will it be possible to arrive at an acceptable interpretation.

It was the Abbé Charles Glandelet — one of the prominent and guiding figures in the fraternal association — who explained in detail the liturgical content of *La Ste. Famille.* In his memorandum of 1689, the *Eclaircissement sur l'Institution de la Deuotion, Feste et Office de la Sainte Famille — establie dans le pays de la Nouuelle France,* Glandelet refers to

> the office which is *composed* (sic) of Psalms which are partly from the Holy Scriptures, and partly from the Holy Fathers of the Church ... the Antiphones, the Responses, and the Versets are mainly those which have been adopted by the church for the particular Offices of the Mysteries and Feasts of Our Lord, the Holy Virgin, and St. Joseph, which are celebrated during the course of the Year; and if there are found others, they

are drawn from the Gospel which bears on the Mysteries of the Holy Family; even the Orations of the Day of Circumcision and that of the Octave of Epiphany; the mass, similarly, contains nothing but the words which are either in the Holy Scriptures or the Church; there is nothing but the hymns and the Prose which have been made following the orders given since the commencement by Mgr. the former Bishop of Quebec, and which moreover explain the Mysteries of the Holy Family according to the Gospel ... one can say that this office is not new in its content since it is taken (drawn) from other offices and mysteries, but only in its *form*₅.

Glandelet's explanation relates to the *first* version of the ritual as requested by Mgr. de Laval in 1684; it is proof that the liturgy (that is, text and music) had been assembled, or "drawn", from other Offices. Even the melodies of the first Sequence, *Summae Deus Majestatis,* and of the undiscovered hymns then in use, must have been borrowed from other sources. Such adaptation was, with more or less gratifying results, common practice in the Roman liturgy. One need only look at any liturgical book to realize the extent of borrowed melodies, interchangeable texts and adapted tunes.

From 1664 to 1684 the celebrations of *La Ste. Famille* had been conducted with the liturgy belonging to the Feast of the Annunciation, while the hymns had been borrowed from the Christmas services. But when in 1684 Mgr. de Laval elevated the ceremony to the level of a first-class Feast, four Quebec priests were assigned to the task of providing the ceremony with its own liturgical text. The four ecclesiastics (Louis Ango de Maiserets and Henri de Bernières from the Seminary, Claude Dablon and Martin Bouvart from the Jesuit College) embarked immediately on their work but after some preliminary attempts considered themselves incompetent to cope with such a dignified and important assignment. With honest self-effacement and with the approval of Mgr. de Laval, they decided to turn to a renowned and celebrated religious poet, the Abbé Jean-Baptiste Santeuil, of the equally renowned Abbey of St. Victor in Paris, submitting to him their literary venture and requesting his criticism and revision.

In historical accounts of New France, such as this chronicle of music, one may frequently encounter apologetic explanations concerning the cultural poverty, caused by "geographical isolation" or "disdainful neglect" from the mother-country. It is therefore to the lasting credit of the Church that neither isolation nor neglect prevented her enthusiastic servants from edifying the worship of the Lord with the best means available. And Santeuil, the famous poet, was not only the "most capable poet of our century [6]" but he had also enjoyed the admiration of his contemporaries, from the great Bossuet, the Condés, the Bourbons and other aristocrats, to Louis XIV himself, who bestowed visible signs of royal favours on the admired poet [7].

In soliciting the literary contribution of the great Santeuil, Quebec was to receive a few crumbs of the cultural achievement that had been a landmark of France's *grand siècle*. In striking contrast, however, the laudable efforts of Quebec's religious leaders did not include the musical aspects, or extend to any musical contemporary of the great laureate of religious poetry. While it is true that the celebrated and admired Henri Dumont had died exactly at the moment when Mgr. de Laval encouraged the local bards to seek the help of the great Santeuil, there remained many composers of religious music in France, whose contributions of original music to *La Ste. Famille* would have meant a distinction and an honour for the colony, as well as an incentive of cultural importance, equal to the literary contribution.

Santeuil, in the charming and flowery style of the time, expressed his gratitude for the honour bestowed upon him: "he corrected and rendered in a more elegant style the *Prose* and the hymns, returning them to the gentlemen, thanking them for the light which they had given him through their work, praising their thoughts, and avowing that if he indeed had added some matter, it was merely to obey their wishes, and that he had been charmed by what he had received on their behalf[8]." In spite of such modesty, Santeuil has definitely been credited with the writing of the Sequence, *Summae Deus Majestis,* and he must also have had some hand in the preparation of the hymns.

In addition to the *Eclaircissement,* and in the same year (1689), Glandelet prepared the liturgical manuscript of the *Missa in Festo Sanctæ Familiæ*[9]. The manuscript contains the text of the *Proprium*[10], and is also the oldest extant copy of the Mass in the form in which the ritual had been conducted following its transfer in 1684 from the second Sunday after Epiphany to the third Sunday after Easter. Curiously enough, although the liturgical structure with the new text is definitely later than 1684 (the inclusion of the double *Alleluia* instead of a Graduale indicates the post-paschal formula), Glandelet asserts that the new text had already been in use for "seven or eight years", in other words, since 1681 or 1682 or, at any rate, some years prior to the change from the winter season to the time of spring.

The *Missa in Festo* ... contains only those items proper for the Feast of *La Ste. Famille,* not the chants of the *Ordinarium.* Hence there is among the vocal items of the *Proprium* a special *Introitus, Alleluia, Offertorium, Communion* and, of course, the *Sequence.* The recited or spoken parts of the *Proprium* include the *Oratio, Lectio, Evangelium (Gospel), Praefatio* and *Post-Communion,* all of which form part of Glandelet's manuscript of 1689. The final and partly revised version of 1702 as well as the printed editions of the early 1800's include in musical notation some of the special prayers listed above, which allows the assumption that the basic structure of the Mass has not been changed since 1684, the year when the work on the liturgy for *La Ste. Famille* had begun. On the other hand, neither *Sequence* nor hymns were accepted into the later versions and, unfortunately, no trace of these hymns has been found; yet hymns must have been in use if we believe Glandelet, who insisted that they have been composed in accordance with Mgr. de Laval's *mandement* of 1684.

Although the Feast of *La Ste Famille* had since 1684 been celebrated with its own liturgy, new problems appeared. A theological dispute had arisen: the legality and validity of the Devotion came to be questioned, and the allegation that the Church had never, through the Holy Council or otherwise, consented to the designation "Sainte Famille" caused serious embarrassment in Quebec. The *Eclaircissement* of 1689 was likely inspired by the desire to explain and to justify the very existence of the new Feast, and its author's brilliant polemic, directed at Mgr. de Saint-Vallier (Mgr. de Laval's successor), was intended to prove that everything was legal and permissible.

In addition to the theological dispute, there was also a certain amount of dissatisfaction with the spiritual content of the liturgy. Glandelet's efforts to have the new texts printed provoked criticism from the head of the *Missions Etrangères* in Paris. Clearly, the teamwork of the four Quebec clerics with the famous French poet Santeuil had not found the approval of the Abbé Jacques-Charles de Brisacier, who as Superior of the *Missions Etrangères* was well qualified to render the best possible advice. In a letter of May 3, 1698, the Abbé Jean-Henri Tremblay, Quebec's representative in Paris, advised Glandelet of the need to recompose the whole Office as it did not seem to be wholly satisfactory; it appeared not sufficiently studied nor learned, and it would be useful to examine the new Breviaries of Cluny, Paris, Orleans and La Rochelle in order to find examples of well-composed Offices. And Tremblay already hints at the possibility of meeting a fine poet whom he hopes to persuade to write the *new* hymns and a *new* Prose for *La Ste. Famille*11.

Tremblay's efforts on behalf of *La Ste. Famille* were successful. In May 1700, this capable and faithful agent of the Quebec Seminary in Paris wrote to Glandelet, advising him that he had, in company of M. de Brisacier, visited a pious monk by the name of Simon Gourdan at the famous Abbey of St. Victor, and that Gourdan, "who is a poet as collected and contemplative as Santeuil was dissipated", had the kindness to prepare "very beautiful hymns and a very beautiful prose for *La Ste. Famille* ... albeit that they are a bit long 12."

Tremblay wanted Glandelet to examine the hymns before printing and, if approved, he would then and without fail have them printed during the following January (1701). It is, however, not known whether Tremblay was able to send Gourdan's hymns and prose to Glandelet for approval in 1700. "Unfortunately", he wrote, "I had given them for examination to M. de Brisacier, who mislaid them and had not yet found them again ... I shall do my utmost to search for them before the departure of the boats 13."

Whether or not Tremblay did locate the "mislaid" copies before the departure of the boats, the approved text did not return to Paris until the summer of 1701, and it was not until March 1702 that Tremblay could inform Mgr. de Laval that the Office had at last been printed, *"but not the music14."* And a few weeks later, in his letter to Glandelet of May 28, 1702 he announces: "You shall at least have the Office this year. I had no other printing done but the Office and the Mass, there is nothing of *Notation15.*"

It is interesting to observe these references to the music; twice Tremblay stresses the fact, while the text to the Mass and the Office had been printed, the musical notation had to be omitted, ostensibly because of financial considerations. At the same time, however, his remarks clearly indicate that the music for the Mass and Office was available in Paris and ready to be printed had not the lack of money thwarted the project.

This highly significant item which could well be the key to the problem concerning the music for the Devotion (in particular for the Prose *Sacræ Familiæ)* has escaped the attention of most historians though a notable exception is found in the work of the Archivist of the Seminary at Quebec.

In his learned study of the Fraternity and the Devotion of the Holy Family, the Abbé Provost arrived at the conclusion that, while Tremblay was aware of the existence of music, he had neither time for its perusal and examination, nor money for its printing [16].

But what did the music consist of? What items of the liturgy were ready for printing? And was the music for the Prose included in the unprinted notation? It is exactly at this point in our investigation that the problem of the music for *Sacræ Familiæ* reaches the impenetrable impasse !

Let us recall that all but *one* of the melodies, including the hymns, had been "borrowed" from other liturgies; all but *one* of the chants could be found in notation in the respective liturgical books. The printing of musical notation in conjunction with the text would have therefore been more a matter of convenience for the officiating priest than of necessity. At any rate, since in addition to the other retarding influences the meagre financial resources at his disposal had been further reduced by the fire of November 1701 which destroyed the seminary at Quebec, M. Tremblay came to the regrettable but unavoidable conclusion: "It will not do that the rest (the printing of the music) could be done so soon [17]."

With the printing of the text, Tremblay considered his task well accomplished. The small booklets containing the words of Mass and Office of *La Ste. Famille* including the new text of Gourdan's hymns and Prose, arrived in Quebec during the summer of 1702. And with it returned the music which, because of high cost, had regretfully been omitted from printing.

Unfortunately, neither Tremblay's letters nor Glandelet's correspondence have shed any light on the obscurity that covers the music for *La Sainte Famille*. And Glandelet was certainly well informed and fully aware of all the activities concerning the Devotion. His position as spiritual and administrative director of the fraternal Association, his rank as Grand Vicar of Quebec, and his initiative and tireless efforts on behalf of the affairs of the Devotion suggest a far greater participation in the musical aspects, including the selection of the chants, than is generally admitted.

There was also Louis Ango de Maiserets who, as we recall, had been one of the four ecclesiastics actively engaged in the preparation of the earlier version of the liturgy. He too had been Grand Vicar, then Arch-Deacon, and since 1698 *Grand Chantre* which included the office of *maître du choeur* in the cathedral. And there was Charles-Amador Martin, the *habile chantre* who, from the inauguration of the Chapter of Quebec in 1684 until 1697, had been canon of the cathedral. But while Amador Martin's musical talent has widely been acclaimed, and Louis Ango's musical ability is evinced by the high office which he held for many years, Glandelet's knowledge of musical art has nowhere been mentioned, though such knowledge must have served him in the selection and arrangement of words and music for the Mass *Sacré-Coeur de Jésus*, as the title page of a manuscript reveals: "Première Messe chantée à Québec, aux Ursulines, en l'honneur du Sacré-Coeur de Jésus, en 1700. Paroles et chant arrangés par Mr. le Gr.-Vicaire Glandelet, ancien Supérieur du Séminaire de Québec [18]."

The manuscript contains only the Ordinary, yet the Mass is a typical example of the traditional custom of "borrowed" chants: the *Introit* appears not only in the Masses of Ste. Anne, of N.D. du Carmel, of Ste. Agathe, but also in the liturgy of *La Ste. Famille*, while the rest of the Ordinary is taken entirely from Henri Dumont's *Messe Royale* [19]. It is perhaps not necessary to attach special significance to Glandelet's choice of music for that particular mass, other than noting his preference for the modern style of the *plainchant musical français,* that interesting trend in 17th-century French religious music of which Henri Dumont's *Messe Royale* is indeed such an outstanding example. And it is perhaps coincidental, but nonetheless remarkable, to find some of the characteristic features of the new style in the Prose *Sacræ Familiæ.*.

In his compositions Dumont experimented successfully with the ancient chant, endowing it with a fundamentally musical and highly expressive character, setting it into measured form and enhancing it with modern accidentals. The tendency towards chromaticism is very pronounced and accentuates inevitably the modern tonality. The same modern approach applies to the melodic form of phrases which, although of great beauty and of severe grandeur and dignity are more appropriate for the operatic style of the *grand siècle* than the pure and profound character of the Gregorian chant.

An analysis of the Prose *Sacræ Familiæ* reveals that while its melodic element is unmistakably representative of the *plainchant musical français,* its formal construction is clearly influenced by the traditional Sequence, notably *Lauda Sion.* In true style, *Sacræ Familiæ* contains certain typical features of the Sequence-form, such as syllabic texture and the repetition of the melodic stanza to different text. As in the *Messe Royale,* the melodic concept of the Prose is based on the implied harmonic structure which contrasts the truly monodic character of the traditional Gregorian chant. The frequent use of accidentals, whether actual or implied, replaces the modal character of the ancient hexachord scale with the tonal concept (or key-feeling) of the modern minor tonality.

Of special interest is the change in modality, analogous to modern modulation from the authentic Dorian (or Tonic mi-

Excerpt from Prose " Sacræ Familiæ "

Cependt. cet este nous pensasmes fort a establir
l'office de la Ste famille, et nous allasmes
Mr L. de Brisacier et moy voir un tres R. Relig.
de St Victor nommé M. Gourdan qui est un Poete
auth. recueilly que feu Santeüil estoit dissipé, c'est
lui que Santeüil avoit fait representer a coste du
crucifix a droite et lui a gauche pr faire quatre
vers sur le bon et le mauvais larron. M. Gourdan
a eu la bonté de nous faire de fort belles hymnes
et une belle prose pr la Ste famille. Mais je
les ay malheureusement donné a examiner a M.
L. de Brisacier qui les a esgaré et n'a pu encore
les retrouver. Elles sont un peu trop longues. M.
L. de Brisacier y vouloit diminuer quelq. chose,
mais elles sont belles. Il y en avoit une pr Laude
dans le temps Pascal appliquée a J.C. glorieux
agissant par les ouvriers apostoliques pr procurer
la gloire de son Pere dans la conversion des ames
qui estoit tout a fait belle. Je feray encore mon
possible avant le depart des vaisseaux pr les
chercher et vous les envoier.

Je serois bien aise que vous eussiez vu ces
hymnes avant que de les faire imprimer, et
si vous les approuvier je ne manquerois pas de
faire imprimer cet office pend. l'an ois de l'année
prochain

Letter of Jean-Henri Tremblay, to Charles Glandelet (May 7, 1700) nor) to its corresponding plagal mode (or Dominant). The use of this particular device is quite ancient, and occurred already in the 11th-century Easter-sequence *Victimæ Paschali*; it is likewise a good indication of the solid historical knowledge on the part of the composer with regard to the rules governing Prose writing. On the other hand, the particularly dramatic effect of a melodic sequence (the repetition of a melodic pattern on a graduated tone-level) is clearly a concession to the new style; it is uncommon in true Gregorian chant. Quite significant is the treatment of motivic segments, ingeniously introduced in certain stanzas, sometimes assuming the rôle of a complete quotation of a melodic phrase.

The melodic inventiveness is quite remarkable; the melodic phrases show subtleties of expression, structure and organization, and retain within their organic inter-relationship a notable individuality. As in other instances, a strong feeling for a melodious folksong-type texture tends to suggest a vernacular hymn-tune.

The poetic meter of the text governs the rhythmic element which, however, does not pulsate in the free, oratoric rhythm associated with the Gregorian chant, but rather with the essentially measured rhythm of the *plainchant musical*, faintly reminiscent of the *vers mesuré* of the 16th century. yet the necessity to conform to the poetic meter forced the composer to resort to metric note-values in a somewhat pedestrian and uninspiring monotonous repetition of the trochaic mode-pattern which does not do full justice to Simon Gourdan's finely wrought poetry.

From the historical point of view, the origin of the music for the Prose remains a difficult and largely unsolved problem. The available evidence is not entirely convincing; many questions remain unanswered, and more research is needed to clarify the only existing reference which until now has formed the basis of the historical premises. The composition has indeed caused some confusion even among historians well acquainted with musical matters, who seem to have been satisfied to repeat existing opinions without much regard to musical properties or consequences [20].

Strangely enough, nowhere has the source-reference been subjected to scrutiny; nowhere has the creative ability and musical activity of the composer received probing attention and certainly not any appreciable amount of investigation. Most writers were content to subscribe and to endorse the vague declaration that Charles-Amador Martin had been "a capable singer", and one of 'les musiciens ordinaires de la maison", and that by default he had been appointed both *Préfet du Chant*, as well as *Préfet de la Sacristie*, a distinction which, however, bears no conclusive proof of the ability to compose music [21].

No doubt, Mother Ste. Hélène pondered meticulously the testimony of those "who lived at the time when the Confraternity of the Holy Family was established", and carefully and prudently selected the written material for her *Mémoire*. One can do no better than to give unqualified credence to her *bona fide* intention. Yet the most loyal admirer must admit that the statement with its inherent multiple possibilities tends to confuse the unwary reader and, although no valid grounds can be advanced on which to reject the statement of the thorough and expert annalist of the *Hôtel-Dieu*, it is the lack of critical analysis as well as the disregard for an acceptable interpretation on the part of historians which has led to a superficial and misleading evaluation of the musico-historical episode.

Surely, Mother Ste. Hélène must have been perfectly aware of the assumption implied in her text; as a learned and trained member of the Catholic clergy, she knew those items of the Mass and Office of *La Ste. Famille* that had been borrowed and adapted from the traditional repertory of the Gregorian chants and had, as she asserted, been *composed* (that is, compiled, assembled or arranged) by Amador Martin. She also knew that the melody of the Prose, because of its different and modern style, could only have been of more recent date. But she did not know, or did not tell us, from where that melody originated, whether it had been adapted from a contemporary melody or had indeed been newly composed by Amador Martin, for she did neither refer to the Prose nor unmistakably mention Martin as its composer. Mother Ste. Hélène could have shed some light on the matter; her omission has smothered all hopes of a clarification of the elusive subject.

It remains to suggest with due caution an alternative solution, obviously based on conjecture, but nonetheless being in the realm of possibility. Tremblay's reference to music is to be accepted as proof that all of the designated musical items together with the appropriate text were ready for printing. Neither Tremblay nor Glandelet, however, refer at any time to the music for the Prose, the only piece of liturgy that was to be newly-composed. The prevalence of certain stylistic features in *Sacræ Familiæ* corroborates the assumption that the music had been composed by someone well acquainted with the characteristics of the *plainchant musical français.* And since Messrs. Tremblay and Brisacier had been fortunate to enlist the services of Simon Gourdan, the resident-poet of St. Victor, it is not impossible that another monk at St. Victor, namely the anonymous resident-composer of the venerable abbey could likewise, and in close co-operation with the poet, have supplied the music. Yet none of the music had been printed in Paris, partly because of the high cost of printing and partly because *all but one* item could be found in the traditional liturgical books used in New France. Thus it remained merely to bring or to send the new composition to Quebec, to make and to distribute copies of it among the parishes of the colony. But while no early copies have been located the possibility cannot be excluded that some of these early manuscript copies may have been in the experienced handwriting of the former *officier de musique* and present *Grand Chantre,* Charles-Amador Martin, which might possibly explains the belief that he had been the composer of the music. Canadian historians eagerly acclaim him as the first Canadian composer with hardly any concern for the fact that not a single manuscript in Amador Martin's handwriting has remained as proof of his activity and not a single copy of the Prose, dating from 1702 or 1703, the year of its first performance, has been located. The earliest extant copy of the Office of *La Ste. Famille,* containing the Prose, may well be the very beautiful manuscript in the fine and delicate handwriting of Mother Ste. Hélène. It is an undated manuscript, inserted in one of the liturgical books that are preserved at the *Hôtel-Dieu*[22] and was probably written before Mother Ste. Hélène assumed the heavy burden of Superior of her order in 1732, coinciding with the writing of her *Mémoire*[23].

The foregoing comments need not be construed as unwarranted criticism, although judgement of earlier methods is imperative, but rather as an exoneration of those who in good faith did the spade work for our historical survey. Without their scholarship this study would be deprived of much valuable material for, as Wade says, "scholarship is a cumulative process, with an ungrateful tendency on the part of the labourer of the eleventh hour to disparage earlier workers in the vineyards. But historical truth can only emerge through continual sifting and winnowing of facts and theories in the light of new knowledge and new perspectives [24]."

As far as the music for *La Ste. Famille* is concerned, new evidence can hardly be expected and there is little prospect of new perspectives and new avenues of research, even for those willing to venture into the realm of speculative investigation. Nonetheless, re-consideration and re-examination of all factors involved is still possible and in fact desirable, if only to defend existing views or to provide an acceptable basis for new interpretations.

VII

Decades of Development

SOCIETY IN THE MAKING

The year 1665 was to mark a turning point in the political and cultural history of the young country. In France, Mazarin had died; Louis XIV began to assume absolute and undivided authority, and with determination — and the help and advice of his capable minister Colbert — took the affairs of the colony into his hands. New France rose from trading-post and mission station to colonial dependency, the domain of the monarch. The assertion of royal power strengthened the hand of the civil authorities; it dispossessed the old rights and privileges and eliminated the rule of the Trading Company and even affected the firm hold which the clergy had acquired over temporal affairs. Having the prosperity of Canada at heart, the king was intent on breaking the constant threat of the Iroquois; he was ready to fight and to destroy the barbarous tribes who hindered evangelization, diverted the trade in furs to the English, and massacred French and allied Indians alike. And the king sent to Quebec as his representative Alexandre de Prouville, Marquis de Tracy, and appointed as governor Daniel de Remy, Sieur de Courcelle, with Jean Baptiste Talon as intendant.

The viceroy arrived at Quebec in June 1665 with a pomp such as Quebec had never seen before. With him arrived the regiment of Carignan-Salières which had distinguished itself a

year earlier in the Austrian wars against the Turks 1. Quebec had
prepared a most magnificent reception but the Marquis refused
all honours — mainly because he had been ill during the long
voyage. To the sound of the military music, surrounded by his
young nobles, gorgeous in lace and ribbons, with plumed hats
and leonine wigs, the royal procession climbed the steep path-
way to the Upper Town. Twenty-four guards in the king's livery
led the way, followed by four pages and six valets, while the
Frenchmen shouted with profound relief and the Indians stared
in silent wonder at their new defenders 2.

And with the Marquis and his splendid *entourage* had
come not only noblemen, officers and soldiers, but also "settlers,
horses, sheep, cattle, young women for wives ... all sent out in
abundance by his [the king's] paternal benignity 3."

The people of Quebec were overjoyed, entranced and encouraged. Canadian society began to emerge and to form itself
in the *salons* of the governors and intendants, in the homes of
the dignitaries and principal residents, the government officials
and the rich merchants. Some of the noblemen and officers who
had come with the viceroy stayed; others returned a few years
later, but all had brought with them a pale reflection of French
civilization, a glimmer of the pomp and splendour of the French
court and much of their love for pleasures and mundane entertainment. "Thus a sunbeam from the court fell for a moment on
the rock of Quebec 4." An atmosphere of gaiety and abandon
descended upon New France, and in this liberty of fun and frol-
ic the *petite noblesse* of Quebec celebrated the first ball.

The occasion was the appointment of Louis-Théandre
Chartier de Lotbinière as "lieutenant-general for civil and crimi-
nal affairs" *(lieutenant civil et criminel de la prevoté de Québec)*
at the first provost's court at Quebec. Rarely has a relatively insignificant event, such as a ball, been so often cited in Canadian
history books as this joyful episode, of which we know nothing
more than that it took place in February 1667 because the

Superior of the Jesuits had recorded the event in the *Journal* together with the pious wish "may God grant that nothing further come of it 5." Neither the *Journal* nor any other contemporary source revealed what took place at the ball, who the musicians were or what the music had been. Yet it is possible to imagine the impressive gathering of Quebec's society, including Viceroy, Governor and Intendant, together with the officers of the garrison and the prominent citizens of Quebec. Most of the guests had, as we saw, recently arrived from France and, anxious to please them, their host attempted to make the occasion memorable and reminiscent of similar events in the mother-country. The ambitious desire to maintain the splendour of Versailles and Paris, at least in spirit if not in substance, may have provided the stimulating initiative for the glittering affair; thus it is quite possible to assume that even the instrumental performance of the dance music achieved relatively high standards. But it seems impossible to ascertain whether the musicians were residents of Quebec, or had been recruited from the ranks of the garrison. No further reference to the sinful and ominous event appears in the *Journal* or in other annals of New France. Moreover, the *Journal* and the *Relations,* our faithful and most important sources of information, were soon to reach their final pages. Although they had not been concerned too elaborately with the musical activities and had rarely disclosed any details, their accounts have helped to form an idea of the conditions of music in the early years of Canada. The last entry in the *Journal* dates from June 1668, while the *Relations* ended in 1673 6.

Without these "authentic and trustworthy historical documents 7" we must from now on rely on the scanty information coming to us through a few descriptive accounts of visitors and travellers, through the rare annals of religious communities, or through letters and official correspondence. What in former years had been the meagre record of liturgical music and devo-

tional musical activities is now replaced by frustratingly inadequate references to light and superficial entertainment such as
the balls and dances of the new society. And it is paradoxical
that, while with the increase in population secular musical activities had greatly increased, we know far less about music during
the hundred years from 1663 to 1763 than during the early
phases of musical life in New France.

Most observers agree that life in Quebec during the
second half of the 17th, and in the first half of the 18th centuries
had at certain moments something of the atmosphere of Versailles, especially if the governor was at all inclined to mundane
pleasure. And some of them were indeed anxious to transplant
some of the brilliant and radiant splendour of the Court into the
pitifully inferior and dismal Château St. Louis of Quebec. Particularly under the governorship of the Count de Frontenac,
Quebec's society assumed the allures of a small regal court.
Frontenac himself gave the tone to the elegance and gaiety that
had been without precedent in the annals of the colony. He was
naturally fond of lavish entertainment, banquets and receptions,
balls and dances were frequent, and it is only appropriate to assume that music provided the framework for all these activities.

With all the unparalleled glamour and delight at their
disposal, the ladies of Quebec were overjoyed, and the ladies of
Canadian birth were "lovely, educated, flirtatious, ambitious",
observed Baqueville de la Potherie. "They have spirit, charm, a
fine voice for singing and a great disposition for dancing." In
fact, he considers the females of Quebec neither provincial nor
bourgeois; "they are the true women of the world, even of the
world of Paris [8]."

The Governor ordered a small theatre to be built at the
Château St. Louis and during the winter of 1693-1694 the young
officers, together with some of the ladies of Quebec, performed
two plays, *Nicomède* by Corneille, and *Mithridate* by Racine. It
was an amateur performance, but its success was prodigious

"and so was the storm that followed", remarks Parkman [9]. Quebec was divided into two parties, the wordly and the devout. The love of pleasure by the one was watched with unrelenting vigilance by the other.

If some years before, the Jesuits had reason to worry over the consequences of the first ball, theatrical performances, and particularly with female actors, were still more dangerous. Mandates read from the pulpits, condemnations, sermons and threats to excommunications mark the troublesome accompaniment of this important, comical but significant moment in our cultural history. The situation reached fever pitch with the rumour that the Count de Frontenac intended to have Molière's *Tartuffe* performed. Mgr. de Saint-Vallier launched two mandates on the same day, one denouncing the impious, impure and noxious comedies, the other excommunicating the Sieur de Mareuil, an officer of the garrison, who was reported to play the title rôle, and in consequence "was interdicted the use of the sacraments [10]."

The Bishop is supposed to have offered Frontenac the sum of 100 *pistoles* [11] to prevent the performance of the play, but it is indeed not established that the play was ever performed. Many years later La Tour published a story according to which Frontenac, in order to ridicule the clergy, had founded an amateur company expressly to play *Tartuffe*. He also relates that the Governor, not satisfied with having the play enacted at the Château, wanted "the actors and actresses, the dancers, male and female, to go in full costume, with violins and other musical instruments, to play it in all religious communities, except the Recollects [12]," who had been the Count's special favourites. The story, however, according to Parkman, had never been confirmed by any contemporary writer or document and may possibly be considered as a fabrication to blacken the memory of the governor. At any rate, Frontenac had given the colony a moment of remarkable cultural exploit; no doubt the "violins and other recreations" had, at least for a fleeting moment in our chronicle, arrived at Quebec.

A few years later our annals record another cultural event, the only documented instance of serious secular or semi-religious art music. This rare and precious item concerns the "Soirées musicales" at the residence of Jacques Raudot, the intendant of New France from 1705 to 1711.

In the annals of the *Hôtel-Dieu* of Quebec, Monsieur Raudot is described as an elderly gentleman "full of spirit, endowed with easy and agreeable conversation who could speak well on all sorts of matters" and presumably also about music. His usual entertainment which he liked to share with his guests was a "concert of voices and instruments, making a charming harmony. In his obliging manner", the annalist of the sisterhood continues, "he wants us to listen to that symphony, and many times he sent his musicians to sing the motets in our church, or some parts of the mass on the holy days 13."

The lack of concern for details is disappointing; the narrator confuses musicians and singers, a frequent occurence in our old sources, both *sing* motets in church, and songs of praise and *noëls* at Monsieur Raudot's residence. The instruments doubled the voice parts, thereby contributing to the "charming harmony" and, while as usual no information is furnished about the musicians, we may indulge in conjectures and speculate whether Monsieur Raudot himself participated as instrumentalist. And although we do not know the nature or the frequency of the "Soirées musicales" we appreciate the efforts of the educated gentleman and amateur of good music for having brought one of the loftier manifestations of French civilization to the colony. The gratifying and laudable enterprise of the musical intendant remained an exception, however, and without further consequence in the chronicle of music.

FRENCH MUSIC IN NEW FRANCE

Many authors deplored the lack of documented evidence concerning vocal and instrumental music in the capital of New France during the 17th and 18th centuries. Nonetheless, Ernest Gagnon explains that "no appreciable aesthetical difference could have existed between the music that was played at Quebec and that which was performed in the provincial towns of Western France. Those were the same compositions, the same art, and even the condition of interpretation were almost identical 14." Statements of this sort are touching in their naivety. Suffice it to refer to the musical life in France by pointing to the Academies of Music which existed in the provincial towns of France since the early 17th-century, or to compare the active musical life in the provinces during the *grand siècle* with the inferior manifestations of the art in Quebec. Nonetheless, it may be assumed that a similarity existed as far as the popular music in the rural areas was concerned. There has likely not been much difference between the light entertainment of the *habitant* of Quebec and the country folk of the Bretagne or Normandie who stomped to the rhythm of the *branles* or other popular dances, and to the shrill and high-pitched sound of a *vielle-à-roue,* except that the use of the latter instrument seems to have been extremely rare in the colony.

"What was the music played on the violin two-and-one-half centuries ago?" asks Gagnon, " we preserved the Gregorian chant in notation; we have also preserved our canticles and our popular songs that had come from France; but the purely instrumental music, the music of the uniquely popular Canadian instrument, the violin, is in our days exclusively English, Scottish or Irish; those are the dance tunes, the jigs, the reels, the hornpipes — nothing of which is French 15."

It is indeed astonishing that so little, if anything, has remained of the popular French dance music of the 17th and 18th centuries. The inability to preserve the artistic dance tunes from the mother-country is not merely an example of acceptance of an inferior expression; it is also a sociological phenomenon. True, the untrained and illiterate *violoneux* of the 19th century could not be expected to maintain and cultivate the heritage of classical French Baroque dances, nor the spirited and graceful dance music of the rococo. If after the conquest and during the 19th century he scratched on his cheap fiddle musically inferior reels, jigs and hornpipes, it was not only because his audience preferred the simple, unassuming and popular style of the British folk-dances to the by far more artistic and sophisticated French dance compositions of earlier days, but he had probably never heard the graceful French dance music of the period.

But there had also been a society, which was anxious to imitate "la bonne société de la vieille France", increasingly desirous of the gaiety and vivacity close to the heart of the pleasure-loving French race; and Gagnon lists the pleasures of that society of bygone days as he finds that "there was very much of good quality in that society of the 17th century [16]." He does not explain that this good society was more likely to be found among the middle and lower classes than among the *élite* of New France. As far as the upper class was concerned, Kallmann regrets not to have "detected any positive evidence of the cultivation of secular art among the educated governors and *seigneurs* of New France [17]." His observation corroborates the suggestion brought forward on earlier pages, that the *élite* of New France, the educated fringe of Quebec and Montreal, the transient government officials and military officers, had failed in their responsability towards art and culture in the colony, and that, in effect, their attitude of neglect and disdain for the higher aspects of music had retarded the progress of musical art.

Neither the recording chroniclers of the religious orders nor the narratives of travellers and visitors, neither the letters of Mme. Begon nor the reports of the Governors, have at any time told of memorable musical events. On the other hand, we have records of the early theatrical performances of the classic dramas by Corneille and Racine, we know the paintings which Frère Luc had left, we know when and where balls and dances were held, and we have learned of other and less important historical episodes. But in the large amount of historical references there are only two or three items which indicate the practice of serious art music. In the light of such undeniable facts it is difficult to accept the strange and somewhat irresponsible statements that works by leading members of the so-called School of Versailles, such as for instance Campra, "... were quite frequently performed in Quebec [18]." Needless to say that not the slightest documentary evidence is produced to substantiate such claim. To do justice to the high quality and technical demands of French Baroque music skilled or highly capable performers are required. Indeed, the technical requirements, the nature, type and form of the pompous and grandiose music of Versailles became the very obstacle to importation of French music into Canada. The first task for the student of Canadian musical history is clearly outlined: to investigate French music of the seventeenth and eighteenth centuries in order to discover one of the main reasons why French art music could not and did not blossom on the shores of the St. Lawrence.

Music and art during the famous epoch in French history began, culminated and ended as a thoroughly courtly art, restricted to the privileged estates and far removed and unattainable for the people. From the *ballet de cour,* the favourite pastime of Louis XIII, to the classic operas of Gluck, protégé of Marie Antoinette, French art music was created for the king and the glorification of Versailles. While Louis XIII, himself a fervent musician, singer and composer, inherited the *ballet de cour* and developed the famous *Vingt-quatre Violons du Roi,* the apex of French music came during the long reign of Louis XIV. The King's desire and taste determined the style and form of music and art, of architecture and fashion, and majestic splendour, pomp and magnificence became the symbol of the cult that elevated the anointed King to the divine position of *le Roi Soleil.* And the King commanded the lavishly staged, grandiose and resplendent performances of operas and ballets; his fancy transformed the pure Palestrina-style and lengthy High Mass into a new, shorter but highly dramatic and theatrical service of the Low Mass, the so-called *messe basse solennelle* with its overwhelming combination of soloists of both sexes, double choirs, organs and a full orchestra with trumpets and kettledrums [19]. None of these large-scale forms could possibly have been performed in New France. Apart from the insurmountable physical obstacles in the way of presenting Lully's *tragédies lyriques* or Campra's ballet operas, it would have been quite impossible to find enough musicians, singers and dancers capable of performing such works. But even art music on a more modest scale required the skill of the professional musician, the type of trained instrumentalist who at the very same time, the second half of the seventeenth and early eighteenth centuries, brought musical life in the American colonies to remarkable heights [20].

It is very likely that lute and harpsichord music found its way to the colony. The lute had been extremely popular in France during the 16th and 17th centuries, but gradually the favourite instrument of kings and queens, of statesmen and famous *femmes galantes* of the period became replaced by the guitar with its simpler technique of chord strumming that suited the monodic style of the time. French *clavecin* (harpsichord) music culminated in the first half of the 18th century in the music of François Couperin, called "the Great". The characteristic sound of the instrument, charming, delicate, graceful and frivolous served well the spirit of the rococo and, no doubt, delighted audiences in the salons of New France. Yet the possibility that lute and *clavecin* became a substantial part of Canada's musical life is extremely remote, inasmuch as only rarely have these instruments been registered in one of our most accurate source of information, the notarial inventories. In comparison to the flourishing state of instrumental music in the American colonies, particularly in the Central and Southern states, New France did have little to offer in this field. Again, a glance at conditions in France will help to understand this odd situation.

Instrumental music had never been popular in France; it could not find an independent place in a musical realm that was traditionally attached to opera and ballet, it never was as much practiced as in England, in Italy or in the German-speaking lands. Chamber music and concerto were slow in gaining a foothold, and symphonic music did not become popular until the middle of the 19th century. This factor must be appreciated before we embark on a comparison with the Puritans who brought the rich English viol and consort music to New England, or the Swedes, Germans and Moravians who imported their remarkable musical culture and their instruments to the Central states, or the plantation barons of the Southern states whose love and interest in musical entertainment built opera houses and symphony halls in the early 18th-century. But the French did not care for instrumental music other than that incidental to opera and ballet. Their traditional predilection for vocal music, already discussed on earlier pages, relegated instrumental music to secondary importance, and accounts for the long and proud history of the *chanson* from the early Middle Ages, from the times of the Troubadours and Trouvères to the *Chansonniers* of today.

Hence, early musical life in New France was probably poor in instrumental music but well supplied with *chansons* and songs of all types. This does not exclude some instrumental music for balls and dances performed by some fiddlers and some percussion instrument. The charming Mme. Bégon attended and recorded for posterity the many balls which had become the rage of Montreal in the 1740's. The letters to her son are at times a delightful chatter of local gossip, but nowhere does she mention such prosaic matters as the instruments, who the musicians were who entertained the dancers until the small hours of the morning, nor what the type of music had been to which the guests danced. But even without her help it is not difficult to point to the minuet as most likely the favourite dance at those festivities. Ever since the days when Louis XIV himself introduced the first minuet composed by Lully in 1653, the new dance became most popular all over Europe and quickly superseded the older dances. The popularity of the minuet in France was reflected in the colony and its rustic origin and its relationship to the lowly *branle* suggests that less sophisticated forms of the minuet were also popular with the lower classes. This view is also held by R. L. Séguin who remarks that "... in New France habitant and gentleman dance the minuet — a sign that the art is not held back by social barriers [21]." The suggestion, however, by the same writer that "the quadrille and the minuet share equally in the favour of the *noblesse,* the bourgeoisie and the peasant class [22]" is not correct because the quadrille as a dance form became popular only in the early 19th century.

Mme. Bégon was not troubled with musico-historical thoughts, but she was upset and embarrassed when at the occasion of a visit of the British envoy in January 1749, Monsieur Noyan in his eagerness to dance the minuet after having enjoyed some quantity of wine, tumbled down "en coulant son menuet", while his wig fell to one side and he to the other [23]. At another occasion there was a "grand dîner chez M. le général" but since he was not a dancer he was quite content to have singing instead, hence his guests remained until eleven o'clock singing at the table, but not dancing [24].

And there was no scarcity of songs, of *chansons,* of *airs de cour,* and of the old and beautiful French folksongs. Indeed, singing, this characteristic element of the *nation chansonnière,* came again to the fore, and perhaps even stronger in the geographical and cultural isolation from the mother-country. Most travellers noticed the great love for singing among the French-Canadian, from the *Seigneur* to the lowly *habitant,* and particularly among the women, whose songs, in the words of Peter Kalm, the Swedish traveller who visited New France in 1749, "contain frequently the word *l'amour*".

THE FINAL YEARS

While Mme. Bégon has disappointingly little to relate about the music-making at Montreal's whirlpool of festivities, Montcalm, the famous French general and hero of Quebec, left us a few succinct references to music, lacking in necessary details but enough to conjure up a fascinating picture of a musical life that could have distinguished the French colony. Alas, those were the last days of New France, the musical life was near its end, and Montcalm's despair in the face of overwhelming military odds was matched only by the disgust with which he witnessed a doomed society, blind to the coming disaster in the frantic desire for pleasure and diversion. Montcalm's letters are documents, tragic, accusing and illuminating the darkest moment in the history of New France. But even he could not help being drawn into the spirited and exciting life of *grands dîners,* balls, dances and especially card games — even after a royal decree had forbidden all games of chance. So does he describe the evenings at the infamous last intendant Bigot where "... almost every evening his salons, magnificently illuminated, are filled with ladies in most elegant attire, and officers in their brilliant uniforms; music is made at times, dances are frequent, one always plays at cards and dines afterwards most sumptuously, and these feasts are prolonged very far into the night [25]."

In his terse style he notes on December 16, 1757: "Sunday supper for eighty, many ladies, *concert, lansquenet,* (game of chance) for nine dealers..." and two days later he enters into his diary one of the rare, and also the very last, reference to musical activities: "At the occasion of the concert, performed by the officers and the ladies, the Intendant had assembled a large company. There was as good music as it is possible to perform in a country where the taste for art has not gained much foothold 26." Montcalm viewed the sober facts of the artistic poverty after one and one-half centuries, unlike some of our modern historians who insist on seeing through the golden haze of a distant and romantic past "... the brilliance of seventeenth-century France (that) was to leave its mark on this first period of artistic life in Canada 27."

The implication, however, is clear; French-Canadian society indulged at times in music making. That this was not merely confined to vocal music is shown by other entries in Montcalm's diary in which violins are mentioned. Although vocal music was obviously easier to perform by ladies and officers, the dearth of instrumental teachers and professional musicians must have greatly curtailed instrumental musical activity in the colony. Nonetheless, the existence of instruments in New France is confirmed a few years later in notices and advertisements in the newspapers which announce the sale or the auction of instruments belonging to French-Canadians.

An interesting social distinction is noticeable in the description of musical activities at that time which also leads to conjecture concerning the type of music performed. Montcalm relates that ladies and officers make music while Mme. Bégon's letters do not reveal the identity of the musicians. Montcalm's music-makers were from among the fine ladies of Quebec's society and the handsome officers of the garrison. Their social status was certainly above that of the unknown musicians, and although their musical proficiency cannot be assessed nor compared it is probable that these members of Quebec's elite indulged in music of a more sophisticated nature, perhaps the *clavecin* music of Couperin, some operatic arias or duets or some other examples of the gay, charming and frivolous music of the French Rococo. Mme. Bégon's concern is to relate the social whirl of balls and dances, hence it may be assumed that the performing musicians had been either servants or at best itinerant fiddlers who stayed in the towns only as long as their services were required, playing the favourite and popular dances of their day.

But all this did not matter any longer: the volleys of cannon balls on the morning of September 13, 1759, brought with a shrill discord to an abrupt end the prelude to our musical history. One hundred and fifty years had elapsed since the days of Champlain's founding of Quebec, and there can be little doubt that, except for religious music, the chronicle of our early musical past recorded disappointingly few manifestations of musical accomplishments. As inadequate as the documented evidence of musical events in the first hundred years had been, even greater was the obscurity that had descended upon musical life during the last fifty years in the French colony. Indeed, "... the eighteenth century, except for its final decades, is a rather dark age in the recorded musical history of Canada [28]."

VIII

Music of the People

FRENCH FOLKSONG

Two types of musical expression flourished side by side like wild flowers in the neglected musical wilderness that was New France: the one of primeval origin, primitive and exotic, deeply rooted in the unchangeable bondage of ritual and custom; the other a distant descendant of the *fleur-de-lis,* a reminder of the proud heritage of ancient France and still bearing traces of a great musical era. Diametrically opposed and musically incompatible, yet connected in the similar functional purpose as the expression of the people, here was the meeting place of two cultures, the juxtaposition of tradition and transplantation. Much has been written about French folksong in Canada, and much research has been devoted in recent years to the field of Indian folklore and music ı, yet the very nature of both forms, as well as the lack of substantial musical evidence, precludes satisfactory investigation into the origin and early manifestations of the music. Modern technology arrived too late on the scene to record with electronic means the pure and unadulterated sound of Indian music, nor have folklorists been able to reconstruct the true and original content of the early French folksongs. Both Indian music and French folksong are in great danger of extinction and it is gratifying that in recent years attempts have been made to preserve these two relics of the past from total oblivion.

Few Canadians are acquainted with the historical aspects of music in Canada but many are to varying degrees familiar with at least a small portion of the heritage of French folksong. Such familiarity varies according to racial and cultural backgrounds; it is not limited to one or the other sector of the populace but, in general, does hardly extend much beyond the standard repertory of a few favourite melodies that had been sung at home, taught in the schools, or have remained the cherished components of merry-making. Yet the quantity of folksongs gathered since the early years of this century is enormous; more than 8,000 melodies, and more than 13,000 texts have been discovered, collected and recorded, at first on old-fashioned and inadequate wax cylinders, and in more recent years with the aid of modern recording devices. This amazingly large number of songs had been drawn from the capacious memory of some forty folksingers of Quebec whose repertory seemed indeed inexhaustible. Included in the large collection are, of course, the many versions of the same theme, sometimes only slightly modified in textual and musical content, but very often greatly contrasting in style and texture, in music and words. A good example of this phenomenon is provided by the popular song *Trois Beaux Canards* of which over one hundred slightly changed versions and thirty entirely different tunes have been gathered.

From the musico-historical point of view, the vestiges of ancient French folksong now preserved in the archives of Canada represent items of considerable interest for the ethnologist as well as the student and admirer of folklore, both in Canada and in France. French folklorists were delighted to find the wealth of old French folklore accumulated and faithfully guarded on the banks of the St. Lawrence, in the Gaspé peninsula and in the hinterland of Quebec. They had discovered, as one of them remarked, under the protective cover of the "arpents de neige" the flower of the Gallic folksong still as fresh as at the time of its expatriation from France and they hoped, in the words of Marguerite d'Harcourt [2], to reconstruct, with greater accuracy than had been possible in France, the melodies of the French *chanson*. "It is to be understood", adds the noted French folklorist, "that the character of the melodies remained absolutely French [3]." And none less than Olivier Messiaen expressed the pleasure of the French folklorists in grateful appreciation: "Chantez ces belles chansons de notre douce France (qui n'est pas si douce que ça) et n'oubliez pas de verser une petite larme de reconnaissance pour nos amis canadiens qui nous les ont si précieusement conservées [4]."

French folksong had come to New France with the early settlers from the Normandy and the Ile de France, and with the later emigrant from Poitou, Saintonge and the Basse-Loire. It is estimated that fully nine-tenths of the folksongs collected until now are musical and textual derivatives of the songs that had been brought to New France by the colonists between 1665 and 1673, while only a relatively small number of songs, including those from the Napoleonic era, found their way to Quebec during the 18th and 19th centuries [5]. Even smaller is the number of original Canadian folksongs, particularly as far as the melodies are concerned.

Deprived of the stimulating sources from the mother-country, the *habitant* preserved the precious heritage that had been entrusted to him, handing it from father to son until, some fifty years ago, it reached the last of the capable folksingers, who may well have been "the son of the same illiterate peasant who, in the 17th century, had received the precious depot of our popular treasure [6]."

In the physical and intellectual isolation of the new environment, the richness and beauty of the ancient French folksong filled the emotional needs, served at work and at social functions, remained the cherished souvenir and the jealously guarded property of the singer and, after the conquest of 1759, became an expression of defiance in an even more emphatic and self-imposed cultural seclusion against the British intruders. Far from being an expression of ethnic characteristics, the French folksong as a manifestation of French musical culture and tradition has remained the symbol of a national consciousness. An ever-present patriotic sentiment emphasizes the spiritual link with France; "the singing of *A la claire Fontaine* is almost to raise the flag of old France [7]" while *Un Canadien errant* (Canadian in text only) will not fail to bring tears to many eyes.

But how did the French-Canadian singer guard the precious heritage? The treasures of the French folkmusic retained much of the stylistic characteristics of the 17th century and occasionally preserved in faint traces of modality some of the flavour of its mediaeval ancestry. Yet in the three centuries of sojourn in Canada the ancient French tunes had in the process of oral transmission undergone such changes that their original prototype was hardly recognizable. If the words may be similar or identical, the melodies are entirely or slightly modified, and in most instances there is hardly any resemblance between the old and the re-discovered French folksongs except in the subject matter.

Folklorists explain such process of change and modification as an expression of animated and constantly renewing evolution; they believe that, while folk music is "a heritage of the past, it kept its freshness and vitality thanks to the constant transformations to which it had been subjected in the course of oral transmission [8]."

In exemplary loyalty to their vocation they persuade themselves that a folksong "is distinguished from an artsong not because it had been written without the knowledge of the art but because, instead of being the work of a single individual, the folksong is the complex product of many generations of singers who, after much groping, found the form of expression which suited the spirit of the community 9."

The aureole of "divine origin", of mystic "self-conception" or of "collective creation" which so often distracts from the sober facts, had long been discounted by modern scholars who regard each folksong as the product of an individual, while its "collectivity" is discernible only in the modification by others in the course of decades and centuries 10. But the folklorists deplore the attitude of the learned musician and scholar towards folkmusic; they are in all seriousness convinced "that the best works of folklore are comparable to the works of the great masters 11." On the other hand, they admit that the ephemeral nature of the folksong had been part of its strength. With the advent of printing, the number of folksongs greatly diminished. Their musical inferiority became apparent and their reliance on the time-bound past excluded them from the evolutionary process. One noted folklorist complains of the state of oblivion to which folkmusic became relegated in countries that had been in the forefront of cultural progress and evolution — hence the degree of development correspond to the disappearance of folkmusic 12.

The inevitable process of decline and destruction did not spare the French-Canadian folksong, and Canada, like other nations, had to submit to the universal law which destroys folkmusic, even if the evil should spread in that country much slower than elsewhere 13. Had it not been for the almost incredible, unceasing efforts of the indefatigable Marius Barbeau, our knowledge of French-Canadian folksong in Canada would be extremely limited. It was he who with enormous enthusiasm went in search of the priceless heritage and, although neither trained musician nor musicologist, collected, classified and lovingly annotated the musical remnants of French culture in Canada. Rescued from oblivion, the enormous collection has come to rest in the archives of Canada, awaiting its renaissance.

In his highly valuable efforts, Barbeau had been aided by the fact that the musical and poetical art of the popular French folksong was better and more abundantly preserved on the banks of the St. Lawrence than at their source in the provinces of France, where at all times the music submitted to renewing influences [14].

The claims to the origin of folkmusic are often tinged with romantic imagination and patriotic sentiment. While the sources of folksong are obscured by the passing of time, it is a well known and established fact that the "civilized folksong" — as distinct from aboriginal and primitive music — assimilated the highly advanced elements of church music as well as the superior resources of the educated *élite*. In other words, folkmusic, while contributing its share to the development of music, particularly in the melodic aspect, was greatly influenced by the gradual sinking of art music to the popular level.

This influence from above to below is shown to some degree in the stylistic features which appear occasionally in the French-Canadian folksong; some illustrate the Troubadour style in the verse structure, while in others the textual similarity and the florid style of the melodies indicate the affinity with Trouvère sources. The ethnologist likes to emphasize that a great number of rediscovered and registered folksongs resemble the artistic creations of the chivalrous knights of ancient France and had reached the lower social strata through the wandering minstrel and jongleur. Messiaen finds the striking difference between the French songs of old France and those of Canada in the purity of the Gregorian modes as well as in the neumatic style of some melodies, similar to the ancient ornamentation in the less florid chants of the church [15].

But we must bear in mind that most, if not all, of our *existing* or known folksongs show clearly the features and technical devices which originated in the vocabulary of art music, such as strict meter and measure, clear and regular phrases, well-defined tonality (at times with some reminders of modality), definite structural forms, triadic intervals, etc., and we must also remember that the balanced union of these components did not exist in the Middle Ages. Hence, a folksong as we know it might have been invented not earlier than the 17th century, or undergone such modifications as to render it in the course of years acceptable to our changing musical comprehension. In fact, the published collections of the French-Canadian folksongs show an overwhelming number of *chansons* of the popular type which developed during the 17th and 18th centuries.

Fortunately, our Canadian folksinger was unconcerned with such thoughts; he sang the way he knew best, and the result in the course of years was a gradual modification and frequently stark mutilation of the original song, such as is the very nature of orally transmitted music where neither the strictly enforced tradition nor the discipline of the ritual is involved. The extent of such modification depended largely on the musical interpretation of the singer, his vocal ability and his musical ear and memory. As Mme. d'Harcourt explains, none of the folksingers whom she encountered had been musically trained; they could neither read nor write. Their art varied from one subject to another and they treated the musical prosody (the application of the words to the music and vice versa) with little respect — indeed with great license. The singer felt free to improvise, to improve or to impair; he may have added a few turns here and there to demonstrate his ability and to impress his audience or he may have eliminated notes which his failing voice could no longer produce or his weakened memory no longer retain. He would change the note values and alter the intervallic relationship even within the repeated verses, for he was indifferent to musical meter and unconcerned with musical accents, which he let fall wherever they may. He was, like his French cousin, more concerned with the text — the rest was of less importance.

But while his French cousin could hardly escape the impact of the renovating trends in French secular art music, the almost complete absence of such art music in New France deprived folksong and folksinger of its most stimulating source. It is interesting to observe the disparity in French-Canadian folk-art on the one hand and its musical counterpart on the other. Created under the artistic influence from the mother-country, the former is manifested in the beautiful handicraft, in exquisite wood-carving, in fine silverwork and embroidery, in weaving and the making of furniture, most of which developed into a distinctive Quebec style. In contrast, the strong dependency on the musical resources of French popular art, the persistence in maintaining the French musical idiom or the inability to free itself from it, retarded rather than helped in the development of an indigenous folkmusic; it did not encourage the growth of a characteristically Canadian folksong in a typical Canadian expression. The number of original French-Canadian folksongs is therefore incredibly small; local compositions remained insignificant, and the character of their music differs hardly from the original French songs; they are, in fact, often merely adaptations 16. Thus the settlers of early New France and their descendants of later Lower Canada were content with the rôle of guardians, the curators of an art that had already been forgotten in the country of its origin. And because it had been a moribund art form, nurtured only by the nostalgic sentiment of the older generations, untouched by the renewing and invigorating influences from the pulsating cycle of evolution, the decline of folkmusic in Canada was inevitable. Indeed, folksong, in the usage and function of earlier times, had become a doomed art, irreverently thrown to the artistic garbage dump by the universal crave for the commercially dictated and exploited " popular " music, or at best limited to the local activities of specialized groups. And today's internationally-perpetrated popular music with its modern harmonic structure, its exciting rhythmic complexity and colourful originality of orchestration has successfully replaced folksong as the means of national expression and as the uniting force at social function. The cherished but antiquated reminder of the past has lost its place in the daily life of the population.

INDIAN SONG AND DANCE

The chronicle of musical life in New France cannot neglect another type of folk music current in early Canada; it cannot disregard a musical activity that had existed in the wilderness, a musical expression that was as much of a different type and quality as it had been relatively superior and by far more extensive than the musical manifestation of the Europeans.

The strange and exotic sound of Indian music attracted the Europeans from earliest times. Those who were interested in the customs and habits of indigenous tribes attempted to describe the life of the Canadian Indian as they saw it. They observed the ceremonies, the rituals and the feasts; they listened to the songs and the beating of the drum, and according to their capacity of comprehension were either impressed or indifferent, fascinated or disgusted. The narratives of the early explorers, the descriptions of the travellers, the annals of the chronicler, and above all the writings of the missionaries and the priests, are records of musico-historical value and, just as much as Indian life is inseparably attached to Canadian history, so are the musical activities of the native population part of the chronicle of music in New France.

The musical activities of the Canadian Indian were first observed by Jacques Cartier in 1535 and are recorded in his *Voyages de découverte au Canada.* But investigation of native traits was not relevant to his primary task; his references to music are therefore of a general nature. The first detailed description appears in the *Histoire de la Nouvelle France* of 1609, by

Marc Lescarbot. The inclusion of examples of Indian music in staffless letter-notation render the work of the first historian of Canada particularly interesting to musical research. The *Histoire* has remained amongst the most important early sources of information and has frequently been alluded to in later works. Of equal significance is the work of Gabriel Sagard-Theodat, the first historian of the Recollects in Canada, who had spent some time among the Hurons. A whole chapter of his *Histoire du Canada* is devoted to Indian music and dance, supplemented by examples of music in staff-notation which, for want of other pertinent information, may be considered as the first printing of original Canadian Indian melodies. Of interest are Sagard's naive settings in four-part harmony of the Indian songs collected by Lescarbot. Other instances of printed music, based on Marc Lescarbot's recording, are found in Joannes de Laet's *L'Histoire du Nouveau Monde* of 1660, in the *Histoire de l'Amérique Septentrionale* by de la Potherie. Among the most important documents are the *Jesuit Relations,* which abound with information and description of native music and musicians, including the remarkable transcription of an Indian song by Father Marquette.

The source of Indian music is buried in the fathomless depth of ancient times and theories that attempt to delve into its origin are hardly more than pleasing speculations. Like all primitive music, transmitted orally from generation to generation, it had doubtlessly existed long before the arrival of the white man, but its quality and content, its construction and performance, can no longer be established. Even if musical notation were available, reproduction would be impossible since, more than any other ingredient, the true, stylistic manner of performance is the outstanding characteristic of Indian music. In the written notation this essential feature is lost, no matter how complicated and intricate a system of notation could be invented. The innate and involuntary agitation finds expression in music as in dance and language, and determines the manner of execution, regardless of the immediate purpose or content. Hence it is not *what* but *how* it is done [17].

The study of Indian music commenced in the latter part of the 19th century and resulted in a considerable collection of valuable and interesting material, but it was only with the advent of modern technical devices that exact reproductions of Indian music with all its irregularities of intonation, rhythm and performance could be attempted. Yet modern research can base its findings only on the musical activities of the contemporary Indian; it has to consider centuries of European influence, and to assume deviations from the accomplishments of the unknown historical past.

The complexity assumes even greater proportion when we consider the differences that existed between the various tribes. The presumption that all tribes were alike has long been repudiated. Admittedly, there were common traits and common characteristics, but there were also many differences in their customs and ways of living, in their political and social structure as there were in their musical activities, their folklore and dances, and in their songs. To describe the many festivities, ceremonies and rituals that were accompanied by music and dance would lead beyond the scope of this work ; moreover, it is not intended to embark on a study of primitive art in general and Indian music in particular. Instead it is proposed to illustrate through quotation from the early pages of our historical annals the different opinions and contrasting appraisals as expressed by explorer, priest and traveller. The quantity of available material is not only in stark contrast to the sore lack of references to European music, but affords an interesting and absorbing comparison of the many aspects of Indian music — superior in variety of purpose and complexity of spiritual significance to the musical expressions of Europeans.

From birth to death, music surrounded the Indian, accompanied his actions, and released in the ceremonies, the rituals and the festive celebrations the unrestrained and powerful emotional force which dominated his whole being. Music and dance had a function to fulfill; it was a means of accomplishing definite results and a way of approaching the great Unknown in order to achieve what was beyond the power of the individual.

Every song had a definite purpose and, associated with some tribal custom, was used only for the performance of such a custom. There is rarely any evidence of music for its own sake or as pleasant pastime distraction. From the prayers of thanksgiving and dedication that greeted the new-born child, to the dirges and sombre expressions of mourning, the amazing number of songs is equalled only by the abundance of occasions for musical activities. In comparison with European folk music, the Indian seems to have had a far larger repertory of musical expression as far as type and category is concerned. In contrast to "civilized" folk music, songs about love, work, clothing, gambling, drinking, etc., are not found in the early documents and appear only seldom even in later references. It is noteworthy that, with few exceptions, hardly any of the songs have a personal significance or are reflective of individual mood and feeling; they are mainly group songs or intended for an audience. The Indian connected a song with an appropriate ritual or ceremony; he regarded music-making not as an art but as part of a sacred and mystic rite, whether it concerned the invocations to the deities or the ritual of the steam-bath, and he preserved through careful observance of prescribed rules the time-honoured tradition of tribal customs which had been handed to him by his elders.

Lescarbot recorded his interesting observations: "The use then of their dances is for four ends, either to please their gods (let who will call them devils, it is all one to me) as we have marked in two places before, or to cheer up somebody, or to rejoice themselves of some victory or to prevent sicknesses. In all these dances they sing, and make no dumb shows [18]." The four main categories of songs as described by Lescarbot as well as later writers may thus be tabulated according to the following groups: (1) religious songs; (2) social and communal songs; (3) war and historical songs; (4) songs of healing and mourning. To the main category of *religious songs* belong the dream or vision songs, the mystical songs such as the invocation to the deities, and the dedications and songs of thanksgiving. *Social and communal songs* accompanied the festivities, the *tabagies,* the games and other public events, while *war and historical songs* are encountered not only in preparation for battle but include likewise the saga of a legendary past and of heroic conquest, as well as the songs of present and future deeds of heroism, the songs in praise of the great warriors. In this category will be found the prisoner and torture songs and dances, the scalp songs and, at cessation of hostilities, the highly important symbol of peace, the *Calumet* song. The *healing songs* occupy considerable space in our annals. In addition, the category includes description of songs and dances at the memorial services that were held at certain intervals in honour of the dead. Other songs that have been recorded may be grouped under the heading *miscellaneous songs* and include the songs presumably invented for singular occasions, as well as those that do not correspond to any of the foregoing categories.

Religion, or superstition as the missionaries called it, and music were inseparable. Le Jeune had noticed that natives used the *songs of superstition* in a thousand different ways, since all of their religion consisted "quasi à chanter". Lescarbot had found that their songs and dances were primarily instituted for religious purposes, as indeed Indian music seems predominantly connected to rituals, and to the large number of religious rites corresponds an equally large amount of devotional music. The natives believed in the power of the priest-physician; overawed by the performance of weird witchcraft, entranced by magic dances, incantatory sounds and words which they did not understand, they accepted the mystic rites in solemn reverence. Le

Jeune wrote down part of the text of "a long superstition which lasted more than four hours", but was unable to ascertain the meaning of the words. "I asked for the meaning of the words, but not one of them could give me an interpretation; because it is true that not one of them understands what he sings, except in the songs which they sing for recreation [19]."

The irrepressible Marc Lescarbot believes to have discovered similarities in certain aspects of Indian and European cults. "Our Souriquois do make also dance and songs to the honour of the devil, who shows them their game, and that they think to gratify him; whereof one need not to marvel, because that we ourselves, that be better instructed, do sing Psalms and Songs of Praise to our God, for that he give us our daily food [20]."

Healing ceremonies were a communal affair, the rites being performed by the medicine-men, often assisted by a juggler and sometimes by a group of hired women and girls, but always attended by a large audience that joined in the noisy activities. In one report we are invited to be spectators of the "plus raffinée" sorcery of the land: "The sorcerer enters with a turtle-shell rattle in his hand, half filled with small pebbles ... he takes his place in the middle of a dozen of women who are going to help him to chase the evil, and the neighbourhood is assembled to watch that superstition – for it is nothing else than that – particularly when the magician beats his turtle-shell on his mat, intoning some songs, and the women dance around him to the rhythm of his song and to the noise he makes with his rattle[21]." A similar account was given by Le Jeune who also added some interesting information with regard to the use of the drum in the hands of the medicine-man:

> They make use of these songs, of the drum, of the noise or pandemonium to heal their illnesses ... the sorcerer enters as in ecstatic fury, singing, screaming, shouting, howling, making noises on his drum with all his force; meantime the others howl like he, and make

a horrible pandemonium with their sticks, beating on what is in front of them; they make first their children dance, then the girls, and then the women; the sorcerer blows on the drum, draws it under his chin, shaking and turning it, striking the ground with all his might so hard, you would say that he wants to smash it to pieces; and all the time running around the fire, and in and out of the cabin, constantly howling and bellowing — *voilà*, this is how they treat their sick [22].

The musical aspects did not please one of the annalists; Father Mercier wrote from the Huron country, describing a healing ceremony or *Aoutaenhrohi* feast: "Twenty-four persons were chosen to sing and to perform all the ceremonies; but what songs, and what tones of voices ! For my part, I believe that if the demons and the damned were to sing in hell, it would be about after this fashion; I never heard anything more lugubrious and more frightful [23]."

In the *Histoire du Canada*, Sagard has left us some detailed and vivid description of healing ceremonies among the Hurons. Like Lescarbot before him, Sagard also noticed the attitude of the Indians towards impudent songs: "But most laudable among them is that it never happens that they sing a bad or scandalous song, as is done here (in France); and if a Frenchman sings, and they ask him to explain the words, and if he tells them that the song is about love or some mundane song, they are not content and say *Danstan Tehongniande,* this is not good, and they will not anymore listen [24]."

On the other hand, Sagard is shocked and repelled by the licentious spectacle of another healing ritual that resembled a sexual orgy and he prays that conversion shall prevent such detestable occurrences: "May God abolish such damnable and unhappy ceremony, together with all those that are of the same kind, and that the French who foment them by the bad example, open the eyes of their spirit to see the strict account which they will have to render one day before God 25."

   To judge from the frequency with which the healing ceremonies have been described, it is certain that our chroniclers were interested and fascinated by the weird and often orgiastic rituals, the mystic invocations to the spirit, and the strange incantations that accompanied the medicine-man's procedure. Here more than in any other ceremony was a visual experience of greatest impact on the observer and while some of the writers were utterly disgusted and condemned in unmistakable terms the devilish, immoral and impudent spectacle, others seem to have been impressed by the display of a primordial rite. None of the early writers seems to have found a kind word for the witch-doctor or sorcerer, nor for the "absurd and ridiculous" methods used by the priest-physician. For the pious missionary, the medicine-man was not only a charlatan, an impostor who believed by making enough noise that he could drive away the demons from the sick; he was also the enemy of the true religion, the greatest obstacle in the path to conversion. His power over the natives was very strong, his influence tremendous. He was well aware of the psychological effect which his performance of mystical rites had on the credulous Indian. And he overwhelmed him with his naive means of contortion, of ventriloquism and other simple tricks of the trade, but also with the impressive display of the magical fire dance.

   The consultation of the oracle, a favourite activity of "iongleur et sorcier", consisted of a large inventory of artful deceits. In the words of Le Jeune, "the juggler would howl and sing, constantly varying the tone, whistling in a muffled manner, as from very far, or speaking as if he were in a bottle, or screaming like an owl of the country ... and other similar sounds, disguising his voice so that it seemed to me I heard those puppets which showmen exhibit in France ... in the meantime our sorcerer, who was present, took his drum and began to sing with the juggler who was in the tabernacle ₂₆." But it was only "after a thousand cries and howls, after a thousand songs, after having danced and thoroughly shaken this fine edifice" and, as Le Jeune explains, after three hours of infernal noise, that the invocation of the spirit took place.

Some of the magic secrets of the "sorcerers and jugglers" were revealed to the priests in later years by converted Indians who had previously been actively engaged in healing or other mystic rites. The following "confession" of a former medicine-man is a remarkable example of the importance which the Indian attached to the close union of magic and music. Father Le Jeune was delighted with the conversion of the "new Joseph, which seemed even more considerable since he had conspired for twenty years in the exercise of the *Aoutaenhrohi* or Feast and Dance of the Fire, the most devilish and at the same time the most common cure of the illness which exists in the country ₂₇." This neophyte confirmed all that had already been written before, and he told how at the age of about twenty years he took fancy to follow those who meddled in magic. But he found that he could not endure the fire test, and he learned to pretend and to cover his game as best he could.

> But (Father Le Jeune continues) at the end of some time he had a dream during which he saw himself taking part in one of these dances and feasts, and handling the fire like the others, and at the same time hearing a song, which to his astonishment, he knew to perfection when he woke up. At the first feast that took place, and which was of that nature, he began to sing his song, and little by little he felt himself enter into a state of ecstasy.
>
> He took the hot charcoal and stones with his hands and teeth from the middle of the fire, he submerged his bare arms in the boiling kettle, and all without in-

jury or pain — in one word, he had become master magician. And since then, in the space of twenty years, it happened some times that he took part in three or four Feasts and Dances of that nature on one evening, for the healing of the sick [28].

It is interesting to observe the mystic powers which the Indian attributed to the song. He assured the priest that it is good to burn oneself in order to feel the freshness of the fire in the hands and in the mouth — but all this must take place quickly, and all depends on the *chanson* which one has learnt in one's dream, since otherwise nothing extraordinary will happen. It is also remarkable that the performance of certain songs and dances was granted only to the privileged few who had been admitted to the Brotherhood of medicine-men, and who had pledged to keep secret the holy and sacred mysteries that had been entrusted to them.

Feasts were the great events in the daily life of the Indian; they afforded the only pleasant distraction in his existence. Such pleasure was eagerly sought; hence festivities were arranged for all possible occasions. Father Le Clercq mentions a few of them, such as feasts for war, for peace, farewell-feasts and thanksgiving feasts; there are feasts to celebrate health and marriage; in fact, the feasts are, in the words of our missionaries, a subject without end. All festivities begin with harangues and all end with songs and dances. Participation was not confined to the family or to relatives; the whole tribe, and frequently the neighbouring villages, were invited to attend. They have that hospitality and mutual charity, says Lescarbot, "which had been lost among us since Mine & Thine were born [29]."

The Indian enjoyed singing as well as listening to the historical epics in which the glorious deeds of the past were extolled. Lescarbot, in his usual sly manner, pokes fun at the civilized world: "They sing also in their common *Tabagies* (feasts) the praises of the brave captains and *Sagamos* who had killed many of their enemies. Which was practised anciently in many nations and is practised yet amongst us at this day [30]."

But not only the heroic achievements of the past are glorified in song; the Indian warrior revels in the boasting of his own deeds of valour, recounting his heroism and success, and pointing with pride to the many scalps that bear witness to his prowess. The war songs abound in promises to kill the enemy, to return with many scalps and prisoners, and to enhance the glory of the tribe. With music the Indian prepares for war and with music he proposes peace. And peace is always connected to the *Calumet,* the proverbial peace pipe, and one of the most sacred object known to the Indian. It is used in ceremonies designed to conciliate foreign and hostile nations, to conclude lasting peace, to secure favourable weather for a journey or to bring needed rain. According to La Potherie, the Indians will not embark on any important enterprise before having celebrated the *Calumet* with song and dance. The dance is thus highly honoured and particularly famous, "be it to affirm the peace, or to make reunion for a great war, or to celebrate a public rejoicing, or to honour a Nation which had been invited to assist in the celebration. They also use the Calumet for the reception of some important personalities, as if they would want to give them the *divertissement* of a Ball [31]."

Indian diplomacy was closely connected with Indian music; without the *Calumet* song and dance the peace treaties and conferences could not have taken place. The many references to the *Calumet,* however, seem to indicate that the peace song and dance did not prevent the constant renewal of hostilities. The fragile peace with the Iroquois, established by the Marquis de Tracy in 1667, was often broken and entirely disrupted by the cruel massacre of Lachine in 1689, and it was not until Frontenac's expedition in 1696 that the strength of the "oldest military power of North America" was finally broken. The solemn peace treaty of 1701, to the sound of the *Calumet* songs, put a formal end to the Indian warfare.

The great variety of functional purposes is the most striking factor in the Indian music. The diversity of styles, the peculiarities in the manner of performance, and the variance in musical expression as found among the indigenous tribes, have rendered extremely difficult an even moderately accurate classification of the songs as referred to in Canadian annals of the 17th and early 18th centuries. Moreover, the area of investigation is too large to expect unanimity of opinion among the early narrators. Thus we find considerable variety of viewpoints about Indian music, particularly about the characteristics of the songs, the manner of performance, the quality of voices — together with moral sentiments and other personal beliefs. To this may be added the varied stages of musical knowledge of the observer, the personal taste and the degree of tolerance and objectivity. And finally, the assessment of Indian music, influenced as it was by external conditions and visual impressions, was not meant to be accepted as musical analysis but rather as the literary expression of an extraordinary experience which could not fail to fascinate the public. Except for a few general impressions of Indian songs together with some of the striking characteristic features of native music-making, detailed explanations are lacking in the descriptions, and have indeed been absent in matters of primitive music until the late nineteenth century.

The solo song is definitely established in the songs of the warriors. These songs were the exclusive property of the owner, not to be tampered with and violation of the principle was regarded as grave offense. Similarly certain invocations and incantations were carefully protected attributes of the Brotherhood of medicine-men and sorcerers.

Group singing is often referred to in our historical records. Some accounts note the singing by two voices while others inform us of groups ranging from three to twenty-four singers. The repeated references to "harmonious singing" in groups, however, need not be understood as part-singing in a technical sense. Harmonic feeling was unknown to the Indian and songs were always in unison. This has already been noted in the reports which stressed the affinity of the monodic plain-chant with Indian songs and which enabled the missionaries to adapt Indian words to the canticles and hymn-tunes of the liturgy for use in conversion. References by modern writers to harmonic substance in Indian songs are clear evidence of musical influence from the white race. Such references fail to distinguished between the historical and logical aspects on the one hand and the purely romantic point of view on the other.

There is a marked difference of opinion pertaining to the quality of voices and musical ability of the Indian. Some missionaries found the singing of the natives highly unpleasant, particularly when combined with the noises of the percussive instruments. Le Mercier's devastating criticism, mentioned in connection with the healing ceremonies, is by no means an exceptional opinion among early writers. It is true, however, that at rare occasions the priests acknowledged, as we have seen, the good voices of the Indians. In his primitive manner of singing, without the adornment of variation in tone volume or time element, with irregularities and unconcern for pitch and scale system and with hardly any ornamental devices, there was probably a certain natural freshness, an unsophisticated expressiveness without sentimentality. The civilized European who considered the musical manifestations of the Indians as poor and miserable howl of savages applied merely his individual point of view as measure. Such viewpoint is based on European music with its schematic and well-defined tonal system, its unique quality of melodic expression and rhythmic organization. Indian music was a new and peculiar idiom; it remained an incomprehensible experience for the missionaries, and even their assessment of the Indian's voice was influenced by comparison with European standard and obscured by the distracting components of the ritual. The visual impression of the weird rites, such as the healing ceremonies or the mystic invocations to the spirits, the orgiastic excesses or the pacific *Calumet* dance, impaired their opinion with regard to the accompanying music and, as the ceremonial witchcraft stood in the way of conversion, the missionaries not only rejected the "devilish" rituals together with the harmless, albeit not "angelic" music, they also were sceptical of the musical ability of the Indian.

Modern research has attempted to define the degree of such musical ability. Some writers believe the Indian to be capable of performing involved patterns of polyrhythm; others admit a greatly developed sense of rhythm because of his ability to maintain coherence in spite of the striking incongruity between melody and rhythm. It has also been asserted that the Indian is completely unaware of the conflict between the melody and accompanying drum beat. Other writers suggest that the division into smaller scalic intervals not only allows for greater flexibility and expressiveness in the melodies, but is also proof of a comparatively highly advanced tonal system. Yet there are cynics who say that these phenomena merely show the native's inability to keep rhythm or to sing in tune, or to combine both items. They believe that the deviations from pitch were caused not by the singer's instinctive feeling for smaller intervals than those of the diatonic scale, but by their incompetence to maintain accurate pitch [32]. Primitive music lacks the accurate measure of scale steps; it aims neither at pure or tempered intervals, nor at European triad formation, nor at the intervallic relation of other systems [33]. Its melodies are neither constructed nor conceived, but follow simply and solely the motivation to which speech furnishes the raw material. Thus speech-melody supplies not only the initial means, but likewise becomes suggestive of further elaboration in a melodic concept in which acoustically unequal intervals serve as irregular soundsteps [34]. It is therefore obvious that Indian songs cannot be represented in European diatonic scale notation, and the attempts to tabulate the melodies according to established tone systems are merely convenient but at the same time misleading devices to aid in customary classification. Nonetheless, traces of the pentatonic modes have been found and a fairly large percentage of songs of certain tribes end on tones which provide the ear with satisfactory key notes. And again it must be emphasized that modern research is based on investigation among the contemporary Indian who even on his reservation has not escaped the influence of mass communication.

As far as the Indian of New France was concerned, we can only approximate his musical ability and achievement. If the priests had not much good to say about the artistic expressions of our natives, they changed their mind and tune as soon as the Indian changed his. No sooner had the Indian been converted and commenced to chant the spiritual hymns of the church, no sooner had the native children received instruction in singing the plain-chant at the Seminary at Quebec that the missionaries and priests began to extend lavish praise, mixed with tutorial pride upon the musical activities and the beautiful voices of the neophytes. Some of the references bear clear evidence of the change of opinion about the quality of the Indian's voice and musical ability. The priests claimed that conversion had not merely changed the belief but also the voice of the native, and European travellers and explorers shared the astonishment and pleasure at such miraculous development with the priests and the settlers. Dierville recounts enthusiastically the musical activities among the Micmacs:"I have heard them more than once sing at High Mass and at Vespers in the church at Port Royal — the voices of the women in particular are so sweet and moving that I thought to hear the angels sing the praises of the Lord ... [35]" The good voices of the Micmacs were indeed praised by several writers who concurred with Father Lalemant that "the majority of Indian women have very pleasing and soft voices, which they know remarkably well how to keep in tune in singing 36."

Many years later, Father François Nau raves about the Indians at Caughnawaga and combines sheer delight with some very interesting observations about the splendid voices and remarkable intonation of the natives:

> For our Savages singing is a necessary adjunct, as they are incapable of prolonged mental application, and it is on this account that all their prayers are set to music; really it would be a great pity were it not so, they succeed so admirably. I often wished that Rev. Father Landreau, who is so fond of well-executed church music, could be present at our high masses; it would be a greater treat for him than everything he has yet listened to.
>
> The men who sing the first verses would present for him a hundred-fold of friars in a choir, and the women who respond, would seem to him the most numerous community of nuns. But what am I saying? Neither friars nor nuns have ever sung so well as our Iroquois men and women, they have a voice equally sweet and full, and have an ear so fine, that they do not miss even a half note in all the chants of the church which they know by heart 37.

From all available accounts it becomes evident that the Indian's voice was neither inferior nor more unpleasant than the voice of the untrained European. Not only did the extensive constant use of his vocal chords required from early childhood provide a training of the voice that was rarely found in his European counterpart, but it is interesting to note how relatively little in European music corresponds to the concept, the function and purpose, the value and importance, and many other aspects of music in the life of the North-American Indian. How thorough the training of his voice must have been may also be judged by his amazing capacity for prolonged singing. Our chroniclers are astounded at the duration of feasts and ceremonies and marvel at the incessant singing activities. Lescarbot had referred to the extreme length of funeral rites and Biard found perpetual singing and dancing a native characteristic "for such is the kind of life all these people lead when they are together". Le Jeune had found the superstitious ceremonies lasting for four or more hours and had counted almost the same amount of time for singing in the sweat-bath. Lalemant's report emphasized the allnight duration of the songs of mourning, while other reports refer to healing rituals that occupied three to four consecutive days. Like physical strength, a powerful and durable voice was appreciated as a commendable and worthy attribute. It commanded respect and admiration even for the prisoner in the hands of his captor who, as we have already mentioned, was forced to sing for days and hours as an additional form of torture.

The range of voice probably did not differ from that of European singers and, although Lescarbot's early music examples show an extremely limited range, not exceeding the interval of a fourth, the song of the *Calumet* already contained the considerable range of an octave and a half, or the interval of a twelfth, while many years later Baker found the voice range extending over two octaves [38]. Women's voices are not specifically mentioned, except that the excellent manner and the great ease in the performance of spiritual canticles and sacred hymns is frequently praised by our annalists.

Ornamental devices are rarely found in Indian songs but may unwittingly have existed in the form of primitive attempts at gracenotes, appogiaturas, a sort of trill, etc. The syllabic character of the songs precluded the use of extended ligatures but, on the other hand, the Indian was able to group together a few notes of his song with a type of portamento, particularly in the descending melodic line. Characteristic of the manner of singing, however, were the few typical peculiarities as noted in the references. Falsetto was used by the medicine-man, not necessarily as a musical ornament but rather as a device of deceiving and impressing his audience. The effective growling and humming sounds were known to the natives and certain hissing sounds are noted by Le Clercq.

The fine ear and remarkable memory have frequently been mentioned by various observers. In particular were the women praised for their ability to sing in tune. Such statements, of course, refer only to the singing of European sacred music but may, after deducing a certain amount of exaggeration and pious sentiment, be accepted as evidence of normal capacity for intonation. The enthusiastic appraisals of memory, however, are entirely credible. The absence of a system of notation, the oral transmission and the desire to preserve the traditional songs necessitated, and presumably developed, the ability to retain the melodies together with the text. Even though the words to many songs seem to have been of secondary importance, some Indian tribes made use of mnemonic devices consisting of figures suggestive of the ideas and order of their succession, in order to aid the memory for the text. The missionaries encouraged such artificial aid as a convenient method of learning and retaining the prayers and hymns. We are told that Father Le Clercq of the mission at Miramichi pursued the matter further and invented a remarkable system of hieroglyphics that has survived until our time.

Our sources of information fail in detailed references to the rhythmic element and a few remarks pertaining to this important item of Indian music have already been offered on earlier pages. Some modern observers believe that the Indian is capable of poly-rhythmic patterns in the performance of his songs,

while others have not detected any points of coincidence between the melodic rhythm and the accompanying drum beat.
The melody follows mainly a measured rhythm in which the
time values are multiples or fractions of a fixed unit but which
remains without the regular and reiterated accents. It is therefore
obvious that the regular drum beat does not fit to the free vocal
rhythm, but it is questionable whether this irregularity may be
ascribed to a highly developed rhythmic feeling on the part of
the performer or, as some writers have suggested, simply indicates a complete unawareness of the conflicting aspects. A
strictly rhythmical drum beat provided the background for the
dance songs whereas the melodic line may have been in free
vocal rhythm, or due to its syllabic character in measured time.
Frances Densmore, the authority on Indian music, frequently
recorded songs in duple or free meter against the accompaniment of a triple drum beat without, however, synchro-
nization of the audible components at any point. Also the free
recitation style found in the ceremonial songs of the medicine-
men may have concurred with an entirely independent but regular drum beat. Yet these incantations, similar as they were in
function, as well as in rhythmic and melodic motion, to the
chants of the Catholic liturgy, could not be considered subject to
a strict temporal rhythm.

The drum was essential to Indian music, and references
concerning percussive instruments on the North-American continent indicate a variety of drums, ranging from hand-drums of
different sizes to instruments of such dimensions that demanded
several men to play them. The drums of the Canadian Indian,
however, were of modest dimensions, the size of a tambourine,
as Sagard had reported. In addition to the drum, the Indians
also used gourds and tortoise shells, filled with pebbles, and aug-
mented their percussive activities with striking upon kettles or on
simple pieces of wood. As with all investigations into the vast
and varied aspects of Indian music, a simple definition cannot

be expected since the different tribes differed among themselves in their songs and dances as well as their instruments and their performance — which prompted different conclusions from the various observers.

Wind instruments are rarely mentioned in our annals, but flutes existed among certain tribes. Lescarbot referred to the use of flutes among the Souriquois; Perrot mentioned the instrument in his description of the *Calumet*; elsewhere we read of the Scalp dance that was accompanied by the sound of rattles, tambours and flutes, and La Potherie, describing certain customs among young Iroquois, observed that "the young men freely boast of their loves and their war deeds, they also entertain themselves by playing the flute [39]." An interesting, and probably the earliest extant pictorial representation of a flute-like instrument is contained in the *Raretés des Indes* [40], and flutes are also depicted in La Potherie's *Histoire*. It is likely that some tribes used flutes or whistles to warn against approaching enemies, but claims that such instruments were played by the young men of the village to please the maidens and to express their amorous sentiments are extremely doubtful, at least as far as the early period of New France is concerned.

Stringed instruments did not exist among our Indians and care must be taken not to be confused by generic terms, such as "violons ou instruments musicaux", that were frequently employed at that period. Indian-made instruments are extremely rare, not because the Indian was incapable of making them, but because his concept of music and music-making centered solely around vocal expression and through it to the time-honoured tradition of rites and ceremonies.

Before we leave the discussion of Indian instruments, the account given in 1607 by Captain John Smith, the famous pioneer of Virginia, is interesting for its comparison between the Indians of Florida and those of New France:

For their musicke they use a thick Cane, on which they pipe as on a recorder. For their warres they have a great depe platter of wood. They cover the mouth thereof with a skin, at each corner they tie a walnut, which meeting on the backside neere the bottome, with a small rope they twitch them together till it be so tought and stiffe, that they may beat upon it as upon a drumme. But their chief instruments are Rattles made of small gourdes or Pumeons shels. Of these they have Base, Tenor, Counter-tenor, Meane, and Treble. These mingled with their voyces, sometimes twenty or thirtie together, make such a noise as would rather affright, than delight any man [41].

The Indian could neither express nor comprehend the complexity of his emotion in music alone. The ritualistic character of the dance, intensified by physical agitation, aided in the solution of the problems with which his primitive mind otherwise could not cope. And in the combination of dance and music the Indian expressed his fears and his desires, his joy and his despair. Similar to musical expressions of religious nature, the dances served to propitiate the divinities, to exert magic, or to heal illness. They were part of almost all sacred rites, and accompanied almost all festive celebrations. Song and dance are thus more frequently encountered in combination than in single occurence. With a limited vocabulary at his disposal, the Indian compensated for the lack of oral expression with a considerable application of gesture signs, of bodily contortion, and a vivacity of mimicry. With these extra-musical aids the native accentuated the musical narration where it needed elaboration and emphasis. More than any other feature, these ingenious means of expression characterized the manner of performance and distinguished racial and tribal groups. The gesture signs in particular constituted an important inter-tribal means of communication.

In spite of descriptions in our annals that stress the unrestrained and savage performances, the music and dance of the
Canadian Indian may in general be considered as having been
slow and emphatic, and essentially different from the unbridled
emotionalism that, for instance, earmarks African primitive music and dance. It is in fact, the seriousness of purpose in Indian
dance, its importance and its prominence in Indian life, which
are prerequisites for the understanding and appreciation of the
art among the primitive tribes. Some observers failed to recognize the significance of the dance-ritual and merely found the
activities "toujours très impertinent". But Lescarbot contrasted
the recreational, spectacular, erotic and sensual elements that are
combined in the bodily activities of the civilized man with the
sacrificial aspects in the dances of the natives. He remarked that
while the natives make use of dances at all times, "... lascivious
pleasure has not yet so far prevailed against them as to make
them dance at the pleasure thereof, a thing which ought to serve
as a lesson to the Christians 42." In the light of these words, a
sacrificial dance, described by Champlain, is indicative of symbolic significance and profoundly devotional sentiment with
which the natives paid homage to deity. To the accompanying
songs of the men, "all the women and girls proceeded to cast off
their mantles of skins and stripped themselves stark naked,
showing their privities, but retaining their ornaments of *Matachias* which are beads and braided cords made of porcupine
quills, dyed in various colours 43." Champlain related that the act
of disrobing continued at certain intervals during the dance, and
was later followed by the same action of the men. The whole
performance is permeated with the essence of sacrificial cult but
seemed to have been distinguished by dignity and restraint. Similar ritual dances in the nude by both sexes were often part of
healing ceremonies, performed in the presence of sick persons.
But Sagard had been repelled by one of such sacrificial cults
around the sick-bed, which he described in detail; and he was

particularly shocked and repulsed when at the end of the ritual-istic songs and dance the girls selected their partners with whom they wished to retire for the night, only to recommence that same ceremony the next day 44. Thus with invocations through music and dance the Indian offered to the deity the sacrificial renewal of life in an attempt to restore his health. Sagard did not record the therapeutical effect of the remedy.

The religious character of some dances was expressed in the arrangement of the dancers in circular form — the symbolic recognition of the sun as divinity. Lescarbot remarks that "the dances of our Savages are performed without moving from one place, yet they are all in a round (or very nearly so) and they dance vehemently striking the ground with their feet and jumping up in a half-leap 45." One of the most detailed accounts of the manner in which Indian dances were performed is incorporated in Sagard's description. His report includes not only the particulars of the dance itself, but also an account of the costumes, the masques and the facial painting, as well as the primitive ornaments with which the natives adorned themselves at such occasions 46. Observers frequently compared Indian danc-es with those of France; so did Father Ragueneau report in the *Relations* that: "... most of those dances resemble the *branles* that are danced in France; the others are in the form of ballets, with poses and harmonies that have nothing savage in them, and are according to the rules of art; all these are performed in cadence and in rhythm with the chanting of certain persons, who are masters of that calling 47." Champlain noted that the dances he had seen contained some sort of measure, one of four steps and the other of twelve, which resembled to him the *Trioly* of Brit-tany.

It is also of interest to note the native's reaction to Eu-ropean dance. Clearly a moral and spiritual concept, heightened by the intensity of expression and by rhythmic precision, per-vaded Indian dance movements, and in comparison the relative artistic quality of some Indian dances appears superior to the clumsy and meaningless entertainment of the Europeans. Yet as in the case of European music, the Indian not only enjoyed the visual impression received from the performance of the European dance, but was eager to imitate the movements that were to him strange but appealing.

The custom of providing religious music with words in Indian language instead of Latin text conveniently helped in education and conversion, and instead of "howling noises" the priests enjoyed the beautiful voices of the natives: "The beauty of their voices is exceptionally rare, especially those of the girls, for whom there have been composed, and adapted to the airs of the Church hymns some canticles in Huron language, which they sing in a charming manner. It is a holy consolation, far from being barbaric, to hear the fields and forests resound so melodiously with the praises of God, in the midst of a country which not long ago one called barbaric [48]." The preceding reference indicates adaptation of Indian words to European religious songs but although Father de Quen had already touched on the problem of spiritual text, adapted to Indian melodies, there is no evidence that such procedure had actually been followed. A report by Father Marest is therefore slightly ambiguous since he did not specify the origin and type of the music when he wrote that "these canticles are veritable instructions which they retain more easily because the words are set to airs which they know, and which are pleasing to them [49]." Although it is not unlikely that the missionaries may have used Indian melodies equipped with French spiritual text, it seems more plausible that the reference concerns some hymn tunes which the Indians already knew and which they enjoyed. A similar ambiguity exists in the report by Father André: "In order to animate more and more their fervor, I advised myself to compose some spiritual canticles, which I had no sooner sung in the chapel, with a recorder (since one must do all and everything to convert all of them to Jesus Christ) that they came in masses, big and small 50." The difficulty in interpreting the meaning of the verb *composé* has already been emphasized. Again we are unable to state whether Father André composed the text, or the music, or both. He played the recorder to attract and impress the natives, as had been done by other missionaries and with various instruments. In the *Relations* of 1655 we read that at the end of religious services "we sang some spiritual motets, a small violin *(Poche)* having joined, and harmonizing well with the voices of the Savages 51." And from another entry in the *Relations* we learn of a small, unidentified instrument that had been used at the inauguration of a new mission centre at the Iroquois 52.

The appearance of these instruments in our historical sources, however sporadic, confirms the fairly extensive custom among the missionaries of enhancing the services with some modest instrumental accompaniment. The extent and frequency of these occurrences obviously cannot be ascertained but it is certain that in all instances the priests used small instruments that could be transported easily and even be carried in the pockets of the priest's cassock.

An interesting and slightly amusing episode involving some larger instruments is told by Father Ragueneau in the *Relations* of 1658. In spite of peace treaties and the intermittent cessation of hostilities, the missionary activities among the Iroquois were not free of danger. In former years the priests ventured singly or in pair to their task but it was often thought advisable to aid them with an escort of soldiers and even with such precautionary measures escape was the only and most frequent alternative that could save the priests and their escort from torture and death. Through a converted Indian, reports Father Ragueneau, the Europeans learned of a conspiracy which the treacherous Iroquois had conceived against the white men and "black robes". He also disclosed the counter-scheme through which the Europeans under the eyes of the suspicious natives accomplished their escape and of the preparations which even included secret construction of canoes.

In order to divert their attention, "we invited", relates our chronicler, "all the Savages who were near us for a solemn feast, where we employed all our ingenuity, and did not spare neither the sound of the drum nor the musical instruments to lull them to sleep with such innocent charm".

The Europeans make a "festin à tout manger" in true Indian style, and "he who presided at the feast made the flutes, trumpets and drums play in order to entertain during the long repast, and to excite the convivial company to dance; ... the Savages sing and dance *à la Française*, while the French dance *à la Sauvage;* ... presents are distributed to those who play best their rôle, and who make most noise, in order to muffle by that the noise which some 40 Frenchmen make outside with the transport of all their equipment".

With all the preparations for the escape completed, the Indians had in the meantime gorged themselves with all the enormous quantities of food, which they had not dared to refuse in order not to offend the Spirit as well as the young Frenchman in whose behalf the feast had been held. But at last the young man released them from the sacred duty "to eat all", and he undertook to soothe them into sweet slumber with the sweet sound of a guitar: 'I am going to play for you a sweet instrument so that you fall asleep, but do not get up tomorrow until very late, and sleep until you will be awakened for the prayers [53]." And the escape was thus effected.

Most of the observers, priests and travellers observed Indian life and customs with keen interest; they recorded in their reports a variety of subjects and described in vivid terms their impression of the ritual ceremonies they had seen and the songs and dances they had witnessed. Yet they were neither skilled musicians nor sufficiently trained in musical matters to be of help in our research; hardly anyone succeeded in noting down the actual melodies and none was interested in a more thorough and detailed discussion of the musical aspects involved. Le Jeune, for instance, frankly admitted his musical incompetence 54, while de Quen, the accomplished singer and musician, criticized the performance but did not deem it important enough to investigate the strange manner and musical substance of the songs. Dierville, the noted French traveller and botanist of the 17th century, is remembered for the discovery of certain species of North American plant life which bear his name, as well as for many interesting accounts of Indian music and music-making, but he, like so many others, failed to record form, structure, rhythm and other musical devices in native songs.

It remained for Lescarbot to have attempted the first authentic recording of Indian songs 55 and, while we are grateful to the gifted and inquisitive Frenchman for the historically valuable document of primitive culture, it is regrettable that he did not denote the melodies in staff-notation but rather in the vague and incomplete letter-notation. Nonetheless, his unique efforts exerted some influence; frequent references were made by later writers to his descriptive accounts and musical notation of the song; the inclusion of music examples became an impressive feature and, no longer satisfied with simple letter-notation, several writers adapted the songs to staff-notation.

The most prominent instance of such adaptation appeared in Sagard's *Histoire du Canada,* in a chapter entitled *"Des dances, chansons & autres ceremonies ridicules de nos Hurons".* "Having described a small sample of a Huron song", explains Sagard, "I thought it appropriate to describe also a part of another song which happened one day in the cabin of the great *Sagamo* of the Souriquois, in praise of the Devil ... as we learn from L'escot [Lescarbot] who claims to have been oral witness 56." Sagard unmistakably referred to the songs collected by Lescarbot. yet the printed harmonization in the *Histoire du Canada* is still a favourite pitfall for unwary historians who, misled by the chapter-heading, believe the music to be of Huron origin, collected and recorded by the Recollect historian himself, when in effect Sagard had not collected a single melody. Moreover, historians did not notice that, in the process of harmonization, Sagard also included the songs of the Indians of Brazil which Lescarbot used as comparative examples of primitive music. None of the many discrepancies are explained in modern versions of Sagard's *Histoire*; thus we find the songs of the Souriquois of Port Royal together with the Indian melodies of Brazil classified as Huron music.

While Sagard cannot claim credit for the earliest printed notation of Indian songs, his adaptation of the Souriquois melodies represents the first harmonization of indigenous music. In the strange idioms of Palestrinian harmony and a-cappella four-part setting, the primitive songs are quite out of place and whoever was responsible for the work succeeded in obliterating and in obscuring the originality and spontaneity of the primitive melodies.

The significance of the Souriquois songs and their harmonic adaptation by Sagard is historical rather than musical. The first musically important Indian song in staff-notation dates from 1673. It is a *Calumet* song, apparently from the Illinois Indians, and is recorded in the manuscript *Récit des voyages et découvertes du Père Jacques Marquette de la Compagnie de Jésus en l'année 1673* [57]. A considerable amount of ambiguity and controversy surrounds the narrative, in particular Father Marquette's authorship of the *Récit*. The established belief, which had ascribed to the renowned missionary-explorer the important document of his expedition to the Mississippi in 1673, had in 1927 been challenged, and the writing attributed to Louis Jolliet, Marquette's companion on that expedition [58]. Other controversial issues concern Marquette's ordination as priest, as well as his

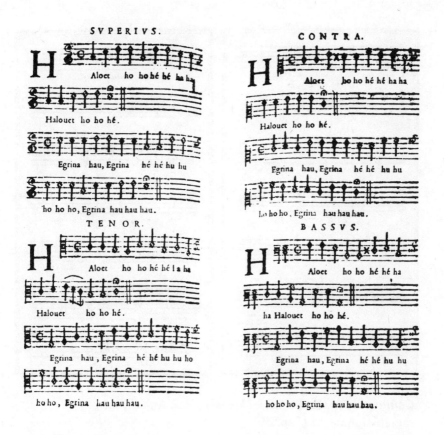

Songs of the Souriquois (G. Sagard, Histoire du Canada)

Calumet Song (La Potherie, Histoire de l'Amérique septentrionale, v. II, p. 20)

personality which received either highest praise and admiration, or had been thoroughly derided and ridiculed.

It is neither our intention nor within the scope of this study to join a debate that has continued for more than forty years. Our concern is the *Calumet* song and its recording in the manuscript *Récit* of Father Marquette. Who recorded the song? Was it Father Marquette himself? Or could it have been Louis Jolliet? The unsolved problem of authorship bears upon the musical notation, yet there can be little doubt that the recording could only have been done by a skilled musician with a particularly fine ear for pitch and a thorough knowledge of musical craft. This is no longer the naive and primitive music of the Souriquois but a highly developed and singable melody. Even though the written notation cannot reproduce the true characteristics of Indian music, the recorded example of 1673 is amazingly similar to the material collected with far more efficient electronic means in our time.

On their expedition to the Mississipi, Marquette and Jolliet had received a triumphant welcome at Peouarea (Peoria), and it was there that they heard, saw and described the *Calumet* song and dance and one of them recorded the music. It is not known whether Father Marquette possessed the musical faculties required for such a complex undertaking, but we know that Jolliet had received as good a musical training as Quebec of the 1660's could offer, that he had been an accomplished organist and, according to some, also a fine harpsichord player (he is supposed to have studied the instrument during his first visit to Paris in 1667 at the age of twenty-two). In short, he was certainly one of the few talented and promising musicians New France had produced. Is it not perfectly logical to assume that the talented musician replaced for a moment the famous explorer and cartographer (and future *Hydrographe du Roi*) and, instead of drawing up maps of the newly discovered territories, Jolliet drew the staff-lines and recorded through staff-notation the song which he had heard and which he had retained in his memory? Whether he had written the notes at the request of Marquette or to satisfy his own musical interest is of less importance, but it is fortunate that he left the manuscript with his companion since on his return to Quebec all his papers were lost when the canoe in which he was travelling capsized near Montreal. Our assumption is based on circumstantial evidence, but is supported by the fact that the notation is found in the *Récit* of the *first* expedition of Marquette and Jolliet in 1673, and not in the manuscript in which Father Dablon, the Superior of the Jesuits at the time, had given the important details concerning Father Marquette's second and last voyage to the land of the Illinois in 1675, and in which Jolliet had not taken part.

From a musical point of view, the analysis of the *Calumet* song offers an interesting study of Indian music. It is remarkable for its musical content and far more advanced than the earlier Souriquois songs. The division into sections is significant as well as indicative of the manner of performance. The ternary structure resembles a modified A-B-A form, with a repeated opening section, an extended middle part and a small coda-section. The melodic range is surprisingly developed and extends over a distance of eleven tones, presumably in the high baritone register. Many devices figure in the song and confirm the characteristics of Indian music; some are less obvious, while others emphasize distinctly the typical and frequently observed features. Auxiliary notes appear with less frequency here than in Lescarbot's examples, but a number of additional ornamental notes are introduced into the melodic line. The intervallic relation is similar to earlier examples, but contains in addition the intervals of the fifth and the extremely rare scale step of the seventh as well as the implied chord of the ninth. The scale formation resembles a modified arrangement of the Phrygian tonality, with a remarkable alternation in modality between the various sections.

While conjunct movement is still predominant, the disjunct motion is more pronounced than in previous examples. Descending motion, a characteristic of primitive music, is clearly outlined in this song, in particular in the middle or recitation section with its highly interesting melodic line. The rhythmic element throughout the entire song is of such variety as to defy clear definition; it is apparent, however, that the recorder of the song was perfectly aware of the different time values. As had been suggested before, the rhythmic characteristics of Indian music, as corroborated by more recent research, seem to have been in the irregularity as well as in the independence between rhythm and melody. The percussive accompaniment consisted of single strokes of equal force and interval, which stood often in conflict to the scheme of accents and the rhythmic pattern the Indian had invented for his song. This is clearly demonstrated by the dance steps in strict and equal time, which were entirely independent of the melody. The invocatory type of *Calumet* song suggests a free rhythmic style; it is, however, almost impossible to suggest a fairly authentic stylistic manner of performance. La Potherie remarked on this difficulty to notate sound and rhythm of Indian songs since "they give them a certain turn (when singing) which one cannot well explain by notation, but which nonetheless is quite graceful [59]."

In conclusion it may be appropriate to remark that the musical activities of the North American Indian present an enormously wide field of intricate research and study and the seemingly disproportionate amount of space alloted to Indian music in this work is still far from adequate to do justice to the scope and extent of the subject matter. These few remarks and descriptions and opinions of contemporary witnesses are offered as an indication of the work to be done in this field and the fascination which awaits the scholars who undertake a study of the historical aspects of Indian music in early Canada.

IX

1759

NEW MUSIC IN OLD QUEBEC

The battle on the Plains of Abraham before the gates of Quebec on September 13, 1759 decided the fate of New France and the treaty of Paris in 1763 brought to a close French rule in Canada. While gloom and despair descended on a shattered Quebec, the English conquest soon brought a copious harvest of artistic activities and the beginning of a considerable musical life. It was at first music by the British regimental bands who had arrived with their regiments to serve for a certain length of time in Canada. One of the earliest notices in the *Quebec Gazette* of September 6th, 1764 informs us that on August 25th: "was review'd on the Heights of Abraham, by His Excellency the Honorable Brigadier General Murray, &c... the 15th Regiment ... being about Seven in the Morning, there was a very genteel Breakfast provided ... and after Breakfast, a great Part of the Gentlemen and Ladies, to the Amount of 20 Couple or upwards, joined in a Country-Dance upon the Sod."

These military bands, or some of their members, took part in civil and military functions; they played at balls and dances, supplied the music for entertainment and processions and without doubt joined with the few local amateur musicians in musical representations of a more or less serious nature which began to appear at that time. The Quebec newspapers, particularly the first of them, the *Quebec Gazette*₁, now contribute all the information. We find in the *Gazette* of November 29th, 1764 an advertisement directed at the "Sons of St. Andrew — in the town of Quebec — Purpose to meet at the Concert-Hall, and have a Dance, on the 30th Instant, at 6 o'Clock at Night, where they will be glad to see all the other Gentlemen of the Place." The event being a dance, it seems to have been understood that the ladies were also invited, because we read a few days later that at the "Ball and Entertainment given on the day of the Festival of St. Andrew, patron Saint of Scotland, His Excellency the Governor was present, also the Chief Justice and his Lady, and Every person and Family in the City and Neighbourhood of suitable rank was invited ... all was conducted with great Propriety and Decorum ₂."

The balls and other festivities of Quebec's *élite* of former days now reach the lower social strata, and what had been glittering social events turn into commercially inspired enterprises with less "propriety and decorum" but greater enjoyment for the people. A typical example of such public entertainment is furnished by the notice in the *Gazette* of December 27, 1764: "A Public Ball will be To-Morrow, being the 28th Instant, at the CONCERT HALL, where tickets are to be had of Mr. DIENVAL (Price One Dollar). N.B. No Body will be admitted without a Ticket." Nothing is known of the type and quality of the dance music played at the balls and dances now appearing in greater frequency. Neither do we know the nature of the processional music — religious or secular — that was played in July 1767 when "... the Masons marched in procession preceeded by a Band of Music ₃." Of greater importance, however, is the notice according to which "the Managers of the *Gentlemen's Subscription Concert*, take this opportunity of informing the Subscribers thereto, that the Performance will, for the future, begin precisely at *six o'clock* ₄." Unfortunately the notice is lacking in details concerning these early Subscription Concerts; we do not know the type of music played nor who the musicians were, but the advertisement remains the definite and undeniable evidence of some remarkable musical events.

Military bandsmen participated in those concerts, their activities enriched the musical life of the town and were sometimes also for the benefit of the musicians themselves, for we note that "on Friday, December the 6th, 1771, at Mr. Prenties's Long Room, will be a Public Concert; after which will be a Ball with Tea, Coffee, and Cards. Tickets to be had at Mr. Prenties's, the Coffee-House, or from any of the Band of the 10th Regiment. Price One Spanish Dollar. The Concert to begin at 6 o'-clock." And we further learn that the concert is for "the Benefit of the Band of the 10th Regiment ... and Each Ticket to admit a Lady and a Gentleman 5."

The Canadians of French descent soon recovered from the defeat; the new life under British domination could not dampen their spirit, and it is in the continuance of their artistic activities that we may presume the manifestations of musical and artistic life that had taken place during the late phases of New France. The New Subjects of His British Majesty were the same French-Canadians who a few years earlier as *Citoyens de la Nouvelle France* had performed the same type of entertainment which they now advertised in the English newspapers:

Spectacle Nouvel et Divertissement Public — *Les Villageoises Canadiennes,* nouvelles Sujettes de sa Majesté Britannique d'un certain canton de la Province de Québec, donneront une Fête, et feront représenter en l'honneur de leur Seigneur, le Lundi dix-huit, Novembre prochain une pièce nouvelle, intitulée LES FETES VILLAGEOISES, Comédie en un acte, qui sera suivie d'un *Ballet de Bergers et de Bergères,* et précédée d'un compliment au Seigneur leur Patron et

Protecteur; entre la Comédie et le Ballet il y aura une *CANTATE* et un *DUO,* qui seront chantés par le Sieur Colin et la Demoiselle Nina, fameux Musiciens du Canada; cette dernière chantera seule un morceau choisi de l'Opéra des *Amours de Vénus* ... L'Orquestre et la Symphonie seront harmonieux jusqu'à une cornemuse; le tout sera terminé par un grand Bal dans le meilleur ordre ... Les Paroles de la Comédie sont composées par le Sieur Lanoux, célèbre Poète du Canada, et la musique de la Cantate et du Duo par le Sieur Zeliot, grand musicien 6.

Behind the grandiose eloquence with which "l'Orquestre et la Symphonie" had been advertised was probably nothing more than one or two violins, a flute and drum, and the *cornemuse,* the bagpipe of the Bretons. Of the *fameux musiciens du Canada* not a trace has remained and they were most likely itinerant musicians engaged for the occasion. Where modesty would have restrained the local amateur performer, customary practice elevated the itinerant "grand musicien" and the "célèbre poète" to the heights of Parnassus. Some amount of exaggeration helped in those days — as well as in ours — to impress the unwary public, particularly when an array of more or less fatuous titles accompanied the boastful advertisement:

THE PUBLIC CONCERT — of Mr. Guillaume de Vaut-Court, Master and Setter of Musick, formerly Deputy Library Keeper to the Royal Academie of Musick at Paris, and one of his Most Christian Majesty's Concerts, will begin at 6 o/clock in the evening, on Tuesday next, the 15th Instant, at Mrs. Croton's Assembly-Room, in the Upper-Town.

Tickets to be had at Mr. Prenties's, and at Mr. Simpson's and Mrs. Crofton's in the Lower-Town, at Half a Spanish Dollar each.

He also informs the Publick, that he has for Sale the Rudiments of Vocal and Instrumental Musick by way of Question and Answer, with Examples of the Variations and Difficulties which occur; he has also composed some Pieces for the Ease of such as love Simple Counterpoint, or the Harmony of Concords; he adapts Musick-Books to all kinds of Instruments and Voices, and has all Sorts of Musick for Concerts to hire, on the most reasonable Terms [7].

James Jeffrey was a clerk in the service of E. H. Derby, a well-known merchant of Quebec. He was born in Salem, Massachusetts, and seems to have come to Quebec soon after the conquest. In his Journal of the year 1775 he recorded that he had gone

to the Seminary to see the scholars of the seminary act the "World Unmasked, and the Ridiculous Consort". Prologue by Doc'r Gill's son, James Gill. Epilogue by Delong's son. The solemn distribution of prizes given by his Excellency Guy Carleton, Major-General and Co.-in-chief of the Province of Quebec, ends the spectacle, and as an addition to this spectacle they had before the play & between each act Fiddling & Fluting by J.Pascaus, a man from the West Indies seek'g business as a fiddler; Thos. Ainslie, His Majesty's collector for this port, tho: three of four vessels was to be cleared, Fiddler; Jn. Gill, a young man & clerk to Mr. Drummond; H. Finley, Postmaster Gen'r & Post-Master of Quebec, tho: post day & no one to attend to the office but a boy w'ch could not give change, fluted; Lt. Layard, 7th Reg't, played on the Bass-viol.

Thus are his Majesty's officers spending their time in this province at this difficult time. I don't know whether to please the Gov'r (who was there w'th a

great number of attendants, gent'm & ladies), or
whether it was to keep in with the Bishops and Priests.
There was a very great crowd of people. The music
began ab't ½ past eleven o'c, P.M. ₈.

Although public concerts had already taken place at
Quebec a few years before, this charming excerpt from James
Jeffrey's diary is among the earliest detailed references to players and their instruments. Where more than a century ago in the
sanctified atmosphere of Quebec's cathedral, the "quatre viols"
had played for the distribution of the "premier prix", we now
find at a similar function three violins, two flutes and a bass-viol
entertaining His Excellency and his guests, and a great crowd of
people. What a pity that Jeffrey did not record in his diary the
titles of the pieces that were played by "His Majesty's officers".
Incidentally, he did not conceal his background — his critical remark recalls the stern attitude of the Puritans towards music —
for "t'was not the time for Canada to dance". Indeed, it was not,
because the American rebel soldiers were ready to march against
Quebec.

Yet Quebec weathered the storm as she had withstood
the onslaughts of the past. The memory of the historical event
was well celebrated a year later:

Tuesday last, being the 31st of December (1776), the
Quebec Militia in Commemoration of the signal Victory obtained over the Rebel Army in their assault on
the City (December 31, 1775) march'd in Procession to
the several Churches, where Sermons were preached ...
In the evening a most elegant Ball and Supper were
given by the Militia, at which were present near 300
Ladies and Gentlemen. An excellent Band of Musick
was provided on this glorious occasion ... at Seven, an
Ode written on the Occasion was perform'd, after
which Dancing commenc'd. In a word, the Gentlemen

who acted as Managers exerted themselves in such a manner, that it was universally allowed to be the compleatest Entertainment of the Sort ever known in this Province ⁹.

MUSICIANS, MERCHANTS, MUSIC MASTERS

While France supported the American rebels, the loyalty of the French-Canadian militia, of the French-Canadian *élite* and the clergy saved the colony for England — and we will soon see how some of the Frenchmen who had volunteered for the American cause contributed in the end to Canada's cultural history, together with some Germans who had joined the British in Canada against the American revolutionaries. One of those new arrivals was Friedrich Heinrich Glackemeyer, who seems to have been a highly capable professional musician and whose activities influenced and enriched musical life in Quebec to a great extent. In spite of a large amount of information, it has not been established when and why the young **Glackemeyer** left his native Germany, but it is known that he became band master in one of the German mercenary regiments which had come to Canada during the early years of the American revolution, and it is not impossible that he arrived together with the regiment under the Baron Von Riedesel in 1776. The latter appears to have appreciated Glackemeyer's work as teacher of his daughters and also offered him a position as organist in his hometown in Germany. Glackemeyer left us a note :

I was teacher of music to the family Riedesel, in the winter of 1783 ; was lodged and treated with the greatest politeness and civility. My two pupils were misses Augusta and Fredericka, who would have made great progress, had they had a better instrument than a miserable old spinet which they had bought of the Revd. Mons. Noiseux, curé at Beloeil, at present Grand Vi-

car at Three Rivers, there being only one piano in
Quebec. I have yet in my possession an excellent rec-
ommendation from General Riedesel who granted me
my discharge from the army, accompanied with a considerable present in guineas, and an offer if I would go
with them to Germany, I should have the place of an
organist in the city of Lanterhack of which I had the
gift, but I declined the offer, having no inclination to
return to Germany [10].

And Glackemeyer remained in Quebec for the rest of his
long life (he was born in Hanover, Germany in 1751 and died in
Quebec in January of 1836), a highly respected citizen, twice
married and father of eighteen children, a fine teacher and musician, a member of those ethnic groups who emigrated to the
New World and whose contribution to the artistic life, both in
the American States and in Canada, had been of notable value.
Glackemeyer was the first of a number of German band masters
and musicians to come to Canada during the next forty or fifty
years — the "German period" as Kallmann has called it — and
who brought with them a highly developed musical culture,
based on a tradition that was far more profound than the superficial musical expressions of the French, or the shallow level of
English music at the end of the 18th century. The situation is
comparable to the development of music in the central colonies
of America after the arrival of the Swedes, the German and the
Moravians, with their contributions to the musical scene.

Glackemeyer began to import instruments and printed
music and established himself as teacher "on the Piano Forte,
Guittar, Violin, Flute, Singing in French and English at 24 Lesson for one Guinea, and One Guinea Entrance [11]." In addition
he played the violoncello, the organ, the clarinet and most likely
some other instruments. It was quite normal that musicians
would turn to teaching and selling music and instruments just as
music dealers would become teachers. In all cases the alternative

provided a welcome source of additional revenue. Glackemeyer had soon realized that teaching was hardly possible, considering the scarcity of instruments, except for the odd "miserable spinet". He therefore embarked on the importation of musical instruments, and the firm of F.H. Glackemeyer was inaugurated.

Meanwhile other music dealers were busily advertising their wares and, judging from the large quantity of material offered for sale, the demand must have been gratifying. The merchant of musical paraphernalia had been a necessary factor in musical life as well as a good indicator of musical development as musical activities could to some extent be observed in the success or failure of the music trade. The advertisements mirror significantly the prevailing trends. As early as 1772 this notice appeared in the *Gazette:* "Just imported from London, and to be sold Wholesale and Retail, by James Sinclair, at his Store in the Uppertown of Quebec, the following Goods, on the lowest Terms (for Ready Cash Only)" and at the end of a long list of various items we find: "Best Roman Fiddle Strings; Fine and Common Violins, and German Flutes, *together with Sundry other Articles, Too tedious to mention* 12." Glackemeyer advertises in November 1788 "Two new excellent Piano Forte's, with a neat leather cover warranted to be of the best tone, and to stand tune a long time". And he also has for sale a large quantity of harpsichord music, "a choice collection of Songs neatly Bound", a few operas, presumably in piano score, together with "a collection of Divine Music" as well as "Military Music fit for Bands, compleat by several Masters". He carries "bassoon and Hautboy reeds, Fiddle Pegs and Bridges" in addition to "strings for Harpsichord, Pianoforte, Guitar, and Violins" and among other items also "a collection of Country Dances for the years 1787, 1788, with their proper figures."

A perusal of such typical advertisements affords an interesting glance at the musical accessories, small and large, without which musical life could not function. We are often forgetful of the importance of these small details, and do not give much thought to the frustrating experience of having, for instance, a viol without proper strings. If Mother St. Joseph, our viol-playing Ursuline of the 1640's, had been in need of new strings for her viol or rosin for the bow, as she may well have been from time to time, she had to wait a year to replace the missing items or to replenish the stock. Then there was also the difficulty with regard to repair-work and to the maintenance of instruments, be it viol or the organ. In addition, the extreme climatic conditions in Canada represented a particular hazard; they affected the primitive cane flute of the Indian no less than the intricate mechanism of Monsieur Destailleur's bassoon.

Looking at the list of musical accessories, we come across some curious items, and some that, obscured by the passing of time, defy investigation. We read of *Sticcado's*, and *Five-bar-ruling-brass-pens* which Cameron, Stewart & Ross imported to Canada together with the rather superfluous "Opera Glasses", while Angus Grant, another dealer, wishes to sell "Officers Fuzees, fowling Pieces, duelling and pocket Pistoles, and new invented Flutes with 6 Keys 13." A very fine selection of musical oddities is offered for sale by one Fred Wyse of Mountain Street, Lower-Town, together with: "Elegant Piano Fortes by C. Gerock; Violins, Flutes, Flageolets, Organs; also *Musical Walking Sticks*, Pandean Pipes and Aeolians, Violin Strings, and a variety of music, also fishing tackle and an elegant assortment of *Patent Wigs, Ornamental Hair, &c., &c...* 14"

Messrs. Mead Freres & Cie. address themselves to the French Canadian musicians and music-lovers, offering a multitude of musical wares, most of which are indeed items of a distant past:

Instruments de Musique, venant directement de Paris, comprenant un assortiment de Guitares d'Espagne, d'Italie et de Paris, de toute description, Clarinettes B, C, et mi-bémol, d'une qualité supérieure, avec 13 clés; Trombonnes avec clés et cintre additionnel, [pistons and additional crooks], Ophicléides, Cornopeans. etc., avec des échantillons de nouveaux Instruments en cuivre pour la musique militaire, tel que NISCOR, instrument à huit clés, qui est préférable au Cornopean ; aussi le célèbre CLAVICOR où se trouve combiné toute la mélodie de la trompette française, et qui la surpasse en beauté et en force 15.

Not all of the merchants had been successful; some of these purveyors of musical merchandise seem to have had an ephemeral existence, or realising the difficult and specialized nature of the music business may have preferred to concentrate on more lucrative commodities. On the other hand, F. H. Glackemeyer was not only solidly entrenched in Quebec, but in later years extended his activities also into Montreal. His first advertisement had appeared in the Quebec *Gazette* of June 24th, 1784: "FOR SALE/FIVE elegant PIANO FORTES ! arrived in the last ships. Enquire at Mr. Glackemeyer's, in the middle of the Hill; he will dispose of them for a very reasonable price."

Nonetheless, Glackemeyer soon had a formidable and stubborn competitor. We do not know where Francis Vogeler came from, or exactly when he arrived at Quebec. The *Gazette* printed his first advertisement in June 1788: "Just imported in the LONDON, and to be sold by Francis Vogeler, FOUR FORTE PIANOS, with new Music and ruled Music Books, which he will sell cheap for ready cash, or short credits."

Glackmeyer countered with an advertisement in the *Quebec Herald and Universal Miscellany* of November 24th, 1788, splendidly decorated with a woodcut showing a "Piano Forte", and offering the material as cited before, as well as his services as repairman and piano-tuner. But the courageous Vogeler was

as enterprising as his commercial rival and always ready to out-
bid the latter. Where Glackemeyer had imported only "Two new
excellent Piano Forte's", Vogeler, in his advertisement in the
Quebec Herald, offered three and also "A very excellent Tenor
with case", together with the best strings, etc., and an enormous
amount of printed music, including works by Bach, Haydn and
Clementi, in company of Stae's *Idées de Campagne* (accompanied by violin, cello and two horns) and together with
the works of other forgotten composers of the time, such as
Schulthesius, Billington, Mislewececk, Venturini, Mancinelli and
others. Where Vogeler advertises "an elegant BIRD ORGAN",
Glackemeyer is not to be outdone, and he offers the public:

> an ORGAN, indefinitely superior in excellence to any
> ever imported into this Province. The various Harmo-
> nic and Mechanical powers of this Magnificent Instru-
> ment may be imagined, when it is stated that several
> instruments of Music perform with it, by self-moving
> machinery; and when in motion form a complete
> Band in perfect concert, playing the newest and most
> celebrated tunes. Although external embellishements
> are but a secondary consideration, yet it may be prop-
> er to observe that the grandeur of this is worthy of the
> internal mechanism. It will be of no avail to expatiate
> further on its qualities as it possesses throughout end-
> less attractions, and will be found to produce a never-
> failing source of recreation. The lowest price is 80
> Guineas [16].

And Vogeler, following Glackemeyer's example, informs the
public that he will "put in tune on the shortest notice, and reasonable terms", all kinds of musical instruments, and he is prepared to give instructions on the "Piano Forte, Violin, Guitar,
German Flute, and other wind instruments". And Mr. Vogeler
uses the opportunity to "return his sincere thanks to the parents

of those young ladies and gentlemen he has the honour to teach music, for their kindness, which he has experienced for several years past, and he hopes that by his zeal, and endeavours in doing justice to his pupils, they will still be pleased to continue their favours."

Gradually we will lose track of the two hardy pioneer music sellers; their advertisements, although still appearing in the newspapers, are no longer as frequent. As for Francis Vogeler, we know from the annual correspondence with his suppliers in London of his difficulties as merchant of instruments and accessories. In these letters Vogeler apologizes regularly for the bad times which prevent him from remitting part or all of his debts and which are the cause of sales far below expectations. "I earnestly beg Mr. Astor to have a Little Patience", writes Vogeler in June 1819. "I never saw the times so bad since I am in Canada, I did not sell any Article, except a few Strings". And at the same time he submits his orders for new material to the English firm — only to apologize again the following year for the unavoidable delay in remittance:

> I am very sorry to disappoint you in not remitting at present. The times are so bad here in Canada that I have hardly sold one article with the exception of Violin Strings of the last year's importations. If I put them to auction they will not fetch quarter their value, and if you will have the goodness to wait a little longer, I will do my utmost to satisfy you in the course of the Winter, as there are hopes that the times will change, in doing so you will oblige me.

> If convenient I would beg of you to send me the following few articles ... (and here follows a fairly long list of accessories) and also 6 Violins, 6 Plain Flutes, and 3 Ivory tip't Flutes with Silver Key.

If not convenient to send the instruments I beg you
will have the goodness to send the strings only, In
doing which, you will oblige,

> Gentlemen,
> your most obed't
> Hu'ble sev't
> Fr. Vogeler

    The last letter in this collection was dated October 27th,
1820; it reached Messrs. Astor & Co., 79 Cornhill, London on
January 1st, 1821. It is similar in content to the earlier examples
— the somewhat plaintive tale of the small music dealer in Quebec, who after 32 years of serving the muse and the public may
have been aware that music was not a lucrative commodity.

    Fortunes and misfortunes of war had played an impor-
tant part in the cultural evolution. It had caused the "grand
dérangement", the cruel deportation of the Acadians in 1755; it
had brought some ten years later the British soldiers and their
music to New France and, at the time of the American War of
Independence, was responsible for the mass migration of the
Empire Loyalists from New England to various regions of Canada. Fifty years after the fall of New France the population of
Canada had risen from 70,000 in 1760 to some 400,000 in the
first decade of the 19th century. Kallmann explains the development: "The new arrivals, whether from the British Isles, the
United States or Germany, included many who possessed musical training. Although music may have been cultivated in the
homes of the individual *seigneurs* of New France, the impression
is that secular art music developed faster in a few decades after
the British conquest than it had in a century before. Even in
Quebec and Montreal the names of musicians and amateurs are
often English and German and the documents relating to concert performances are usually written in English [17]."

Musical life blossomed at Quebec and Montreal in those waning years of the 18th century. The backbone of this musical development was still the military band, but there were also many other musical events such as recitals by solo performers and private chambermusic activities by educated amateurs. From the occasional reference we may obtain some interesting information about the practice of music among the French population, such as is indicated in the announcement in the *Gazette* of October 13th, 1785: "To be SOLD by AUCTION / On Saturday next at 11 o'Clock, at the late Mr. Destailleur's, in Palace Street, by Messrs. Sketchley & Freeman: Household Furniture; wearing apparel; Table Furniture; *Bassoon with Reeds — Tenor Violin with Strings* — Gold Watch, with various other articles."

Presumably Monsieur Destailleur had been playing the Bassoon and the Tenor Violin, and no doubt there must have been many like him who enjoyed music-making for their own pleasure or who were willing to entertain the public to the best of their ability. A few months earlier someone advertised a tenor violin for sale (presumably Monsieur Destailleur or his heirs tried to dispose of the instrument), as we read in the *Gazette* of March 31st, 1785: "Left at the Printer's for SALE — A Fine Toned TENOR VIOLIN, with a Screw Bow and Case, Price same as it cost, FIVE GUINEAS".

Tenor violins and tenor strings are frequently mentioned in advertisements in the journals of Montreal and Quebec. Yet it is difficult to describe exactly the instrument because of the amount of obscurity that surrounds its origin and development. Many explanations have been offered but most of them are contradictory and none entirely convincing. The instrument is sometimes referred to as a larger viola, having assumed the part of the alto-tenor in the string choir of the Baroque period, between the violins and the bass. Curt Sachs believes that the tenor violin was a five-stringed instrument with ribs of a depth from three to three and a half inches, tuned to F, c, g, d', a' and being intermediate between viola and violoncello 18. Other sources refer to the tenor violin as a member of the *Viola da Braccio* family, with four strings, tuned in succession of fifths below the violin and viola. Michael Kelly, the first *Basilio* in Mozart's *Figaro,* relates in his charming *Reminiscences, anno 1786* that he attended a quartet party in Vienna with Haydn playing the 1st violin and Mozart the tenor 19. The tenor violin seems to have enjoyed a good amount of popularity in England and there is frequent reference to quartet playing of two violins, tenor and violoncello, or in combination with wind instruments and it is therefore understandable that the Canadian music dealers imported tenor violins, strings and other accessories. But the question whether the instrument was a small violoncello or a large viola cannot be answered without more intensive research.

Instruments of various kinds were frequently offered for sale, either in private transaction or by public auction. The first of such offers appeared in the *Gazette* of October 11th, 1764 where we find advertised for sale "... A Genteel Organ, with Five Stops, fit for a small CHURCH or CHAMBER ...". While the owner of this "genteel" instrument does not reveal his identity, the early date of the notice indicates French ownership and presumably French manufacture. Similar consideration could apply to the "excellent Violin" offered for sale in the *Gazette* of December 1767. Pity the poor bandsman whose misfortune, as recorded in the *Gazette* of December 26th, 1782, brings to our attention one of the earliest Clarinet types of the 18th century:

> ONE GUINEA REWARD — Lost on Wednesday morning, 4th Instant, by a River side nearly opposite the Ferry House, Montreal — A NEW *C* CLARINET AND A FIFE in a RED LEATHER CASE — belonging to the 29th Regiment at St. John's. Whoever has found them is requested to send them to John Turner, Junior, Merchant, living near the Barracks by whom the above Reward will be thankfully paid — or —

should they be offered for SALE, 'tis humbly desired
to stop them and give Mr. Turner, or the Master of the
Band of Music, John MacLean, Notice thereof.

At times neither sale nor auction, nor any other attempt was successful even when the instrument-maker enjoyed highest reputation in Europe. The *Gazette* of December 1st, 1791 carried a notice concerning the sale by auction of "a fine Ton'd Single Key
Harpsicord by Kirkman, warranted to stand any stove room ..."
but as there had apparently been no sale a new attempt was
made one week later: "To be sold by private sale at Mr. Cameron's house, An Excellent Harpsicord by Kirkman, and a Patent Piano Forte ... 20"

How much musical entertainment had become part of
the social life is demonstrated by the growing number of public
concerts. The "Gentlemen's Subscription Concerts" of 1770 were
followed by many single events of unknown content or type. We
do not know what happened at the "Concert of Musick, to be
held at the British Coffee-House in Lower-Town on Tuesday
next, the 30th of May, 1780 — where tickets for the same may be
had at one Dollar each — to begin at half past six in the Evening", or who took part in the "*Quebec Concert* to be on
Thursday next, the 31st of January 1782, and to *continue every
fortnight* — the rooms to be opened for the reception of the
Company at 7 o'Clock".

Similar announcements appeared in the newspapers of
Quebec and Montreal and while one cannot avoid the suspicion
that more tribute was paid to Bacchus than to Euterpe there is
reason to believe that musical activities were not confined to the
uproarious rendition of ballads, glees or other popular songs, but
included some instrumental works by the composers of the day.
Indeed, the nature, type and to some extent also the quality of
these concerts seem to have resembled similar manifestations in
the larger centres of North America, and most of them were
modelled on English examples. English music-lovers enjoyed the

popular yet serious nature of the musical style as exemplified in Arne and Boyce and particularly as represented in the popular works for the stage by a long list of fine composers such as Batishill, Hook, Arnold, Dibdin, Shield and others. With nostalgic memories the British immigrant to Canada cherished such old-country favourites as Arnold's *The Maid of the Mill,* Sheridan's *School for Scandal,* Shield's *Ploughboy* and the wealth of catches and glees by Calcott, Dibdin and others. Yet concerts in Canada were not limited to English music only. Before Haydn had arrived in London on his first visit in 1791 the subscription concert season of 1790-91 in Quebec featured some of his symphonies together with music by Bach, Handel, Mozart and many others. It is reasonable to assume that the London orchestra, manned by professional musicians, was well prepared to do justice to the symphonies of the great composer. On the other hand, the *Quebec Subscription Concerts* united amateur, bandsman and other kindred souls for an evening of entertainment and pleasure, and players and audience were not as much concerned to have a perfect performance but to have a performance at all. It must have been a great disappointment to player and public alike when circumstances beyond control, ranging from inclement weather to political storms, may at times have caused the cancellation of an evening's musical entertainment. Yet even the postponement of a concert is an *ipso facto* confirmation of musical activities, an example of which is furnished by the notice regarding the concert which had to be postponed for unknown reason: "The Public are most respectfully informed that the *Concert* of *Vocal* and *Instrumental Music* to have been performed this evening at the *Merchants Coffee House,* is deferred until Wednesday next, when it will positively be performed agreeable to the bills delivered before [21]."

Musical pioneers of the type and quality of a Glackemeyer were rare. Those who came after him may have gambled on the growing interest in cultural matters in the rapidly growing

colony or may have wanted to try their luck in the musico-
educational field or in commercial enterprise. Some were successful and remained; others were not and left for greener pas-
tures in the South; some were good teachers, others poor or indifferent — such as had been noticed by the visiting Englishman,
John Lambert, who travelled through Canada in the first decade
of the 19th century. He did not find any cultural activity that
met with his approval; he deplored the lamentable condition of
the arts in Canada, criticized the theatre performances in Montreal and came to the conclusion that "the polite accomplishment of drawing and music are almost stranger in Canada";
and he blamed lack of education and educators for the cultural
deficiencies, the same default that had been noticed by the visiting Frenchman in New France. As far as teachers of music were
concerned, he had only met one who was "a good Violin performer", but he thought the others to be indifferent if not of
very poor quality [22].

There were only a few teachers before the turn of the
century in Quebec and Montreal. The first advertisement appeared in the *Quebec Gazette* in May 1780:

> Mr. *Davis* begs leave to acquaint the Ladies and
> Gentlemen in Quebec, that he intends on Monday the
> 12th of June next to commence teaching the
> *Harpsichord* on the following terms, viz. One Guinea,
> Twenty Lessons, one every day in the Week, Saturday
> excepted — And one Guinea Entrance.
>
> And as there may be several who would be inclinable
> to learn, were they provided with instruments, Mr.
> *Davis* intends having one at his Lodgings, where they
> may depend upon equal attention being paid them as
> at their own Houses ..."

Signor Gaetano Franceschini had been playing a solo on
the violin at a "Public Night [23]" and shortly after he an-

nounced that he proposes to instruct "a few scholars on the Violin and Harpsichord during the Summer season. Entrance for beginners one Guinea, and one Guinea for twelve lessons of one hour each [24]." Evidently he was an Italian who had come to Charleston, South Carolina, sometimes after 1773 and who appeared there in concerts of the St. Cecilia Society and also in "benefit concerts" of his own. Some of these concerts terminated with the favoured custom of a dance or a ball. And Signor Franceschini advised the ladies that "carriages will be provided for them after the ball [25]." He seemed to have remained in Charleston until 1783 when his name appeared on concert programmes in Philadelphia and New York, which might well indicate an excellent reputation as a violinist. His visit to Quebec, however, was of short duration, probably only during the spring and summer of 1784, as is apparent from the wording of his advertisement. We do not know whether he had much success with his scholars; his name does not appear anymore in Canadian newspapers.

There was also Mr. Mechtler who had in July 1787: "respectfully informed the Public that having entirely quitted the business of the Theatre, intends to settle in this town, where he means to teach the *Violin* and *Harpsichord,* and assures those Ladies and Gentlemen who he may have the honour to attend, that they may depend on the strictest care and attention [26]."

Alas, Quebec's fine Ladies and Gentlemen do not seem to have fully appreciated Mr. Mechtler's art; he left Quebec and went to Montreal, where two years later the *Montreal Gazette* prints the following notice: "Mr. *Mechtler* / begs leave to inform the Ladies and Gentlemen of Montreal that he has settled himself in this city as MUSIC MASTER, and intends to teach the FORTE PIANO, HARPSICHORD and VIOLIN: he therefore flatters himself that he will meet with encouragement from those Ladies and Gentlemen who may please employ him, etc., etc. [27]."

Montreal may indeed also claim the credit for having housed the first school of Music and Art. In June 1789 Mr. Charles Watt of London opened a school for "teaching young Ladies and Gentlemen vocal and instrumental music ... and also Drawing, Etching, Engraving on any kind of metal, etc. [28]."

Monsieur Jouve, Bandmaster and Professor of Music, arrived at Quebec in August 1791 with His Royal Highness, the Duke of Kent, and offered "that he will teach (either abroad or at his own lodging) Vocal Music, to play the Harp, on the Violoncello, and the French Guitar, which last Instrument is very easy to learn and very pleasant, as in a very short time one may learn enough to accompany the voice with it [29]." His appeal for students does not seem to have been successful. He therefore advertised "that he will give a Vocal and Instrumental Concert for his own benefit" and for that of "several Ladies and Gentlemen being desirous to hear the Harp [30]." Jouve could count on the participation of local artists, such as Mrs. Allen who sang an "Arietta of the Soldier, tired of War's alarm", and of Messrs. Glackemeyer and Bentley who joined with Jouve in the rendition of vocal music. It must have been an impressive concert, to gather from the programme, with music by Gluck, Gretry, Piccini, Rhen, Desaides and — Jouve. The Band of the Royal Fusiliers of the 7th Regiment played, and also provided the obligatory cannon for the "Ariette de la Mélouranie, avec tous les instruments et le canon obligé". Nonetheless, the public of Quebec was probably not too enthusiastic and, as in the case of Mr. Mechtler, it is again the *Montreal Gazette* which informs us that "Monsieur Jouve, Professor of the Harp and Guittar, and Musician to His Royal Highness Prince Edward, has the honour to acquaint the Public of Montreal that he intends giving a Concert of Vocal and Instrumental Music for his benefit ... etc., etc...

That was in August 1792, and it was also the last sign of Mr. Jouve; perhaps he returned with His Royal Highness to England?

CONCERTS IN QUEBEC

If Quebec had not been too kind to the Mechtlers and Jouves, the city, thanks to the initiative of Glackemeyer and kindred souls, could boast of regular subscription concerts, beginning in 1790 and continuing at least for a few years. Unexpected delays, "and the time required for the preparation in the rooms", had made it necessary to postpone the first concert to the 15th of November, but here is how the *Quebec Herald* recorded the great musical event:

> On Monday evening the Winter Concert commenced at Free-Masons-Hall, it is to continue every Monday Evening for twenty-four weeks. His Honor, Major-General Clarke, our Lieutenant Governor, added sanction to the Concert with his presence, and enlivened the female part of the auditory by his affability and attention.

> The Concerts are supported by subscription: From the genteel manner in which the first was conducted, the convenience of the Hall, and musical abilities of the gentlemen institutors, we augur a few pleasing hours weekly to the Amateurs of Apollo.

Then, as now, some press reporters, knowing nothing about music, were more interested in the affability and attention with which His Honor "enlivened the female part" ! While we lack information about these early concerts — we know the programmes of later performances — the few notices in the newspapers allow us to form a fairly good picture of the organization that was behind this amazing and highly gratifying musical endeavour. In the best tradition of musical societies, the subscribers had been asked to "chuse a *Treasurer* and *Committee* agreeable to the *Rules*", and they had chosen as Treasurer one John Rotten, but they forgot to make rules to "preserve decorum", for this letter appeared in the *Gazette* of January 1792:

A Subscriber to the Concerts hopes that the Managers will give themselves some trouble in future to prevent the confusion and noise that prevailed last concert night, by number of gentlemen talking loud during the music — — — if there are any rules for the concert they surely require silence during the performance. If there are no rules, it is high time that some should be formed to preserve decorum, and till rules are formed it may be recommended to those gentlemen who distinguished themselves so loudly last Concert night not to be ashamed to imitate the example of His Excellency Lieut. Governor General Clarke and His Royal Highness Prince Edward.

There were twenty-five concerts during that season of 1790-1791, indeed a remarkable achievement. One hundred and four subscribers (slightly more than one-half per cent of Quebec's population) had paid twenty-five shillings for one season, or one shilling for each concert. At the end of the season, John Rotten prepared the financial statement, a fascinating document of conditions in the small musical world of Quebec:

SUBSCRIPTION CONCERT	May 12th 1791		
Cash received from one hundred and four suscribers	130	0	0
Paid as follows	'		
To Mr. Franks for his Rooms, for fire and candles	37	10	0
To seven hired Performers	49	0	0
To copying musick, ruled paper and to extra hired Performers	5	3	6
For delivering the Tickets and collecting the money	3	17	6
For the use of a Piano Forte	3	10	0

To Mr. Kutcheon for making an Orchestra, musick stands, sconces, and for putting up and taking down the Orchestra at different times	8	0	0
To Mr. Moore for printing tickets, rules and advertisements, &c.	3	9	0
To a servant for receiving the tickets at the door and attendance at supper	2	11	3
Balance paid by order of the managers to Mr. Taylor to be distributed to the poor	27	18	9
	130	0	0

John Rotten, Treasurer

While thirty shillings had to be paid for rent, heat and light, the seven hired performers (probably the musicians of the regimental band) received five shillings and sixpence as remuneration for each concert. Mr. Franks' rooms must have been fairly large to hold an audience of more than one hundred as well as an orchestra of somewhere between fifteen and twenty players. Mr. Kutcheon, the ingenious carpenter, had made a movable orchestra platform, as well as the music stands and the candleholders and there was also a servant who, in addition to looking after the tickets at the door, served at the supper which presumably was tendered the performers and some committee members after the concert. As was usual in those days, there had not been a conductor in the modern sense, but the necessary direction was given either from the Leader of the violins — the modern Concert-master — or from the piano or harpsichord player. Quebec's enthusiastic amateur players and amateur listeners must have derived great pleasure from these concerts, as well as from the knowledge that their efforts also brought some laudable charitable results.

Unfortunately there are gaps in our records; the newspapers do not carry reports or financial statements about concert life during the season of 1791-1792. But we meet the "Subscription Concerts" again in a new surrounding — the Free-Masons' Hall — on November 15th, 1792:

> The first Concert will be this evening: *Act First* — — — New Overture, Pleyel — — — Songs, Dr. Arnold ... Concerto, 5th of Avison, opera 4 — — — Concertante, clarinett and Bassoon, Devienne. *Act Second* — — — Haydn's Grand Symphony in D — — — Quintett (two violins, two tenors and violoncello) Pleyel — — — Glee, (Hark, the hollow woods resounding) four voices from the opera of Robin Hood — — — New Finale, Gyrowetz.

> The committee informs the subscriber that the concerts during the season will begin precisely at half past seven o'clock.

This is a typical programme in which the eternal music of the great masters shared the honours with the time-bound and forgotten compositions of the contemporary favourites. Yet, while some of the latter are difficult to trace in historical sources, an astonishingly high standard prevailed in the choice of music.

The programme of the second concert contained the Concerto Grosso no. 2 by Corelli and a "New Symphony" by Haydn and, although we find in later performances such unknown quantities as "Opprimate Contumaci" by Bifiri, or the chorus "Here we Sons of Freedom dwell" by Dr. Samuel Arnold, the British composer, organist of Westminster Abbey and founder of Glee Clubs, there was also music by Bach, Handel (Overture to Occasional Oratorio, Saul, etc.), Mozart (Piano Concerto), Arne, Stamitz, Dittersdorf, the indispensable and undethronable Pleyel, and of course the inevitable Glees. The latter had become the highly favoured entertainment in England, and were also popular in Anglo-Canadian circles. But the golden age of English musical history had come to an end; particularly the later part of the 18th-century was what one writer had called the "gloomiest period in our [England] country's musical history. Musical taste was at a very low ebb; glees and ballads were produced in profusion, but little music of lasting value ₃₁." And the Canada of the 1800's received little inspiration and stimulus from a musically impoverished England, just as music in New France had not been engendered by the rich musical resources of the *grand siècle*. The causes were different ; the effect remained the same.

Nonetheless, it was sincerity of purpose, the enthusiasm of the amateur, and the devotion to music that marked the beginning of the new era; musical art enjoyed a short but active development. The subscription concerts continued unabated; the programme of the eleventh in the 1792 series did not substantially differ from earlier or later ones – the Concerto Grosso no. 8 by Corelli was followed by the Glee by Dr. Arne ("Which is the properest day to drink ?") – and the subscribers are again asked to nominate a treasurer and committee for the ensuing season. The new season started on December 5th, 1793 and, before the year had ended, a remarkable event in the history of music in Canada had taken place, the performance of Handel's music to the "Messiah". Admittedly, it had not been a complete presentation, containing also other works, but the ambitious programme was mainly dedicated to the great oratorio:

> Act First ---Overture to the Messiah, Handel ---Recitative 'Comfort ye my people' ---Chorus 'For unto us a child is born' ---Air 'He shall feed his flock' ---Concerto, Avison ---Chorus 'Lift up your heads oh ye Gates'
>
> *Act Second* - - - Prelude (Pastorale) and Recitatives 'There were shepherds abiding in the fields' and Chorus 'Glory to God' - - - Air 'Total Eclipse (And Darkness shall cover the Earth)' - - - Duett 'Oh lovely

peace' - - - Concerto, Corelli - - - Grand Hallelujah Chorus[32]

During the declining years of the 18th century the subscription concerts were not as frequently advertised as before. One of the last announcements had been accompanied by some discordant notes: "The Subscribers in general and the Gentlemen of the Orchestra particularly having been much incommoded at the last Concert, the Committee feel themselves compelled to inform the Public, That unless a stricter attention is paid in future, the Concerts must of necessity be discontinued [33]."

While Quebec was basking in the glory of remarkable musical achievements, Montreal enjoyed artistic activities equally extensive but with emphasis more on light music or musical comedy. There was also a greater participation of the French element, be it as audience, as performer or as in the following case, as beneficiary:

A CONCERT/For the Benefit of/Mr. DUPLESSY/ Will be performed at Mr. Franks's Assembly Room Vauxhall, on Friday evening the 2nd of Nov., of Vocal and Instrumental Music. The concert will be concluded with a piece of Harmony, in which will be introduced the favourite Air of *Ma Chère Amie.* After the Concert will be/ A BALL/ The Concert to begin precisely at Seven o'clock [34].

And so the musical life in the two cities of the former French domain continued to grow, sometimes at a slower pace, but frequently at an accelerated speed, particularly when towards the middle of the 19th century theatre or opera companies from England or the United States arrived. But at the turn of the century there are still the many announcements in the newspapers which tell us of the local musical events, those with no further intent or purpose than the love of music-making, while in others the prospect of a pecuniary reward loomed high in attraction. There were never enough musicians or singers. In the *Quebec Gazette* of March 1797 the Commanding Officer of the King's Own at Montreal promises "great encouragement" for two or three good musicians who are wanted for the King's Own Infantry, while a few years later the English Church is looking for "twelve boys of respectable parents, and eight young men of good characters" to build up the choir. And the chronicle of our musical life after nearly two hundred years in colonial environment continues to be written in these small episodes, the charmingly unimportant incidents and insignificant events that form, similar to James Sinclair's musical wares, a long list of items "too tedious to mention". Nonetheless, in the final count the balance sheet of attainment does not any longer appear so dismally deprived of creditable musical manifestation.

MUSIC AND THEATRE

The chronicle of French-Canadian musical achievement in the last decades of the 18th century must take into account the participation of the French population to the theatrical life in the new Canada under British rule, since theatre performances were always accompanied by some sort of musical contribution. In ordre to appreciate this contribution it is necessary to remember the clerical attitude in Catholic New France towards music and the theatre, particularly since the stormy events of 1694 resulted in a ban on public performances of the "sinful" plays of Molière, such as "Tartuffe" and others. The "Tartuffe" incident had made the clergy aware of the potential dangers inherent in theatrical performances, and it is due to the success of clerical vigilance that, except for some occasional student performances in colleges or other educational institutions, no theatrical performances are recorded over a period of almost seventy years, from the days of Frontenac to the arrival of the British garrison. But Molière returned to Canada — albeit on the shoulders of the British officers. Indeed, the initiative to perform on stage came from the officers of the garrison, most of them fluent in French, who presented in the original language and with great success such masterpieces as *Le Bourgeois Gentilhomme, Le Médecin Malgré Lui* and *Les Fourberies de Scapin.* Captain William, the director and principal actor, would have preferred to see the female rôles played by the young ladies of Montreal, but the *Canadiennes* feared possible scandal and the young English girls were either too scared or not capable — the risk was in either case too great. At any rate, there it was: the classic French comedy, played in 1774 by Englishmen in the first theatre of Montreal, situated in the house of the notary Antoine Foucher ₃₅.

The first theatre in Quebec featured the works of lesser known playwrights. According to an announcement in the newspaper a series of performances seem to have been offered to subscribers and one of those performances was advertised as follows :

> " On Wednesday next, the 14th Instant, will be Performed for the Subscribers, the Comedy of the BEAUX STRATAGEMES. To this will be added a Piece in TWO ACTS, consisting of VOCAL and INSTRUMENTAL MUSIC.
> N. B. Wanted to borrow, or hire, for the THEATRE, a *Harpsichord, Piano Forte, or Spinet.* It will be kept in good order and returned safe. ₃₆"

The *Juvenile Theatre* of Quebec announced that "for the benefit of two distressed orphans will be performed on Thursday the 30th instant, the Comedy of the IRISH WIDOW, with Singing between the Acts, and the Entertainment of the GHOST ... ₃₇" Such obviously exciting fare was not to be offered at the College St. Raphael in Montreal, where in 1776 the students presented the biblical tragedy *Jonathas et David,* or *Le Triomphe de l'Amitié.* The author of this edifying piece was a French Jesuit, Père Pierre Brumoy, who has also the honour of having had his play printed in one of the earliest Canadian editions, published by Fleury Mesplet and Charles Berger of Montreal 38. It speaks well for the quality of instruction at the College St. Raphael that such theatrical performances seem to have been a permanent affair, for we learn of other and similar events, such as the performance by students of the *Sacrifice d'Abraham* in the presence of the General Haldimand, the Governor of Canada. In Quebec a group of young French Canadian amateurs performed with great success the classic and contemporary French stage repertory for an enthusiastic audience. Beaumarchais' *Barbier de Séville* received its first Canadian performance only a few years after its *première* in Paris in 1775, while his *Mariage de Figaro* of 1784 was played only one year later in Montreal. If the quality of acting may not have satisfied a critical and sophisticated public the *Quebec Gazette* supported the efforts of the young Canadian actors in a very significant manner:

> It is with no small satisfaction that we remark the inoffensive pleasure felt by the public, on seeing the laudable efforts of a few Canadian Young Gentlemen to amuse themselves and the public, in a rational way, by dedicating their leisure hours to theatrical exhibitions; those hours which youth but too often employ to far worse purposes. Whatever rigid preachers may say, theatrical amusement, far from having an immoral tendency, tend to raise the mind above the sordid passions of every denomination; to say nothing of their effect in qualifying youth for the world, by the ease, confidence and grace they inspire 39.

This was an unequivocal rejection of clerical interference, a courageous reply to episcopal exhortation against immorality and sinful pleasures of the stage; and it is also evidence of clerical vigilance and concern which since the early days of New France has been characteristic of Quebec. Encouraged by public acclaim the Canadian Young Gentlemen continued to present Quebec with their type of histrionic art. The quality of these performances may be judged from the somewhat apologetic acknowledgement in the *Gazette:*

> On Wednesday the 2nd inst. the Canadian Young Gentlemen closed their theatrical campaign with the Comedy of the *Barbier de Séville.* They were honoured with the presence of General Clarke and a numerous and brilliant assembly of Ladies and Gentlemen both English and Canadian. If it be considered that the efforts of these young Gentlemen are purely the result of nature; barely their own ideas of characters and things, unassisted by example or any previous acquaintance with stage artifice; if to this be added the scantiness of their wardrobe, scenery, decorations and stage, we think it will be doing them no more than justice to say they wore the sock with ease, humour and even with *éclat.* As they were pleased to entertain the public *gratis* we can do no less on the part of the public than to make this small acknowledgement [40].

The proximity of the American States was bound to affect cultural activities in Canada. English theatre companies played already in the early 70's in New York, Boston and Albany, and the first of these companies arrived in 1776 in Montreal to perform the highly popular play by Goldsmith, *She Stoops to Conquer.* The year 1787 was particularly prodigious for Montreal's theatre-goers; the Edward Allen Company announced in the *Montreal Gazette* of March 1st, 1787 that on "Friday Evening next, will be presented a New Comedy, call'd FOLLIES OF A DAY, or the MARRIAGE OF FIGARO. To which will be added a New OPERA (never performed here) call'd the POOR SOLDIER, with the Original *Overture* &c. &c. as compos'd by Mr. Shield." As a sort of programme note, the following information was offered : "The Musical Entertainment of the POOR SOLDIER, to be performed at the THEATRE on Friday Evening, is universally allow'd to be the most pleasing Musical afterpiece ever exhibited on the Stage, and notwithstanding it had a run of Sixty odd Nights the Season it was wrote, has been repeated at least twenty times every Season since, at the Theatre Royal in Covent Garden." A few months later the Edward Allen Company gave a number of performances in Montreal after having played at Quebec. The announcement read :

> By permission of His Excellency Guy Lord Dorchester for a few evenings, the Theatre in Mr. Proulx's Room, will be opened on Monday next, with a *Comedy* (in four Acts) alter'd from Dr. Goldsmith's SHE STOOPS TO CONQUER or the MISTAKES OF A NIGHT, and the Entertainment of the CITIZEN. With a PROLOGUE by Mr. Moore and a Poetic Tale, call'd the FARMERS BLUNDER by Mr. Allen. These Pieces were performed by Command of His Royal Highness Prince William Henry at Quebec, and received with his particular approbation [41].

Theatrical entertainment became a regular feature in Quebec and Montreal. Weekly performances took place in both languages, the English stage tending towards the light comedy while the French Canadian Gentlemen Amateurs, unconcerned of clerical misgivings, played Molière, Marivaux, Régnard and other classics of French comedy. The light entertainment presented by the English theatre was indeed in obvious contrast to the high quality of works performed by the French groups. This contrast had been noted by at least one indignant citizen of Montreal who in a letter to the editor of the *Gazette* complained that humour and ridicule are often abused by licentious writers who are "turning objects which were serious, and characters which were sacred, into derision. Hence it may be affirmed of

English Comedy in general (for exceptions there are) that, to the eternal disgrace of our stage, obscenity is too often substituted for Wit, and Ribaldry for Humour ... In the hands of a libertine, Comedy will corrupt; in those of a well-disposed writer, it will amuse, it will instruct." "Hence", continues our critic, "it has always been observed, and justly, to the honour of the French nation, that their Comedy is a school of manners, while ours has been too often that of vice." And he refers to the comedies of Molière and "other eminent Comic writers, such as Régnard, Dufresne and Marivaux, whose compositions are strongly marked with chastity and decency", and he draws the corollary "that the French stage, by a proper selection, may be rendered subservient to Religion and Virtue". [42]

But if the English theatre did not present works of a higher quality it nonetheless gilded its frivolous comedies with music by way of preludes, postludes and also in form of arias interspersed in the performances. Characteristic of such presentations with music are also the references to performances in London which could not have failed to impress the audience. Announcements in the journals invite the public to attend: "The Grand Historical Pantomime Call'd *The Death of Captain Cook* with the original music as performed at the Theatre Covent Garden and Drury Lane, London, which is descriptive of the manners and customs of OWYHEE in the Pacific Ocean - - - and with a characteristic Dance and Procession, and the Marriage ceremony peculiar to that Country. All to conclude with the Assassination of Captain Cook and the Funeral procession ... [43]" An evening's entertainment must indeed have been satisfying, if not in quality at least in the quantity of amusing diversion. Here is a typical case: "Comedy — I'LL TELL YOU WHAT, after which a FANCY DANCE, to be followed by the Farce of DEVIL TO PAY, or the WIVES METAMORPHOSED, between the Acts, a SONG by a LADY." The quality often left much to be desired, and the critic found that "the after piece (Devil to

Pay) had it been presented by professional performers ought to have been hooted. But we shall in the present case draw a veil over it . . . 44" Such critical remarks appear more frequently than before on the printed page: "Charity being the sole motive for the exertion of the Gentlemen who pay their addresses to the enchanting Thalia, we shall, while we omit the errors, recommend true deserts (!) . . .", and elsewhere we read that ". . . the theatre on Saturday evening was graced with the assemblage of the principal beauties of Quebec, and the Comedy of the WEST INDIAN, with the entertainment of the DIVORCE, were represented to the satisfaction of the spectators, except for a few snarling critics, who had been paying their *devoirs* to Bacchus. The four first Acts of the WEST INDIAN would not discredit a London Theatre, but towards the [scene of the] *Catastrophe* owing to some mistakes a veil clouded the former excellence... 45."

Musical interludes were not only songs, including the "new Vauxhall song, compos'd by Mr. Hook," but also one-act farces, consisting of music, dancing and singing, such as the interlude called "the *Wapping Landlady, or Jack in Distress,* in which will be introduced the song of *Sweet Willy O !* by a Lady 46." The favourite duet *"How sweet is the woodland"* and a *hornpipe* followed Thomas Otway's famous tragedy, *Venice Preserved* — "and the whole to conclude with the Chorus of God Save The King 47."

Stage plays of all sorts with or without music continued to enliven Quebec and Montreal in the last decade of the 18th century. For the promoters of the light muse the uppermost consideration was the entertainment aspect without much regard for either the literary values or the quality of acting. Letters to the newspapers emphasise the poor state of theatrical affairs, as in the case of the writer who suggests that "theatrical representations, especially those of the Comic kind, have ever been the delight of Societies in the least degree refined. The vanity of

Man, gratified with the Mirror held up to the view of his Neighbor, in the contemplation of his foibles, seems to forget the language addressed to *his* heart. Each man laughs at his neighbor's burden, which he sees hanging at his breast, while the sack that contains his own infirmities is pending, unheeded, at his back." Annoyed with the incompetent acting, with "sneaking haughtiness and smooth-tongued folly" he suggests that

> if these truly *comical* (not Comic) performers were to appear with a barrel about their necks ... they might succeed. Hurt at these performances the writer of this Letter wishes to make a proposal to the Public ... It is proposed, that a number of dancing Bears, flying Fishes and red Elephants — together with swimming Bulls, dancing Dogs and wooden Puppets, be collected from all parts of the *habitable* World, *for the amusement of this Town* — Natives of whatever clime, they shall be welcome ... and they shall perform while three thousand Cats, all together from the precints of this City, shall unite their harmonious voices, to please the Spectators, between the Acts 48.

Nonetheless, whatever took place between the acts (or plays) seems at time to have been pleasant enough to cause the editor of the *Montreal Herald* under the heading "Better late than never" to apologize to "those Gentlemen who have afforded us so many rich treats from the ORCHESTRA of the AMATEUR THEATRE. Their selection of Music cannot fail to please, being chosen from the best Composers, and the execution of which have both astonished and delighted ... 49"

While thus the English theatre in the 18th century suffered from many ills, there were in the early years of the 19th century the occasional attempts to scale the glorious heights of the Shakespearean drama. What may have been the earliest known public performance of Shakespearean plays in Canada took place in Montreal in 1808:

On Thursday evening last the persevering diligence of
Mr. Prigmore enabled him to open the New Theatre
and present to a full house the popular and diverting
play "The Taming of the Shrew" ... The piece was
judiciously chosen, the parts well cast, and the principal characters supported with propriety. But a criticism
is not intended — All excellence is relative; and the
critic who goes to the Montreal Theatre to trace the
analogy between that and those of Drury Lane or Covent Garden, to look for correct representations of general nature, or feel in their full force those emotions
which our immortal Shakespeare intended to excite,
loses all fastidiousness in the contemplation of the individual, who is at once the Manager, the preceptor of
the subaltern actors, and the principal performer in
the Drama 50...

Shortly after Mr. Prigmore presented the *Tempest*, and in May
of the same year also *Hamlet*. Between the play and the costu-
mary *Farce* was the usual musical interlude, sometimes only a
song ("the much admired Comic Song, called *The Sprig of
Shelala*") but occasionally also some instrumental music, the
popular *Battle of Prague* by Kotzwara, or the overture to *Lo-
doiska* by Cherubini. The "persevering diligence of Mr. Prigmore" did not allow him to rest on his success in Montreal and he
intended to gain more fame by extending his activities to Quebec. The whole company, covered in heavy furs and travelling in
large sleighs, left Montreal for Quebec probably in the winter of
1809. But the sleigh-train never arrived there; buried under
mountains of snow, or devoured by wolfs as legend will have it
— nothing was ever again heard of Mr. Prigmore and his troupe.

In later years other theatre companies made their ap-
pearances, either as travelling group or as resident company
gathered under the leadership of a capable individual devoted to
the histrionic art and some monetary reward, and providing the

grateful public with some cultural events. Such an event took place in Quebec on April 7th, 1817 when under the patronage of His Excellency, Lieut. Gen. Sir John Coape Sherbrooke the "Amateurs of the Garrison" performed part of *Henry IV.* Perhaps a complete performance was thought to tax actors and public too much, hence the shortened version of the drama was "followed by the Farce: *Love à la Mode*". Of interest to our study is the performance of *Macbeth* in Montreal on May 4th, 1818:

> Mr. Turnbull respectfully informs his friends and the public, that his benefit will take place on Monday Evening, May 4, 1818, when will be represented a celebrated Tragedy in five Acts, written by William Shakespeare, called MACBETH, with new Scenery, Dresses and Decorations; together with the original Music, Incantations, Songs and new Choruses composed by Locke. To which will be added, never performed here, a Grand Serious Comic Pantomime, in two acts, with Scenery, dresses and decorations, called DON JUAN or the *Libertine Destroyed.* Interspersed with Songs, Duetts, and Choruses. Music by Hewitt [51].

The English Theatre continued in more or less similar manner well into the 19th century. In its beginnings it had more often than not been of low artistic quality not only in its literary but also in its musical aspects. In the 19th century theatrical endeavours continued to follow the popular trends of England without, however, attaining the standards of professional achievement. Yet there was a substantial amount of exciting enthusiasm and refreshing spontaneity in these meagre cultural manifestations which exonerated much of the unavoidable weaknesses and shortcomings.

Of course, there had sometimes been the devastating criticism by visiting Englishmen, such as John Lambert, mentioned earlier, who had the misfortune of attending stage performances of the worst kind, with actors as bad as "the worst of those in

English touring companies", (moreover, they have the audacity to charge the same price as the theatres of London), and in fact there were hardly any actors "who did not massacre the most beautiful scenes of our great poets". As evidence of the deplorable state of the theatre he refers to the custom of young men playing female roles, the only actress being an "old, semi-virtuous, antiquated female whose inebriate interpretation of the great heroine often enchanted the Canadian public 52." The object of this cynical and censorious comment was the *Brobdingnag theatre*, managed by the Ormsbys whose conception of art and artistry seems to have been lacking in its most fundamental elements. Apparently Mr. and Mrs. Ormsby encountered some sort of opposition, which made them resolve to take leave of Canada after the next performance, only to change their intention after the next performance and to announce the presentation of "A Comedy — never performed here before — call'd BOTHERATION — or a THREE YEARS BLUNDER — to which will be added the Celebrated Pantomime of the Death of GENERAL WOLFE, or the *Conquest of Quebec*, etc. etc. ... 53" A year later the Ormsbys are still in Quebec, (having changed from *Brobdingnag* to *Patagonia*), and in usual fashion announce that in the "Patagonian Theatre ... will be presented a Comedy in two Acts, Called: *Raising the Wind*, also a Farce in one Act called *The Contrast*, or the *True Born Yankee* ... etc., etc.", after which performance they will "take leave of Canada". At the same time Quebec's French population was invited to attend at the Théâtre Patagon two comedies by Molière, *Les Fourberies de Scapin* and *Le Médecin Malgré lui*. A *nota bene* obviously referring to earlier disturbances by an over-enthusiastic audience advised the public that only honest and decent persons will be admitted 54.

French theatre had already in the 1780's become an important factor in our cultural development. A group of young Frenchmen met in the large studio of Louis Dulongpré, a successful painter and able musician, and in this artistic atmosphere a contract was drawn up which stipulated that Monsieur Dulongpré furnish the "Théâtre de Société", as the new establishment was called, with three decorations painted on canvas, viz., a room, a forest, and a street, together with the great curtain. And it was further stipulated that he be in charge of lighting, advertising, the music and the hairdresser, the tickets, the guardians — in brief, the painter-musician became managing director of the new enterprise.

Louis Dulongpré had arrived in the New World on board a vessel that carried supplies from France to the Americans as aid in their fight against the English. After the war he visited Montreal and decided to stay there. At first he tried his luck as music teacher and, like most of them, found teaching not exactly a rewarding profession. His friends encouraged him to develop his apparent aptitude for painting and for portraiture in particular. Soon his reputation was established and his financial situation thoroughly satisfying. Unfortunately, his musical activities are nowhere mentioned; they could, however, not have been very extensive considering the great demand on his talent as portrait painter (he is supposed to have painted more than three thousand five hundred portraits), as well as the time required to fulfill his obligations towards the *Théâtre de Société.* It was he who in his capacity as general factotum placed in November 1780 the first advertisement with the *Gazette: "Théâtre de Société* / Mardi, 24 du courant, il sera donné à la Salle de Spectacle, chez M. Dulongpré, une représentation du RETOUR IMPREVU / Comédie en Deux Actes & en prose, de Mr. Régnard; / Suivie des / DEUX BILLETS / Comédie en un Acte & en prose, mêlée d'Ariettes, / Du Chevalier de Florian / La Porte sera ouverte à Six Heures, & à Sept la Toile sera levée. Messieurs les Acteurs Prient les Dames d'y venir sans chapeaux, ni autre coiffures qui puissent empêcher de voir commodément." The second representation was announced in the *Gazette* of December 24th; "Théâtre de Société / Mardi, 29 du courant, il sera donné à la Salle de Spectacle, une représentation du / LEGA-TAIRE / Comédie en 5 Actes & en Vers, par Mr. Régnard; SUIVIE des / DEUX CHASSEURS & LA LAITIERE / Opéra Comique en un Acte, en Prose, par M. DUNY. Musique de M. ANSEAUME. Entre la Comédie & l'Opéra, il sera dansé un / BALLET / Les Acteurs réitérent leurs instances auprès des Dames, en les priant d'y venir coiffées de façon à ne pouvoir empêcher les personnes derrière elles d'y voir commodément."

As can be seen, the two programmes include music, either as part of the comedies, such as *Les Deux Billets* by Jean-Pierre Claris de Florian (1755-1794), or in the Ballet of which, however, we lack any further detail. Of interest is the reference to the *opera comique, Les Deux Chasseurs et la Laitière.* An obvious printer's mistake assigned the music to Anseaume, and the text to Duny, while in reality the reverse is true. Egidio Romualdo Duni (1709-1775) was born in Italy, had been choir-master at Naples, went to Paris, became director of the *Comédie Italienne* and wrote a large number of *opéras comiques en français,* the text for which had been provided by a number of librettists, among them Anseaume.

The success of the *Théâtre de Société* was above expectations, the entertainment was enjoyed on all levels of Montreal's society; but a proposed social distinction threatened to disturb the peace and harmony. This is how one apprehensive and resentful individual warned of class distinction and waved the banner of *égalité;*

Un Citoyen observe

(1) Que quelques uns de ses compatriotes se proposent de donner cet hiver quelques représentations théâtrales;

(2) Qu'il y en a parmi eux qui ont proposé de n'admettre dans le parterre qu'un très petit nombre de personnes de *haute* extraction ou de race noble:

Il remarque là-dessus

(1) Que le projet d'acter est bon, & que le théâtre ne peut qu'inspirer du goût dans cette nouvelle colonie;

(2) Qu'il ne remplira pas cet objet, s'il est si resserré; qu'il ne fera tout au plus qu'exciter la haine & l'animosité résultantes ordinairement des *sottes distinctions*;

ET C'EST TOUT 55.

COLAS ET COLINETTE

Some years later, in 1795, the *Théâtre de Société* was still active; the location had changed; some of the repertory was new and included such items as *Le Barbier de Séville* by Beaumarchais; *Le Mari Devin* by Destouches and Molière's *Médecin Malgré Lui*.

But it is not because of Molière and Destouches that the *Théâtre de Société* is remembered in the annals of music in Canada. On January 14th, 1790 the Montreal audience was treated to a rare event, the first performance of the first comedy with music, written and composed in Canada. It was a brief and modest advertisement in the *Montreal Gazette* of January 7th, 1790 which announced that on: "Jeudi 14 du courant il sera donné à la Salle de Spectacle une représentation du / MEDECIN MALGRE LUI / Comédie en 3 Actes & en Prose par *Molière*; Suivie de *COLAS & COLINETTE* ou *LE BAILLI DUPE*, Comédie en 3 Actes & en Prose, mêlée d'Ariettes; Pièce & Musique nouvelle." We could not locate any further announcement, criticism or other remark about the first performance, but it may be permissible to quote the report of the first presentation in Quebec, which took place in January 1805, fifteen years after its Montreal *première*:

Theatre — On Tuesday evening was presented a French Opera, called the *Bailli Dupè*, or *Colas & Colinette*. The Dialogue, Songs and Music by Mr. QUESNEL, of Boucherville.

This is perhaps the first piece of the kind that has been written and performed in this province. The dialogue, the songs and music are, we understand, the composition of M. Quesnel, and as a colonial production, it possesses considerable merit. It rarely happens that the Poetry and Music are composed by the same person. It was the union of these two arts that gave to the operas of Rousseau a Superiority over those of his contemporaries, and impressed his audience with the most powerful emotions of sympathy.

Like his friend Dulongpré, Joseph Quesnel had reached Canada by serving as a volunteer in the American War of Independence. Born at St. Malo in 1749, he went to sea at an early age, sailed on many oceans and touched on many ports from India to Brazil, and in 1779 found himself in command of a vessel that carried provisions and munitions to the American revolutionaries. Captured by an English frigate, his ship was brought into Halifax and he was taken to Quebec where Sir Frederick Haldimand, the Swiss-born Governor-in-chief of Quebec, who had known his family, granted him freedom and naturalization papers, and Quesnel, finding the Canadian way of life to his liking, decided to stay. The *Corsaire Malouin* became shopkeeper and general merchant in the quiet small-town atmosphere of Boucherville. In 1780 he married Marie Deslandes and by her had thirteen children, one of whom carried the family name as far west as British Columbia 56.

Kallmann says that Quesnel had been described as "a gentleman of cheerful temperament and nice tastes, who was happy in promoting the happiness of another people", and while it is certain that he fascinated the townspeople of Boucherville with the colourful stories of his adventurous voyages, he may also have overawed and impressed them with his taste for literature, art and music. It is said that on all his earlier voyages he had never abandoned the treasured companions of his artistic spirit and his leisure times: the works of Molière, Boileau, Lafontaine, and a violin. Thus even in the artistically deprived atmosphere of the small town Quesnel found inspiration for his artistic muses, and he devoted his free time to the writing of poems, epistles, comedies and also some music. In fact, it has been claimed that in addition to his literary works Quesnel composed "several symphonies for large orchestra, quartets and duos, and several motets and other pieces of sacred music composed for the Parish church of Montreal 57." Unfortunately, no trace of the music had been found nor have these claims been substantiated. There exist, however, the vocal parts of two of his comedies, *Lucas et Cécile* and *Colas et Colinette*, together with the second violin part of the latter. On hand of these few parts Godfrey Ridout re-composed *Colas et Colinette* and even arranged an overture based on some of the melodies.

The story of *Colas et Colinette* centres around the usual plot in the manner of Molière's stage plays. It involves a young orphan girl (raised by the kindhearted and generous country squire), whose sentimental attachement to Colas, the village swain, is requited by the young bucolic lover's affection. But there is also the Bailiff, an old and rich bachelor, whose passionate interest in the young girl leads to the usual flurry of subterfuges, intrigues and complications, until in the end he finds himself completely duped in his schemes, while the young lovers receive the blessings of the noble squire. The characters are, as Kallmann says, the stock figures of French and not Canadian village society.

The music to *Colas et Colinette* is of the charmingly naive type, the insignificant and amateurish imitation of a style that had begun with Rousseau and became highly popular with

Philidor, Monsigny and Gretry. Their music is filled with the aristocratic spirit of the time, based in essence on the music of Lully and Rameau and oriented towards the simple, natural and honest qualities which since Rousseau have been the earmark of *opera comique*. But the true style of French *opéra comique* was created by Egidio Duni, the Italian who appropriated the spirit of French light music and soon became the example to be followed by genius and amateur, and by those who rallied to the cause of French music. Quesnel was thoroughly French in his cultural manifestations; the pleasant and refined personality as which he is depicted in historic accounts remained imbued with the Gallic spirit to the end. And as he remained French in all artistic aspects he did neither adapt to the new country nor exert any influence on its literary or musical development. *Colas et Colinette* is French in spirit, in the story and its characters, it could not help but be French in the music as well, and if Quesnel in writing it looked for stimulus and motivation he found it not in his environment but in the nostalgic thoughts about the country of his birth. It is therefore somewhat pretentious to claim more than historical value to this first "colonial production of considerable merit".

French public interest in Canadian affairs had from the days of Cartier to the conquest in 1759 been insignificant, and there was even less interest discernible after the loss of the colony. Nonetheless, for a short moment the French public became acquainted and concerned with a small segment of Canadian life through the pen of the great Voltaire. *L'Ingénu* appeared in 1767 — not as an accusation of French political failure at the loss of Canada nor as a protest against harsh British rule in the former French territory, but rather as the satirical story of the misadventures of a Huron Indian (who is not a savage but the abandoned son of a French nobleman brought up in a Huron village), lost in the morale and customs of French society. So much did the story arouse interest and compassion that Marmontel adapted it for an operatic libretto, called it *Le Huron*, and Gretry wrote the music. The first performance in 1768 was a tremendous success; it established Gretry's fame as composer of light opera, and it remained for forty years in the repertory of the Paris Opera. It is regretable that this work with its textual connection to Canada has received less, if any, attention than *Colas et Colinette*.

   Quesnel did not criticize his environment nor did he compare Canadian life with that of his youth. But he had a good eye for the cultural and other weaknesses of Canadians, whether in his play *L'Anglomanie* or *Le Diner à l'Anglaise* where he ridicules the desire of certain French-Canadians of the upper class to imitate English manners, or whether in his autobiographical poem, *Epitre à M. Généreux Labadie*, where he sadly complains about the uncultured, uncivilized and ungrateful Canadian. And he deplores the fact that the Canadian, in contrast to people all across the globe, does not appreciate true talent; he regrets that in this country where the spirit is even colder than the climate, his talents are lost in the present but, he hopes, will be recognized in the future. As far as musical life is concerned, he noted that Canadians sing old drinking songs at the dinner table, and in church some old motets accompanied by the organ whose pipes are missing. He admits that his music is neither elegant nor exciting, and he advises those who look for greater musical satisfaction to go to London to hear Handel or to Paris to enjoy Gretry.

   Joseph Quesnel died in Montreal in July 1809. The obituary in the *Quebec Gazette* expresses the universal regret:

   Died — in this city [Montreal] on the 2nd instant, after a short illness, JOSEPH QUESNEL, Esquire, of Boucherville, aged 58. He saw the approach of death without dismay, and recited several times the following concluding verses of some moral stanzas written by himself two years before:

Hélas ! Que sert de regretter
Les instants de ce court passage;
La mort ne doit pas attrister,
Ce n'est que la fin du voyage.

Concerts became regular features in the last decades of
the 18th and the early part of the 19th century, and while these
events were more remarkable for the variety of music and instruments than for their artistic value they set the stage for the increasing interest in musical activities. In addition to the small
group of "Gentlemen Amateurs" who had united in the pursuit
of musical pleasure and social entertainment, a new attraction
arrived on the musical scene: the solo performer, the artist of
many talents and forerunner of the great virtuoso of the European romantic period, or the descendant of the medieval *jongleur* and purveyor of musical entertainment. Coming usually via
the American States, some of these self-anointed masters of the
dazzling *roulades* of larynx and phalanges left the unwary and
inexperienced public spellbound with the magic of their musical
showmanship.

Some appeared on the fledgling Canadian concert stage
advertising their artistic wares in most eloquent terms and after a
number of performances disappeared without leaving any further trace. Some sailed under their own banner while others
quite obviously preferred the glamour attached to a foreign
sounding name, be it French or Italian, in order to impress their
public. Yet it is the content of their concert programmes, wherever available, which indicates to some extent their musical
prowess and artistic standard. Most of the music listed belonged
to the lighter type and lesser quality, and it may well be assumed that the ability of the performer did not greatly surpass
the level of the music performed. But there was an uncritical
and grateful public, craving for pleasant entertainment and duly
impressed by these colonial manifestations of culture. More important, however, was another less ostentatious yet more signifi-

cant sign of growing musical art. The aftermath of the American revolution had brought a large number of British emigrants from the New England States to Canada and among them "were men of good education and refined taste 58." One of them seems to have been the later Chief Justice of Lower Canada, Jonathan Sewell, a New Englander by birth, whose musical interest and considerable skill as amateur violonist enriched musical life in Quebec well into the early decades of the 19th century. Together with the illustrious commander of His Majesty's Forces, His Royal Highness the Prince Augustus, and in company of the ordinary musician, teacher and music merchant, Frederick Glackemeyer and other enthusiastic music lovers, Jonathan Sewell became the leader of a society of musical amateurs and introduced chamber-music of the finest quality and by the greatest masters to Quebec's musical scene 59.

It is not at all curious to note that the joys of chambermusic were shared by these enthusiastic musical amateurs rather than by professional musicians. Not only did Canada in the late 18th and early 19th century lack the trained and skilled professional but chambermusic has always been the undisputed domain of the devoted amateur, except in cases where the technical requirements of the music exceeded the capabilities of the player. The activities of these devoted amateurs were, however, not limited to the private and intimate pleasures of chambermusic. It may justifiably be assumed that Judge Sewell, Frederick Glackemeyer and their musical friends, together with some of the military bandsmen participated in the orchestral concerts of the 1790's, and that the music for these subscription concerts as well as for the private chambermusic evenings may have been imported by our resourceful music dealer. Moreover, Glackemeyer imported not only music for string quartets or for larger orchestras, he also brought to Quebec symphonic music in the customary arrangements for various instruments. Some of this music became the property of his son, Edouard, a music lover, accom-

plished flutist and Notary by profession, although it had been
said that he considered his professional commitments secondary
to his musical activities. Part of that music consisted of a number
of famous symphonies and overtures, ranging from Haydn, Mozart and Beethoven to Pleyel, Winters, Méhul, Rossini, Paer, von
Esch, and other long-forgotten minor composers, and arranged
by Hummel and others for Flute, Violin, Violoncello and Piano.
Glackemeyer jr. listed and numbered the music, and had it
bound in separated volumes according to instru-
ments [60] Kallmann also explains that Sewell became the leader of
a string quartet in which the notaries Campbell and Glackemeyer "... took the second violin and flute parts respectively,
and J. Harvicker played the cello." And he goes on to say that
"one may speculate that the second violinist took the viola part
and the flautist one of the violin parts [61]." This is an unlikely
suggestion since the viola parts in the quartet music of the classic
masters frequently descends past the lower limit of the violin.
The extant collection of Glackemeyers music mentioned earlier
furnishes an indication to the type of music performed. Humble
and modest as these manifestations may have been they became
the backbone of musical life to such an extent that the development in the early decades of the 19th century may well be
considered as the beginning of our musical history.

X

Coda

In the preceeding chapters an attempt has been made to trace the development of music in Canada from its modest beginnings at Port Royal to the modest yet remarkable achievements in the early 19th century. The road to artistic and cultural accomplishment had been long and wearisome, made difficult and at times almost insurmountable by many factors, by climatic conditions no less than by priorities of political, economic and social nature; by disinterest in the physical and cultural growth on the part of those entrusted with the guidance and leadership of the colony no less than by insufficient education on the part of those who tilled the soil and built the new land. Two more glaring factors may be added: the courtly and exclusive quality of music in France during the *grand siècle* and the stern and forbidding attitude of the religious leaders of the colony towards artistic manifestations of a secular nature. Indeed, these two factors contributed more to the cultural poverty than "pioneer conditions", lack of education and leadership or other considerations. The attainments of the *grand siècle* could not be transplanted into the musical wilderness of New France nor was secular art and music allowed to flourish under the watchful eye of the clergy.

What is the conclusion to be arrived at? Is it that the colonial enterprises are not fertile grounds for cultural development? Is it that pioneer conditions are not conducive to the pursuit of artistic endeavours? Or that any other than rudimentary education is neither possible nor desirable in colonial environment? The answer to these and similar questions is found in the comparison with the amazing musical achievement in New Spain in the 16th century, in the splendid artistic accomplishments in the Southern States and in New England and in the enviable success of European musical life transplanted into the central colonies. The problems connected with our slow cultural development are unique in colonial enterprises on the North American continent, since nowhere else has education, art and music been deprived of their rightful place within the context of a well-planned colonization.

To provide an impartial historical account of more than two centuries of musical art in Canada is a difficult task. It becomes a precarious undertaking if partisan or biased opinions becloud the issues. What some consider splendid accomplishment appears to others merely as insignificant events that were frequently supported by weak claims or in extreme cases even based on fictitious accounts [1]. If claims to Amador Martin's alleged composition are hardly convincing in the light of musico-historical research, the references to the music of the School of Versailles, the erroneous assumption with regard to instruments at religious ceremonies, or the unsolvable mystery of the lost symphony by Calixa Lavallée [2] are examples of conjectural opinions lacking in substantiated evidence, as indeed no other aspect of our cultural past had received so little attention or been subjected to less careful investigation than the musical history of early Canada. In his interpretation of the facts the historian does not attach unwarranted blame nor indulge in undeserved praise; he is not concerned with comparison *per se* but aims at discovery and examination of cause and affect. Yet a judiciously balanced evaluation of all factors concerned cannot avoid disappointment as it proceeds to illuminate the inadequacy of our musical past. The audacious attempt to collect the episodes and incidents and to relate the scattered fragments of our musical chronicle to the wider context of our general history might well be considered a tedious exercise in tautology by those who somewhat justifiably believe that Canada's musical history begins in the twentieth century or at the earliest with the arrival of the British entertainers after 1759, while others may be disturbed by the impact of sober historical facts which are bound to upset preconceived ideas and patriotic sentiment. Two-hundred years of musical history had come to an end — the end of a beginning, the end of a neglected chapter in our chronicle. Whatever the conclusion, the present work was intended to rescue from oblivion the few remaining vestiges of early Canadian musical life.

NOTES AND BIBLIOGRAPHY

Preface

1. Helmut Kallman, *A History of Music in Canada, 1534-1914*, Univ. of Toronto Press, Toronto, 1960.

I
Introduction

(Unless otherwise stated all translations are by the author.)

1. Marc Lescarbot, *Histoire de la Nouvelle France*, ed. Tross, Paris, 1866, vol. 1, p. xv. "For not having the violins and other recreations in New France there is no need to complain, since it is quite easy to bring them there."

2. Present-day Annapolis County, Nova Scotia.

3. Lescarbot, *op. cit.*, "il n'y a point les violons, les masquerades, les danses, les palais, les villes et les beaux batimens de France." v. 1, p. xv.

4. "Je suis comme le public, j'aime beaucoup mieux la paix que le Canada, et je crois que la France peut être heureuse sans Québec." Letter : Voltaire to Choiseul, September 6th, 1762. Public Archives of Canada, Ottawa.

5. Pierre Biard, *Relation de la Nouvelle France, de ses Terres, Natvrel dv Païs & de ses Habitans*, in *Jesuit Relations and Allied Documents*, v. III, p. 21. "Le Capitaine Thomas Aubert, Dieppois, y fit voile, l'an 1508 & en ramena des Sauuages du païs, lesquels il fit voir auec admiration & applaudissement à la France." (See also *Dictionary of Canadian Biography*, Toronto, 1966, I, p. 72).

The arrival in France of the first North American Indians with their costumes, arms and most likely their songs and dances caused not only great excitement and admiration but also seems to have stimulated the choreographers of the famous royal ballets. An illustration in H. Prunières, *Le Ballet de Cour en France,* (H. Laurens, Paris, 1914,) entitled "Musique de l'Amérique" shows an amusing entry of "American" music in the ballet *La Douairière de Billebahaut,* in which "four Indian bagpipe players lead onto the stage a truly exotic lama pulling a Chinese gong chime." (M. Bukofzer, *Music in the Baroque Era,* W.W. Norton Company, New York, 1947, p. 143).

6. Marie de l'Incarnation, *Lettres,* ed. Richardeau, Tournai, 1876, lettre à son fils, XCVIII, 30 août, 1650 ; v. I, p. 429. "... que ni nous ni tout le Canada ne pourrons subsister encore deux ans sans secours ... si ce secours manque, il nous faut ou mourir ou retourner en France."

7. Francis Parkman, *The Old Régime in Canada,* Little, Brown, and Company, Boston, 1886, p. 400.

8. *Memoire touchant le Canada et L'acadie,* envoyé par M. de Meulles, 1684, Archives Nationales, Colonies F3/2, Paris. (Jacques de Meulles, Intendant of New France, 1682-86.) "On a toujours regardé le Canada comme vn païs qui estoit au bout du Monde, et comme vn exil qui povvoit presque passer pour vne mort ciuuile. Et aussi comme vne retraitte que plusieurs miserables ont cherchée jusques à present pour se mettre à couuert de leurs crimes ; son nom mesme fait voir qu'il a esté consideré comme peu de chose, puisque A Canada en Espagnol veut dire icy rien. Et je ne doute point que les Espagnols qui ont les premiers decouuert cette terre, et qui ont entré d'abord dans le fleuue St. Laurens bordé de fort hautes Montagnes couuertes de neiges cinq ou six mois de l'année, n'ont esté obligez de dire que ce païs icy ne valoit rien."

9. Gabriel Sagard-Theodat, *Histoire du Canada* (Paris MDCXXXVI), ed. Tross, Paris, 1866, v. I, p. 173-74. English translation as quoted in F. Parkman, *Pioneers of France in the New World,* Little, Brown, and Company, Boston, 1890, p. 392. "Il se faut aussi estudier à la douceur & monstrer une face ioyeuse & modestement contante, & chanter par fois des Hymnes, & Cantiques spirituels, tant pour sa propre consolation, le soulagement de ses peines, que pour le contentement & edification de ces Sauuages, qui prennent un singulier plaisir d'ouyr chanter les louanges de nostre Dieu... plustost que des

chansons profanes, contre lesquelles ie leur ay veu quelquesfois monstrer de la repugnance. O bon Jesus, qui condamne les mauvais Chres-
tiens chanteurs de chansons dissolues & mondaines."

10. *Nouveaux voyages de Mr. le baron de Lahontan, dans l'Amérique Septentrionale,* 1703-04, Amsterdam, MDCCV, lettre VIII, p. 68.
"J'ai passé en Ville le reste de la mauvaise Saison, & j'ai passé le plus
desagréablement du monde. Vous avez au moins en Europe les diver-
tissements du Carnaval, mais c'est ici un Carême perpétuel ... c'est trop
peu pour leur zèle que d'excommunier les masques ; ils les poursuivent
comme on poursuivroit un Loup, & après avoir arraché ce qui couvre
le visage, ils vomissent un torrent de bile contre ceux qui s'étaient
deguisez."

11. Chrestien Le Clercq, *Premier Etablissement de la Foy dans
la Nouvelle France,* Paris, 1691, I, p. 478. "Pour leur representer la ge-
henne où estoient les consciences de la Colonie, de se voir gouverné
par les mesmes personnes pour le spirituel et pour le temporel." See
also F. Parkman, *The Jesuits in North America,* Little, Brown, and
Company, Boston, 1890, p. 158.

12. *Mandements des Evêques de Québec,* ed. H. Têtu & C.-O.
Gagnon, Québec, 1887, v. I, p. 311. "... ceux qui ont des tableaux ou
représentations lascives, ceux qui composent ou débitent de mauvais
livres, vers ou chansons ; les femmes qui par leur nudité scandaleuse
d'épaules et de gorge portent les autres au péché."

13. *Ibid.,* p. 171. "... il est d'une grande importance pour la
gloire de Dieu et le salut du prochain que M. le Gouverneur et Madame la Gouvernante ... tiennent ferme, non-seulement pour ne point
aller en des maisons où se feraient des assemblées de bal et de danse,
mais encore pour interdire de la leur l'entrée à ces sortes de diver-
tissements ... cependant comme l'âge et la vivacité de mademoiselle
leur fille a besoin de quelque divertissement et récréation, l'on peut
user de condescendance en lui permettant quelques danses honnêtes et
modérées, mais avec les personnes de son sexe seulement, et en la présence de madame sa mère, de peur qu'on ne se licencie à des paroles et des chansons peu honnêtes, mais non en la présence des hommes et des garçons, ce mélange de sexe étant à proprement parler ce
qui cause les inconvénients et les désordres du bal et de la danse."

14. Mgr. H.-M. Dubreuil de Pontbriand, *Lettre Circulaire aux curés de l'Acadie*, in *Mandements* ... v. II, p. 15.

15. Paul Le Jeune, *Relation de ce qui s'est passé en La Nouvelle France en l'année 1637* (Rouen, 1638), p. 63. "... composée d'âmes d'élites, & bien choisies, & d'autres bien basses, & bien ravallées."

16. *Ibid.*, p. 21. "... on se veut resiouïr & on tombe dans l'excez ..."

17. Mason Wade, *The French Canadian, 1760-1945*, The Macmillan Company of Canada Limited, Toronto, 1955, p. 3.

18. Paul Henry Lang, *Music in Western Civilization*, W.W. Norton & Company, New York, 1941, p. 216.

19. H. Kallmann, *op. cit.* p. 6.

20. *Relation du Voyage des Dames Religieuses Ursulines de Rouen à la Nouvelle-Orleans*, ed. Gabriel Gravier, Paris, 1872, p. 89.

21. F. Parkman, *The Old Régime...*, p. 397.

22. *Loc. cit.*

23. P.H. Lang, *op. cit.*, p. 428.

24. John Tasker Howard, *Our American Music*, 3rd ed., Thomas Y. Crowell Company, New York, 1946, p. 22.

25. H. Kallmann, *op. cit.*, p. 51. See also P.-G. Roy, *La Famille Glackemeyer*, in *Le Bulletin des recherches historiques*, XXII, p. 195.

26. J. T. Howard, *op. cit.*, p. 30.

27. Juan de Torquemada, in "Monarquia Indiana", as quoted in Robert Stevenson, *Music in Mexico*, Crowell, New York, 1952.

28. Variously called Petrus de Mura, de Moor, Van der Moere.

29. Elisabeth Begon, *Lettres au cher fils*, 1748-1753, Hurtubise, Montréal, 1972, letter December 9, 1748, p. 44. "Le croiras-tu, cher fils, que cette dévote Mme Verchères a fait danser toute la nuit dernière ? Nos prêtres vont joliment prêcher : le jour de la Notre-Dame, dans l'Avent, donner le bal ! Ce qu'il y a de beau, c'est que demain, il y en a un chez Mme Lavaltrie, après-demain chez Mme Bragelogne. Voilà de quoi désespérer M. le curé."

30. Mason Wade, *op. cit.*, p. 30.

31. Charles Le Beau, *Avantures du Sr. C. Le Beau ... ou, Voyage curieux et nouveau, parmi les sauvages de l'Amérique Septentrionale*, Amsterdam, 1738, v. 1. p. 67. "... si dans le Canada, les Missionnaires connoissent tous leurs Paroissiens, d'autant qu'ils ne sont pas en trop grand nombre & s'ils tâchent de les édifier par leur piété qu'ils poussent jusqu'à la bigoterie : d'un autre côté, les jeunes Libertins que l'on y envoye de Paris, ne leur portent pas trop de bon example, ne s'amusant qu'à caresser leurs Femmes, leurs Filles ; chantant des chansons abominables, en un mot poussant la malignité de leurs débauches jusqu'à l'excès. C'est ce que j'ai vu, & ce qui fait qu'on ne comprend pas qu'elle peut être l'idée de la Cour de France, en envoyant de pareils Débauchés, qui n'étant pas propres à labourer la terre, sont obligés, pour pouvoir vivre, d'aller dans les Côtes chez les Habitans, où, sous prétexte d'y être Maîtres d'Ecole, ils font plus de mal que de bien."

32. F. Parkman, *The Old Régime ...*, p. 392. Charlevoix also adds a list of shortcomings he had noted with the Canadians, and although he found them pious, religious and brave he saw among them avarice, ingratitude, impetuousness, lack of respect for parents, and above all lack of education and general knowledge. He remarked on the provincialism of "a society which had no news of its own and received that of Europe once a year when the ships came in the spring." (Wade, *op. cit.*, p. 2).

Lahontan, whose cynical comments and anticlerical attitude has always been a controversial issue, thought that the people "... lack the knowledge of literature ... are presumptuous and full of themselves." But he also saw them as enterprising, vigorous, indefatigable, "... and in need of nothing else but education." (Parkman, *op. cit.*, p. 388).

The Intendant Hoquart reported in 1736 that all the education which the children of officers and gentlemen receive consists merely in a few subjects, "... and hardly do they know how to read and write, they are ignorant of the rudiments of history and geography, and it is desirable that they become better instructed." *(Op. cit.*, p. 366). The Intendant had also found the Canadians, in particular the country-people vindictive, self-interested, not at all truthful, volatile and very much attached to religion. *(op. cit.*, p. 389).

Towards the end of the French régime, Bougainville, who had accompanied Montcalm to Quebec, described the *habitant* as "loud, boastful, mendacious, but also obliging, civil and honest ..." *(loc. cit.)*, and confirmed that there was little concern for the education of the young. In his assessment of the people, the renowned navigator noted the cleavage between Frenchmen and Canadians, and he arrived at the conclusion that "... it seems we are of a different nation, even an enemy one." (Wade, *op. cit.*, p. 43.)

    33. Wade, *op. cit.*, p. 50.

    34. *Les Ursulines de Québec*, C. Darveau, Québec, 1878, v. 2, p. 349. "Tous les hommes éminents de l'époque, ou à peu près, en France, semblent avoir méconnu l'importance des événements qui se passaient en Amérique, et le Canada fut non-seulement negligé, mais même regardé comme un obstacle à l'alliance de l'Autriche... Notre pauvre peuple ressentait avec amertume cette triste vérité, que le roi Louis ne se souciait plus du Canada ! ... il est plus facile de concevoir que de décrire les sentiments des Canadiens ... ils avaient bien senti l'indifférence toujours croissante du gouvernement dans les dernières années ; mais savoir que la France les abandonnait !"

Chapter II

1. Jacques Cartier, *Discovrs dv Voyage fait par le Cappitaine Iaques Cartier,* (Rouen, 1598) ed. Tross, Paris, 1865, p. 49 & 54. "vne partie des femmes qui ne passerent, lesquelles estoyent iusques aux genoux dans la mer, savtans & chantans ... & tous les hommes se mirent à chanter & danser en deux ou trois bandes, & faisans grands signes de ioye pour nostre venuë ..." ("... a group of women who were knee deep in the sea, jumping and singing ... and all the men began to sing and dance in two or three groups, and made great signs of joy at our arrival ...").

2. *Ibid.,* p. 22.

3. *Ibid.,* p. 26. "... print ledict Cappitaine vne paire d'Heures, et tout hautement leut mot à mot la Passion de nôtre Seigneur ..."

4. *Loc. cit.,* "Ce fait, ledict Cappitaine commanda sonner les trompettes & aultres instrumens de Musique, dequoy ledict peuple fut fort rejouï. Apres lesquelles choses nous prinsmes congé d'eulx & nos. retirasmes."

Pierre Marquier is the only member of Cartier's crew listed as "trumpeter", yet there was more than one trumpeter who had taken part in the expedition. Cartier explained that his craftsmen and mariners had built the first *fort* on the North American Continent near Stadacona, "... tout clos de grosses pieces de bois plantées de bout joignant les vnes aux autres & tout à l'entour garni d'artillerie, & bien en ordre pour se defendre contre tout le païs." And the Captain "... fit renforcer le fort tout à l'entour de groz fossez larges & profonds avec porte à pont-leviz ... et fut ordonne pour le guet de la nuyt pour le temps advenir cinquante hommes à quatre quars & à chascun changement desdicts quars *les trompette sonnans* ce qui fut faict selong ladicte ordonnance." *(Brief Recit & succincte narration, de la nauigation faicte es ysles de Canada, Hochelaga, & Saguenay & autres ...* Paris, 1545, p. 67).

Cartier's reference to the night watch indicates the presence of more than one musician. Trumpets, fifes and drums were the well-known and traditional accessories to military display, hence the reference to "other musical instruments", presumably alludes to some of these instruments. The presence of musician-soldiers seems to have been customary. In the chronicles of the ill-fated Huguenot colony in Florida, Menendez, the Spanish conqueror of French Florida declared in his account of the victory in 1565, that he had saved the lives of "the fifer, the drummer, and the trumpeter", while all the other Frenchmen, including their courageous leader, Jean Ribaut, had been "put to the knife." (as quoted in Parkman, *Pioneers of France in the New World*, p. 144).

5. The devotional ceremony referred to in Cartier's annals is of considerable musico-historical interest as it represents the first religious procession in Canada. It is also the earliest recorded evidence to specific liturgical music, as well as to the singing of the ritual of the Mass. "Nôtre Capitaine ... fit porter vne image et remembrance de la Vierge Marie contre vn arbre distant de nôtre Fort d'vn trait d'arc le travers les neiges et glaces et ordonna que le Dimanche ensuivant l'on diroit audit lieu la Messe, et que tous ceux qui pourroient cheminer tant sains que malades iroient à la procession chantans les sept Psaumes de David, avec la Litanie .. Et la messe dite et chantée devant ladite image ..." (Lescarbot, *Histoire de la Nouvelle France*, v. II, p. 354). For a description of the procession see also Parkman, *Pioneers* ... p. 213.

6. See Parkman, *Pioneers* ... p. 216ff.

7. Marc Lescarbot, *Histoire* ... v. II, p. 503. "... noz plats voloient d'un bout de la table à l'autre, ... quelquefois aussi nous avions des calmes bien importuns durant lesquels on se baignoit en la mer, dansoit sur le tillac, on grimpoit à la hune ; nous *chantions en Musique.*"

8. *Ibid.*, p. 527. "... pour avoir l'œil à la maison, et maintenir ce qui restait de gens en concorde."

9. H. H. Walsh, *The Church in the French Era*, The Ryerson Press Toronto, Toronto, 1966, p. 59.

10. The first religious play was the *Comedia de Adan y Eva,* performed in Mexico City in 1532. See Leonard Ellinwood, *The History of American Church Music,* New York, 1953.

11. Marc Lescarbot, *Les Mvses de la Novvelle-France* (Paris MDCXII) ed. Tross, 1866, p. 28.

"O Neptune true, to Thee we pray
For safety from wild water's dance ;
To our hopes thy scepter sway
That we may meet again in France."

12. According to the renowned ethnologist Marius Barbeau, Lescarbot adapted the melody of a French folksong, *La Petite Galiote de France* as music for the stanza. (See Kallmann, *A History of Music in Canada,* p. 9). There is, however, no conclusive evidence to support such claim, nor has the basis for the arbitrary assumption been revealed. Although adaptation of existing tunes to new text has been a common device, there is no proof that the musically trained and educated Lescarbot resorted to such procedure. Unexplained remains also the reference to four-part harmony *(en musique à quatre parties)* which clearly contradicts the monophonic style of the folksong.

La Petite Galiote de France is quoted in *The Theatre of Neptune in New France* in a translation by Henrietta Taber Richardson. The tune appears in notation without Lescarbot's text, but with the following comments : "The music of the song is added through the courtesy of Mr. Marius Barbeau of Ottawa ; the form of Lescarbot's song is so nearly that of *La Petite Galiote de Fance,* sung to-day, that it seems probably that it was sung to the same music". From a musical point of view, however, it becomes quite obvious that in adaptation Lescarbot's verse would suffer from the shackles of a clumsy rhythmic, melodic and formal arrangement, as the text is neither in form nor meter close to the structure of the melody.

13. cf. Paul Henry Lang, *Music in Western Civilization,* W. W. Norton & Company, New York, 1941, p. 253ff.

14. "The term denotes a late 16th century French practice of setting poetic texts to music in a rhythm which reproduces exactly the strong and weak syllables of text, by giving the former the exact double duration of the latter." *(Harvard Dictionary of Music,* p. 790).

15. Lescarbot, *op. cit.*, v. I, p. 145. "... car en vain habitera-on en vn païs s'il n'y a de quoy vivre ... il y a assez de prisons partout sans en aller chercher si loin."

16. *Ibid.*, v. II, p. 553. "Ce seroit chose longue de vouloir minuter tout ce qui se faisoit durant l'hiver entre nous ..."

17. *Ibid.*, v. II, p. 553. "But I will relate that, to keep us merry and cleanly, concerning victuals, there was an order established at the table of said Monsieur de Poutrincourt, which was named *l'ordre du bon temps*, the order of good time (or order of the mirth) at first invented by Monsieur Champlein, wherein they (who were of the same table) were every one at his turn and day (which was in fifteen days once) Steward and Cater. Now his care was that we should have good and worshipfull fare, which was so well observed that (although the Belly-Gods of these parts do often reproach unto us that we had not *La Rue aux Ours* of Paris with us) we have ordinarily had there as good cheer as we could at *La Rue aux Ours,* and at far lesser charges."

"Mais je diray que pour nous tenir joieusement et nettement quant aux vivres, fut établi vn Ordre en la Table dudit sieur de Poutrincourt, qui fut nommé *L'Ordre de Bon-Temps*, mis premièrement en avant par le sieur Champlein, auquel ceux d'icelle table estoient Maitres-d'hotel chacun à son jour, qui estoit en quinze jours vne fois. Or avoit-il le soin de faire que nous fussions bien et honorablement traités. Ce qui fut si bien observé, que (quoy que les gourmens de deça nous disent souvent que nous n'avions point là la ruë aux Ours de Paris) nous y avons fait ordinairement aussi bonne chere que nous sçaurions faire en cette ruë aux Ours et à moins de frais."

18. *Ibid.*, v. II, p. 558. "... et me souvient que le 14, de ce mois par vn Dimanche apres midi nous nous rejouïssons *chantans Musique* sur la riviere de l'Equille." This reference is confirmation of musical activities beyond the recorded evidence. In its specific context the remark implies to some degree the quality and type of singing. In 16th century terminology *chantans Musique* refers almost exclusively to the singing of *chansons savantes*, the serious poetic creations of epic-lyrical nature, as opposed to *chansons populaires*, the rustic, bawdy and impudent songs. The distinction is carefully observed in the early collections of chansons, published during the 16th-century, in which clearly marked categories separate the *chants de Musique* (or *chansons musicales*) from the popular *chansons amoureuses et rustiques*. (cf. F. Lesure, "Ele-

ments populaires dans la chanson française" in *Musique et Poésie au XVIe Siècle*, Centre National de la Recherche Scientifique, Paris, 1954, p. 170).

19. Lescarbot, *op. cit.*, v. III, p. 655. "Mais vn jour m'allant promener en noz prairies le long de la riviere, je m'approchay de la cabane de Membertou, et mis sur mes tablettes vne parcelle de ce que j'entendis, qui y est encore écrit en ces termes ..."

20. *Loc. cit.* "I'ecoutay attentivement ce mot *alleluya* repeté par plusieurs fois, et ne sceu jamais comprendre autre chose. C'est ce qui me fait penser que ces chansons sont à la loüange du diable, si toutefois ce mot signifie envers eux ce qu'il signifie en Hebrieu, qui est : Loüez le Seigneur."

21. *Harvard Dictionary* ..., p. 682.

22. Jean de Léry, *Histoire d'vn voyage fait en la terre du Bresil, avtrement dite Amerique*, Geneve, 1578.

23. Lescarbot, *op. cit.*, v. II, p. 535. "Le sieur de Poutrincourt ayant pris terre à ce port, voici parmi vne multitude de Sauvages des fiffres en bon nombre, qui joüoient de certains flageollets longs, faits comme des cannes de roseaux, peinturés par dessus, mais non avec telle harmonie que pourroient faire noz bergers : et pour montrer l'excellence de leur art, ils siffloient avec le nez en gambadant selon leur coutume."

24. The noted Jesuit historian, François X. Charlevoix, paid tribute to Lescarbot whom he considered "... un esprit cultivé par l'étude ... c'est à cet Avocat, que nous sommes redevables des meilleures Memoires, que nous ayons de ce qui s'est passé sous ses yeux ... on y voit un Auteur exact, & judicieux, un Homme, qui a des vues, & qui eut été aussi capable d'établir une Colonie, que d'en écrire l'Histoire." (François X. Charlevoix, s. j., *Histoire et description général de la Nouvelle France*, Paris, 1744, 3 vols., I, p. 185).

Parkman agrees with Charlevoix that Lescarbot had left "one of the best, as well as earliest records of the early settlement of North America ..." ; he also endorses the opinion that the French *Avocat en Parlement* had been equally capable to build up a colony as to write its history. "Lescarbot was no common man", says Parkman, "Not that his abundant gift of verse-making was likely to avail much in the woods of

New France, nor yet this classic lore, dashed with a little harmless pe-
dantry, born not of the man, but of the times. But his zeal, his good
sense, the vigor of his understanding and the breadth of his views, were
as conspicuous as his quick wit and his lively fancy." *(Pioneers ...* p.
258ff).

It had also been said of Lescarbot that while a Catholic in
name, he was a Huguenot at heart. Indeed, the reading of the scriptures on Sundays at Port Royal must have greatly pleased and satisfied
the Huguenot element at the colony, as it was based on a Genevan
translation of the Bible. It is also known that neither he nor his friend
Poutrincourt were admirers of the Jesuits. Nonetheless, the renowned
French Church historian, Georges Goyau, is firmly convinced that Lescarbot, through his writings and actions, proved beyond doubt his ad-
herence to the Catholic conscience. (Georges Goyau, *Les Origines Religieuses du Canada,* Fides, Montréal-Paris, 1951, p. 52ff).

For a detailed biographical information see the article by Father R. Beaudry in *Dictionary of Canadian Biography,* p. 469.

25. The Souriqouis, also called Micmacs, were the early inhabitants of present-day Nova Scotia. A branch of the Abenaki tribe, they
belonged to the populous family of Algonquins. In 1606 they had as
leader (or *Sagamo)* a centenarian, called Membertou, whom Father
Pierre Biard later described as not only the "greatest, most renowned,
and most redoubted savage since many centuries, but also a veritable
homme d'esprit". (cf. also Parkman, *Pioneers* ..., p. 293).

26. Lescarbot, *Les Mvses ...,* p. 30.
"Must we forsake the beauty of this place
And bid farewell forever to its grace ?
Inconstancy ! Accused we stand
In building France in the new land."

27. F. Parkman, *Pioneers ...,* p. 274.

28. Marc Lescarbot, *Relation dernière de ce qui s'est passé au
voyage dv Sievr de Povtrincovrt en la Nouuelle-France depuis 20. mois
ença,* (Paris, MDCXII), Gabriel Enault, Paris, 1929, p. 16. "Mais il faut
premierement batir la Republique, sans laquelle l'Eglise ne peut estre.
Et pour ce le premier secours doit estre à cette Republique, & non à ce

qui a le pretexte de pieté. Car cette Republique estant établie, ce sera à elle à pourvoir à ce qui regarde le spirituel."

29. *Ibid.*, p. 39. "... oyans fort devotement le service divin, lequel estoit ordinairement *chanté en Musique* de la composition dudit Sieur [Poutrincourt]." This reference is considered by Kallmann as evidence of the "earliest example of composition in America north of Mexico." (Kallmann, *History...*, p. 14).

30. See article in *Dictionary of Canadian Biography*, p. 99. Jean de Biencourt de Poutrincourt. Baron de Saint-Just, governor of Méry-sur-Seine. Lieutenant-governor of Acadia, commander of Port-Royal ; soldier and colonizer, native of Picardy ; fought in the Catholic ranks during the wars of the League, and was later attached to the services of Henri IV. Joined his former companion-in-arms, de Monts, in 1604 on the expedition to colonize Acadia ; returned to France in 1607, but sailed again for Acadia in 1610. After destruction of Port Royal in 1613, went back to France ; because of Jesuit complaints was imprisoned, but regained liberty, and after one more unsuccessful journey to Port Royal in 1614, returned to France where in 1615 he died on the battlefield of Méry. He is buried at Champagne, where a monument in his honour preserves the memory of the noble pioneer of Port Royal.

31. *Jesuit Relations and Allied Documents, 1610-1791*, ed. R.G. Thwaites, Cleveland, 1896-1901, 73 vols., II, p. 37. Some doubts had been expressed with regard to Biard's narrative which was not always accurate in details. Many of the French at Port Royal were Huguenots or their sympathizers and not many treated Biard with esteem and respect. However, it is not important whether the men, as Biard said, really sang the sacred hymns of the Catholic liturgy rather than the Huguenot psalms or just ordinary folksongs. More significant is the fact that the Jesuits and their noble patrons at the French court, far from satisfied with their subordinate rôle at the heretic settlement of Port Royal or with the monetary rewards of their financial investments in Poutrincourt's commercial enterprise, decided to look for greener fields and to establish another, more devoutly Catholic colony at Saint Sauveur along the coast to the south.

Chapter III

1. Samuel de Champlain, whom many have fitly called the Father of New France, began his career as a Huguenot soldier and ended his adventurous days as Governor of the colony. He had been sailor and fur-trader, historian, artist, architect, botanist and diplomat, and it seems that this "true man of the Renaissance" lacked only music in the long list of accomplishments. But if music is missing, Champlain's literary qualities are amply manifest in his accounts of travels and explorations while his artistic penchant gained him a place in books on early Canadian art. He illustrated his narrative of an earlier voyage to the West Indies and Mexico with 62 quaintly primitive drawings of flora and fauna, as well as of Indian life and customs; he made many sketches of his exploratory travels in Canada, and, according to a Jesuit priest, is supposed to have painted "quelques pauvres images", apparently of religious content, which perished in the fire that destroyed the Church of Notre-Dame de la Recouvrance in 1640.

2. Chrestien Le Clercq, *Premier etablissement de la Foy dans la Nouvelle France,* Paris, 1691, p. 56.

3. Some of those songs could have been the folk-melodies of ancient France, so frequently claimed to have descended from the Troubadour and Trouvère songs of the chivalrous period. Others may have been the artful serious chansons of the time, those written by Janequin, Sermisy, Costeley, Le Jeune or others, but most of them would have belonged to the repertoire of the lighthearted and frivolous chanson characteristic of the era of sensuality and hedonism.

4. See note 9 on p. 258.

5. Le Clercq, *op. cit.,* p. 125. "Quelques uns même d'entr'eux, un peu plus avancez dans l'instruction récitoient les prieres, en chantant avec nous de leur mieux."

6. Gabriel Sagard-Theodat, *Histoire du Canada*, ed. Tross, Paris, 1865, p. 26.

7. Parkman, *Pioneers of France in the New World*, p. 419.

8. *Ibid.*, p. 426.

9. *Loc cit.*

10. Francis Parkman writes : "No religious order has ever united in itself so much to be admired and so much to be detested. Unmixed praise has been poured on its Canadian members." (*The Jesuits in North America*, Little, Brown, and Company, Boston, 1890, p. 13).

11. "Thus was New France to be forever free from the taint of heresy. The stain of the infancy was to be wiped away. Against the foreigner and the Huguenot the door was closed and barred ... If instead of excluding Huguenots, France had given them asylum in the west, and left them there to work out their destinies, Canada would have never been a British province, and the United States would have shared their vast domain with a vigorous population of self-governing Frenchmen." (Parkman, *Pioneers...*, p. 430).

Parkman merely repeated what many years earlier had been expressed by Canada's renowned historian and man of letters, François-Xavier Garneau. Indeed, Garneau clearly states his views on the cause of many ills that plagued the French establishment in North America since the days of Cartier to the present time : "Si Louis XIII et son successeur eussent ouvert l'Amérique à cette nombreuse classe d'hommes [Huguenots], le Nouveau-Monde, compterait aujourd'hui un empire de plus, un empire français." (*Histoire du Canada depuis sa découverte jusqu'à nos jours*, 1ère éd., Québec, 1845, v. 1, p. 155).

With sincere regret Garneau complains, "De quel avantage n'eût pas été une émigration faite en masse et composée d'hommes riches, éclairés et laborieux, comme l'étaient les Huguenots, pour peupler les bords du Saint-Laurent ou les fertiles plaines de l'Ouest ? Du moins ils n'auraient pas porté à l'étranger le secret des arts de la France, et nous ne serions pas, nous Canadiens-Français, réduits à défendre pied à pied contre une race étrangère notre langue, nos lois et notre nationalité." *(ibid.,* p. 250). While from the pen of the erudite Franch-Canadian historian this expression of patriotic sentiment deplores by implication the inferior cultural level of the early emigrant, he is disturbed by the policies of Crown and Church, demonstrated by the indifference and egotism of the former and the "pernicious influence over colonial policies and colonial destiny" of the latter (*ibid.*, p. 41).

12. More than other European colonizers the French were anxious to spread their own civilization among the natives. Parkman had remarked that "Spanish civilization crushed the Indian ; English civilization scorned and neglected him ; French civilization embraced and cherished him " ; (Parkman, *Jesuits* ..., p. 131). Garneau had already expressed his opinion with regard to colonial enterprise : "Si nous voulions exposer en peu de mots les motifs qui ont amené les Européens en Amérique, nous dirions que les Espagnols y vinrent pour chercher de l'or, les Anglais, la liberté politique et religieuse, et les Français pour y répandre les lumières de l'Evangile". (Garneau, *Histoire* ...., 3ième éd., v. 1, p. 222).

13. Paul Le Jeune, *Relation de ce qui s'est passé en la Nouvelle France en l'année 1637*, (Rouen, 1638), p. 223. "Ie prononçois doucement le *Pater*, ou le *Credo*, que i'ay dressé quasi comme en vers pour le pouuoir faire chanter ; ils me suiuoient mot à mot, l'apprenant fort gentiment par cœur, en ayant appris quelque couplet ou strophe, nous la chantions, en quoy ils prenoient vn grand plaisir."

14. Idem. *Relation ... 1633*, (Paris, 1634), p. 112. "*Nous finissons par le Pater noster* que i'ay composé, quasi en rimes en leur langue, que ie leur fais chanter ... C'est vn plaisir de les entendre chanter dans les bois ce qu'ils ont appris."

15. *Ibid.*, p. 137. "I'en pris seulement six ou sept auec moy, ie les fis chanter leur *Pater* en Sauuage dans le Nauire : nos François y prenoient grand plaisir."

16. *Loc. cit.*

17. Le Jeune, *Relation ... 1637*, p. 66. " C'est vne douce consolation de les entendre chanter publiquement dans nostre Chappelle le symbole des Apostres en leur langue : Or afin de les animer d'auantages nos François en chantent vne Strophe en nostre langue, puis les Seminaristes vne autre en Huron, & puis tous ensemble en chantent vne troisième, chacun en sa langue auec vn bel accord."

18. *Ibid.*, p. 63. "Ie ne crois pas qu'il s'en trouue aucune dans le sein de la nature qui produise des espics de froment, pour n'auoir

receu que de la graine de chardons. Ce miracle neantmoins se fait assez souuent en la nouvelle France."

19. Le Jeune, *Relation ... 1636*, p. 146. "Ie confesse ingenuement que mon cœur s'attendrit la premiere fois que i'assistay à ce diuin seruice, voyant nos François tous réjoüis d'entendre chanter hautement & publiquement les loüanges du grand Dieu au milieu d'vn Peuple barbare."

20. Le Jeune, *Relation ... 1635*, p. 26. "Ils prient celuy qui a tout fait, leur donnera-il ce qu'ils demandent? Or comme nous tardions trop à leur gré, assurément, disoient-ils, il ne leur veut pas donner : voyla ils crient tous tant qu'ils peuuent (nous chantions Vespres pour lors)."

21. Le Jeune, *Relation ... 1636*, p. 268. "... qu'en signe de réiouissance, & d'amour mutuel les vns les autres, on fist danser quelques-vns de nos ieunes gens au son d'vne vielle, que tenoit vn petit François."

22. *Le Journal des Jésuites*, ed. Laverdière et Casgrain, 2nd ed., J.M. Valois, Montréal, 1892, p. 40. "Ensuite on fit le seruice, où la passion fut chantée à trois, sçauoir : de M. de St. Sauueur, euangeliste, & de M. le prieur qui faisoit le synagogue, & de moy. Ie pensé pour lors que le P. de Quen eut mieux fait que M. de St. Sauueur pour cet article."

23. *Loc. cit.* "... auec les mesmes ministres que le iour precedent ; il me sembla de rechef que pour l'*Exultet* le P. de Quen l'eut mieux chanté."

24. *Les Ursulines de Québec*, C. Darveau, Québec, 1878, 2 vols., v. I, p. 24. "Ce fut donc le 1er août 1639, que l'on vit s'approcher de nos rives cette sainte troupe si longtemps désirée, et c'était au son des canons, des fifres et des tambours, que ce petit renfort prenait possession du poste que le Seigneur leur avait assigné sur les bords du St. Laurent."

25. Joseph Le Ber, *Départ pour le Canada en 1639*, Dieppe, 1939, p. 37. "On est tout ravi d'entendre nos Mères, tous les festes et dimanches il vient des gens pour ouir vêpres que l'on chante ... Il y a du plaisir de voir les sauvages & sauvagesses auprès de la violle, quand on en joue ils sont ravis."

26. *Les Ursulines de Québec,* letter Sœur Anne de Ste. Claire, p. 40. "Elle [Mother St. Joseph] est maîtresse de nos petites séminaristes, qu'elle aime comme une mère aime ses enfants. Après le catéchisme elle leur apprend à chanter et à toucher, sur la viole, des cantiques spirituels : parfois elle les fait danser à la mode des sauvages."

27. Marie de l'Incarnation, *Lettres,* ed. Richardeau, Tournai, 1876, 2 vols., letter, Sept. 3, 1640, XXVIII, p. 71. "Le nom d'Agnès lui convient très bien, car c'est un agneau en douceur et en simplicité ... Elle a fait de très grands progrès auprès de nous, tant dans la connaissance des mystères, que dans les bonnes mœurs, dans la science des ouvrages, à lire, à jouer de la viole."

28. *Ibid.,* letter XXXI, Sept. 4, 1640, p. 90. "... et jamais je ne me sentis si forte. Si en France on ne mangeait que du lard et du poisson salé comme nous faisons ici, on serait malade et on n'aurait point de voix ; nous nous portons fort bien et nous chantons mieux qu'on ne fait en France."

29. *Ibid.,* letter CCII, v. 2, p. 429. "Nous voilà néanmoins encore ... Dieu nous veut en Canada pour y assister les filles, tant Françaises que sauvages. Et en vérité les premières seraient pires que les dernières, s'il n'y avait ici des Ursulines pour les élever et les cultiver."

30. *Les Ursulines de Québec,* v. 1, p. 130. "... se glissent parfois dans nostre chœur, & là se plaçant de part & d'autre, tenant chacune vn liure en la main, elles se comportent comme nous faisons pendant nostre office, elles chantent l'*Ave Maris Stella* & le *Gloria Patri*, faisant les mesmes inclinations qu'elles nous voyent faire ; & comme elles ne sçauent que cet hymne par cœur, elles le chantent vingt & trente fois sans se lasser, s'imaginans qu'elles font une prière bien agréable à Dieu, cette innocence est rauissante."

31. Marie de l'Incarnation, *Lettres,* letter CLXXXVIII, v. 2, p. 372. Also letter CXCIV, v. 2, p. 396.

32. *Les Ursulines ...,* v. 1, p. 39. "Ce bon Père disait chaque semaine une messe votive en son honneur. Il avait composé quelques motets que nous chantions après l'élévation."

33. Dupont-Ferrier, *La vie quotidienne d'un Collège Parisien,* Paris, 1925, v. 1, p. 293.

34. Barthélemy Vimont, *Relation ... 1642*, Paris 1643, p. 38.
"Nous n'avons point icy d'autres ennemis que nous mesme, le reste est
peu de chose. Les procès, l'ambition, l'auarice, la saleté, les désirs de se
vanger qui sont les demons de l'europe, ne paroissent quasi point icy,
nos bois ne sont pas propres pour allumer leurs feux."

35. *Loc. cit.*

36. Vimont, *Relation ... 1640*, p. 85. "Ie n'aurois pas creu qu'on
eut peu trouuer vn si gentil appareil, & de si bons acteurs à Kébec."
"... ce pauvre peuple se viennt rendre à Iesus Christ & de iour en iour."

37. *Correspondance de M. Tronson aux Messieurs du Séminaire
de Montréal*, 1676, Bibliothèque des Sulpitiens, Paris, Tome XIII.

38. *Ibid.*, letter no. 302, June 4, 1686, folio 436. "Je ne fais pas
mesme de difficulté que pour l'accomplissement de vostre musique
vous ne vous serviez du luth que la providence vous a fait trouver à
Montréal Je scay l'inclination que vous y avez eue autrefois : mais
qu'elle sera assez rectifiée pour ne vous point faire de tort quand vous
ne iouerai que dans l'Eglise, et que vous ne vous en servirez que
comme d'un instrument non pas pour exciter les passions mais pour
porter à la dévotion."

39. *Loc. cit.*, folio 440.

Chapter IV

1. *Jesuit Relations and Allied Documents 1610-1791*, ed. R. G. Thwaites, 73 vols., Cleveland, 1896-1901.

2. Léon Pouliot, *Dictionary of Canadian Biography*, I, p. 455.

3. *Les Ursulines de Québec*, v. 1, p. 137. "Nos Méres, en effet, écrivaient tous les ans des mémoires dont on retrouve encore les restes précieux dans quelques-unes des Relations. Mais lorsque M. Cramoisy, libraire de Paris et imprimeur, reçevait ces écrits des RR.PP Jésuites, il en retranchait souvent les plus belles pages."

4. *Loc. cit.* "Suffit que Dieu sache avec quel amour nous servons nos neophytes. C'est assez que Lui seul connaisse ce qui se passe en cette petite maison sans qu'il soit produit aux yeux des hommes." (See also Marie de l'Incarnation, *Lettres* ... CLXXXVI, v. 2, p. 365.)

5. *Le Journal des Jésuites*, ed. Laverdière et Casgrain, 2nd ed., J.M. Valois, Montréal, 1892.

6. *Ibid.*, p. v. "... pouvaient être utiles non seulement aux membres de la Compagnie de Jésus, mais encore à tous ceux qui plus tard voudraient étudier à fond notre histoire."

7. *Ibid.*, November, 1645, p. 14. "Le 27 mariage de la fille de Mons. Couillar auec le fils de Iean Guion : Le P. Vimont assista aux nopces ; il y eut deux violons pour la premiere fois."

8. *Ibid.*, ..., December, 1645, p. 20. "Le 1er coup de la messe de minuit sonna à vnze heures, le 2nd vn peu deuant la demye, & pour lors on commença à chanter deux airs ; *Venez mon Dieu* &c, & *Chantons Noel*, &c. Mons. de la Ferté faisoit la basse. St. Martin iouit du violon ; il y auoit encores vne fluste d'alemagne, qui ne se trouua pas d'accord quand se vint à l'Eglise."

Uncertainty surrounds the carols mentioned in the *Journal*. *Venez mon Dieu* could not be traced, and there is little evidence to support the assumption that *Chantons Noel* is identical with the ancient carol *Chantons Tous à la Naissance* as has been claimed by some historians. Equally much doubt covers the claims concerning the carol *Mortels*, sung at Midnight Mass of 1646. The text to that carol has been found in the *Nouveau Recueil de Cantiques à l'usage du Diocèse de Québec*, compiled by the Abbé Daulé, and published at Québec in 1819. In this collection of liturgical songs the carol *Mortels* is to be "sung to the air *Après le cours heureux*" which in turn had been adapted from a 17th century vaudeville song, entitled *On dit que vos parents sont autant de Centaures*, from the vaudeville called *La Trompette*. In an attempt to unravel the complicated maze of adapted or original text and music, Myrand discovered that the text to this canticle had been written by the celebrated hymn writer, the Abbé Pellegrin, and appeared in a collection under the title *Cantiques spirituels sur les points principaux de la religion et de la morale chrétienne, composées sur des airs d'opéras, de vaudevilles très connus et sur les chants de l'Eglise*. (See Ernest Myrand, *Noels Anciens de la Nouvelle-France*, Québec, 1907, p. 48).

9. See also p. 98-99.

10. The latter assumption is supported by the fact that throughout the Middle Ages, the Renaissance and deep into the Baroque period the transverse flute *(flûte traversière)* was a typical and widely used military instrument that had been associated particularly with Germany ; hence it became known as the German flute.

11. A year later the weather had been so mild that little or no heating was required but the musical programme at Christmas 1646 included neither viols nor out-of-tune flutes. *(Le Journal* ..., December, 1646, p. 74).

12. *Dictionary of Canadian Biography*, p. 119.

13. *Loc. cit.*

14. Jérôme Lalemant, *Relation* ... *1650-51*, p. 174. "On a commencé cette année vn Séminaire, où les enfans sont en pension sous vn honneste homme qui en a pris le soin, où ils apprennent à lire & à écrire, & où on leur enseigne le plainchant, auec la crainte de Dieu ... sans cela nos François deuiendroient sauuages, & auroient moins d'instruction que les sauuages mesmes."

15. *Le Journal* ..., December, 1646, p. 74. "Le iour de la Conception vn soldat nommé de Champigny, natif de Fontainebleau, fit abiuration de son heresie auparauant la grande messe. Ce mesme soldat sçachant la musique, & pouuant chanter vn dessus, nous commençasmes le iour de St. Thomas à chanter à quatre parties."

16. *Ibid.*, ..., June, 1647, p. 90. "Enuiron ce temps on commença à chanter la messe haute tous les Dimanches & Festes à Québec, nous sentans assez forts pour le faire, & la façon ordinaire qu'on la chantoit, auec vn *Veni Creator, Gloria, Credo & O salutaris hostia,* n'estant pas reguliere & estant capable de choquer ceux qui viennent de nouueau (de) France, qui s'attendent de trouuer au moins en quelque lieu de la nouuelle France vne messe de paroisse."

17. Father Lalemant recorded on St. Ignace's day in July 1647, "... the Hospitallers gave a collation to the musicians at my request ..." ("Les Hospitalières donnerent la colation aux musiciens à ma requeste"). (*Le Journal* ..., p. 92).

18. *Ibid.*, ..., May, 1648. "... à Monsieur le Gouverneur & plvs honnestes gens au refectoire ; aux musiciens à la petite sale, aux matelots dans la menuiserie, & le reste, soldats, à la grande sale ; cela alla bien."

19. *Ibid.*, January, 1649, p. 129.

20. *Ibid.*, March, 1660, p. 278.

21. *Loc. cit.* "Le P. Dablon n'est point propre pour chanter seul vn *Exultet.*"

22. *Ibid.*, April, 1661, p. 294.

23. See *Dictionary of Canadian Biography*, p. 244. See also Goyau, *Origines Religieuses...*, p. 237.

24. *Le Journal* ..., April, 1661, p. 295. "L'vn disant *S. Petre* & l'autre *sancte Paule,* & nos FF. ne sçachant à qui respondre."

25. *Ibid.*, April, 1661, p. 294. "*Multa ibi peccata, scilicet* ... on n'auoit pas preueu ce qu'on y debuoit chanter."

26. *Ibid.*, December, 1648, p. 119. "... La messe de minuict fut precedée des matines, qui furent dites pour la 1re fois ... On sonna le dernier vn quart d'heure devant, & on finit vn quart deuant minuict, & ce quart fut employé heureusement à vn petit *entretien*, qui ne s'estant

fait que par hasard, fit voir que c'estoit vne chose à faire auec dessein. On chanta les troisièmes psalmes des nocturnes en *faux-bourdon*, & les responds du dernier nocturne *en musique :* en l'eleuation, musique auec violes, & pendant les communions ..."

In its historical context *faux-bourdon* designated a 15th century compositional technique of part-writing in which the melody, usually a plainchant or hymn-tune, had been placed in the upper part, moving together with a lower part, the *contra*, in intervals of a sixth or octave. In addition, an unwritten improvised middle part followed the melody in exact intervallic relation of a fourth below.

27. *Ibid.*, ..., December, 1657, p. 228.

28. *Loc. cit.* "Le P. Superieur dit la messe de minuict, qui fut chantée en musique qui ne valut rien. On oublia à chanter le *Te deum* au commencement."

29. *Ibid.*, March, 1660, p. 276. "... on commença en musique par le *Pange lingua*, après quoy immediatement les religieuses chanterent vn motet court du St. Sacrement, ensuite la musique recommença l'*Iste Confessor*, après quoy immediatement les religieuses chanterent vn motet du Saint, après quoy la musique reprit le *Domine saluum fac regem*, à la suite duquel Mons. de Bernieres officiant dit le verset & les 3. oraisons correspondantes ; après quoy les religieuses deuoient chanter quelque chose pendant l'encensement & la benediction, ce qu'elles ne firent pas, pour n'en auoir esté suffisamment aduerties. Le tout fut conclu par vn *Laudate Dominum* chanté par la musique. On en fut fort satisfait, & la chose parut belle & deuote ; toute l'eglise estoit remplie."

30. *Ibid.*, July, 1648, p. 113. "... excepté qu'à faute de musiciens & de prestre, les Religieuses seules chanterent vespres ..."

31. *Ibid.*, March, 1647, p. 80.

32. The Superior registered the cultural event in the *Journal :* "Le dernier iour de l'an, on representa vne action dans le magazin, du *sit*. Nos Pères y assisterent pour la consideration de Mons. le Gouuerneur, qui y auoit de l'affection & les sauuages aussy, sçauoir, les PP. de Quen, Lalement & Defretat ; le tout se passa bien, & n'y eut rien qui put mal edifier. Ie prié Mons. le Gouuerneur de m'en exempter." (*Le Journal* ..., December, 1646, p. 75).

33. See page 192.

34. Cf. Jean Béraud, *350 Ans du Théâtre au Canada Français*. Le Cercle du Livre de France, Ottawa, 1958, p. 17.

35. *Le Journal* ..., June, 1646, p. 52.

36. *Ibid.*, March, 1647, p. 80. "A la St. Ioseph, on ne fit point de feu de ioye la veuille comme de coutume ; i'en fus vne partie cause, comme ne goustant guere cette ceremonie, qui n'auoit aucune deuotion qui l'accompagnast ..."

37. *Ibid.*, February, 1647, p. 78. "... pas vn de nos PP. ny de nos FF. n'y assista, ny aussy des filles de l'Hospital & des Vrsulines, sauf la petite Marsolet."

Chapter V

1. Mason Wade, *The French Canadians, 1760-1945*, p. 39.

2. Helmut Kallmann, *A History...*. p. 22.

3. Marie de l'Incarnation, *Lettres*, letter September 13, 1661, CLII, v. 2, p. 192-93. "... en sorte que cet abrégé, qui serait plus propre pour des Carmélites ou pour des religieuses du Calvaire que pour des Ursulines, ruine effectivement notre constitution... Nous ne disons mot neanmoins, pour ne pas aigrir les affaires ; car nous avons affaire à un Prélat, qui étant d'une très-haute piété, s'il est une fois persuadé qu'il y va de la gloire de Dieu, il n'en reviendra jamais, et il nous en faudra passer par là, ce qui causerait un grand préjudice à nos observances. Il s'en est peu fallu que notre chant n'ait été retranché. Il nous laisse seulement nos Vêpres et nos Ténèbres, que nous chantons comme vous faisiez au temps que j'étais à Tours. Pour la grand'messe, il veut qu'elle soit chantée à voix droite, n'ayant nul égard à ce qui se fait soit à Paris soit à Tours, mais seulement à ce que son esprit lui suggère être pour le mieux. Il craint que nous ne prenions de la vanité en chantant et que nous ne donnions de la complaisance au dehors. Nous ne chantons plus aux messes, parce que, dit-il, cela donne de la distraction au célébrant, et qu'il na point vu cela ailleurs. ... J'attribue tout ceci au zèle de ce très-digne Prélat ; mais, comme vous savez, mon intime Mère [Mère Ursule], en matière de règlement, l'expérience doit l'emporter par-dessus toutes les spéculations."

4. Bertrand de La Tour, *Mémoires sur la vie de M. de Laval*, Cologne. 1761, p. 172.

5. cf. Kallmann, *A History* ..., p. 19.

6. *Le Journal des Jésuites*, April, 1664, p. 325. The notice in the *Journal* refers to the organ in the Parish Church.

7. La Tour, *op. cit.*, p. 173.

8. *Le Journal* ..., February, 1661, p. 292.

9. John Tasker Howard, *Our American Music*, p. 18.

10. *Ibid.*, p. 17.

11. *Loc. cit.*

12. *Le Journal...*, February, 1661, p. 291. "Les 40. heures se firent à l'ordinaire de l'an passé ; le Dimanche au salut, l'*Ecce Panis* en plein chan [sic] à l'entrée ... & chanta-t-on le *Pange lingua* auec quelques couplets des litanies du nom de Iesus ; on oublia le *Sub tuum praesidium*, l'orgue ioüa pendant la descente du St. Sacrement & la benediction, & puis on finit par le *Domine saluum fac regem. Item* le lundy par le *Tantum ergo*, & ... Enfin le mardy l'*Ecce panis* en musique ... on donna à gouster au refectoire tous les 3. iours à Pierre Duquet & Fillon, qui auoient assisté à la musique."

The two lay-members of the choir, Pierre Duquet de la Chesnaye and Filion, had been honoured with meals on each of the three feast days. Pierre Duquet had been one of the first pupils at the Jesuit College of Quebec ; he was an "explorer, royal notary, attorney-general, seigneurial judge, etc." (cf. *Dictionary of Canadian Biography*, p. 298). His name appears twice in the *Journal* in connection with his vocal talent which this versatile and esteemed member of Quebec's society contributed to the religious ceremonies. Less is known about Fillon, Pierre Duquet's musical partner, unless he is identical with Michel Fillon, a notary, surveyor and court sergeant, who had come to Canada in 1654, and who played a part in the administrative and social life of the colony. Abbé Provost suggests that there could have been another individual named Fillon at Quebec, "perhaps more skilled in Music than Michel Fillon." (*DCB*, p. 305).

13. *Le Journal* ..., January, 1660, p. 272. "... le Curé auec le Clergé monta au Iubé, où il dit les vespres en Chape, qui furent fort bien chantées en musique."

14. According to Ramsay Traquair, *The Old Architecture of Quebec*, (The Macmillan Company of Canada Limited, Toronto, 1947,) "The Jesuit church in Quebec was cruciform with a spire on the crossing and one tower, apparently never finished, attached to the west end. It had a flat ceiling of carved wood and an octagonal sanctuary. But to judge from Short's drawings, and they are our best record, the Jesuit

church was quite unlike any other in the province of Quebec." (p. 139) The author adds : "Jubé means a gallery, usually at the west end of the church, sometimes in the transepts. French-Canadian churches have nothing corresponding to a roodloft or screen. The term 'gallerie' is rarely used. It is usual and it holds the organ and choir", (p. 142).

15. A. Gosselin, *Henri de Bernières*, Evreux, 1909, p. 78.

16. *Le Journal* ..., November, 1662, p. 314. "Enuiron ce temps, nous receusmes aux pensions François Dangé musicien, & la Marque par charité, ne sçachant que deuenir."

17. cf. *Dictionary of Canadian Biography*, P. 246.

18. *Le Journal* ..., December, 1662, p. 315. "... où les derniers psalmes furent chantés en musique."

19. *Loc. cit.* "Il y eut vn desordre pour les boissons des chantres, ou enfans de nostre seminaire ; ie leur fis donner outre leur biaire vn pot de vin la veuille, & le iour les marguillers aussy leur en donnerent sans que nous le sceussions. Cela enruma Amador, qui ne put plus ensuite chanter les festes, aussy bien que d'autres musiciens, François, d'Anger, &c."

20. *Le Journal* ..., January, 1662, p. 304.

21. *Ibid.*, December, 1663, p. 322. "Le 15. ou le 16. reuint François le musicien, que nous entreprismes de nourir par charité, & Mr. l'Euesque ou la paroisse à luy fournir *vestitum.*"

22. *Ibid.*, February, 1664, p. 324. "... il y eut grande messe icy en musique sur les 7½ ... l'ordre de la musique fut : 1° vn motet en l'honneur du S. Sacrement, puis le petit sermon, puis *l'orgue.*"

23. *Loc. cit.* "Nous priasmes Mess. les Ecclesiastiques d'officier aux saluts, & de dire les grandes messes, à l'issue de laquelle on les inuitoit, tant eux que les chantres extraordinaires, de desieuner. Il seroit meilleur de faire desieuner les musiciens ordinaires de la maison deuant les grandes messes, pour puuoir mieux fournir au chan ..."

24. cf. *Dictionary of Canadian Biography*, p. 393. See also Ernest Gagnon, *Louis Jolliet*, 4th ed., Beauchemin, Montréal, 1946, p. 35.

25. As quoted in Ernest Gagnon, *Louis Jolliet*, p. 145. "... un service pour défunt M. Jolliet, en reconnaissance d'avoir joué des orgues à la Cathedrale et paroisse beaucoup d'années. Fait gratis."

26. As quoted in Ernest Gagnon, *op. cit.*, p. 145. "Le feu Sieur Jolliet n'a point payé la mutation qu'il devoit après la mort du d. feu Sr Bissot, parce que la d. fabrique luy en avoit fait remise en consideration de ce qu'il jouoit des orgues et avoit montré à en jouer à plusieurs personnes du Séminaire."

27. *Le Journal ...*, July, 1665, p. 332.

28. *Ibid.*, April, 1664, p. 325. "La Sepmaine Sainte, *Tenebres* à la Paroisse & le seruice solemnel, où la passion *primum* fut chantée par trois diacres ; le Ieudy icy salut auec instrumens comme le matin pour le *Pange lingua* ; ... Il y eut icy, le samedy, salut solemnel ; les 3. festes suiuantes le salut se fit à la paroisse auec les instrumens (*tunc primum*) au iubé proche des orgues ; cela alla bien, excepté que les voix & instrumens sont faibles pour vn si grand vaisseau."

29. *Ibid.*, February, 1662, p. 305. "Ce moys, commencerent les concerts de 4. violes, 1° à l'action des premiers pris, puis à l'oraison des 40. heures."

30. Thurston Dart, in *Musical Instruments through the Ages*, ed. Baines, London, 1961, p. 186.

31. *Mandements des Évêques de Québec*, v. I, p. 36.

32. The Guidonian system of *Hexachord* and *Solmization*, with its divisions of *Hexachordum Durum, Hexachordum Naturale* and *Hexachordum Molle*, had been the intermediary step between the ancient Greek *tetrachord* and the modern *heptachord*, or octave system. It remained unaltered, particularly in liturgical music until the end of the 17th century when chromaticism and modulation had rendered it unsuitable. The various aspects of the hexachord system are convincingly interpreted in the sense as suggested, and references are to be found in standard works on history, styles and form. For special study the reader is referred to Gustave Reese, *Music in the Middle Ages* (chap. 6, p. 149), or the article in the *Harvard Dictionary of Music* (p. 330).

33. A meaningful interpretation of the Latin text is extremely difficult. Many factors have to be taken into consideration before a literal translation can form an acceptable basis for a musical interpretation. Musical styles and contemporary terminology must be taken into account if such interpretation is to clarify existing confusion. Without

any claim to linguistic accuracy, the following interpretative translation is suggested :

"On the days of the Great Feasts, the Mass, Vesper and Even-song are sung in harmony [choir] in the diverse hexachords and complete in all sections, and the organ blends pleasantly with the voices, embellishing wondrously that musical harmony."

In his biography of Mgr. de Laval, the Abbé Auguste Gosselin has given what seems to be one of the earliest translations from the Latin text of Laval's *Informatio :* "Il y a ici une basilique construite en pierres ; elle est grande et magnifique. L'Office divin s'y célèbre suivant le Cérémonial des Evêques ; nos prêtres, nos séminaristes, ainsi que dix ou douze enfants de chœur y assistent régulièrement. Dans les grandes fêtes, la messe, les vêpres et le salut du soir se chantent en musique, avec orchestre, et nos orgues mêlent leurs voix harmonieuses à celles des chantres." *(Le Vénérable François de Montmorency-Laval,* Québec, 1901, p. 217).

The identical text of Gosselin's translation appears also in Gagnon's *Louis Jolliet* (p. 139) published one year later, including the misleading reference to *orchestre.* If Gosselin's fanciful use of that term may be excused with the author's obvious lack of musical knowledge, Gagnon, a trained musician and teacher, not only perpetuates uncritically the error but also implicates the innocent and defenceless Mgr. de Laval. "Il ne faut pas prendre dans son sens moderne le mot "orchestre" *employé par Mgr de Laval* dans les lignes qui précèdent", declares the author of *Chansons Populaires du Canada* and first president of the *Académie de Musique* in Quebec. Indeed, Canada's first bishop had nowhere given an indication of an *orchestre,* not in the Parish Church nor elsewhere ; neither did he merit such misinterpretation of terms which he had never used in the first place. But Gagnon, in blissful innocence and unaware of his mistake, continues to explain to his readers that "... au seizième siècle, on se servait quelquefois de ce mot [orchestre] pour désigner l'ensemble des parties vocales dans un chant harmonisé ; au dix-septième siècle on l'employait pour désigner l'ensemble des instruments qui soutenaient les voix." *(Loc. cit.).*

The obvious misinterpretation of the term *hexachord* and the allusion to an orchestra was, however, not restricted to French historians only. An English translation of recent date is even more in-comprehensible, and less acceptable from musicological standpoint. "On the more important festivals, the mass, the vespers and the Even-tide *Salve* are sung with an instrumental accompaniment in counter-point with viols, and are arranged according to its own style",(see Kall-mann, *History* ..., p 20, translation by E. J. Barnes). This is quite a dif-ferent interpretation and one that completely disregards the musical as-pects at religious ceremonies. It does not take into account the histori-cal as well as musical implications regarding the ritual of mass and ves-pers, nor consider conditions in 17th-century Quebec, but attaches itself to a learned and literal, but entirely unacceptable translation which is far from the actual event. Entirely misunderstood is the meaning of *musice cantatur, hexachordo diversum*, interpreted as "instrumental ac-companiment in counterpoint (!) with viols". Equally extraordinary is the translation of *numero absolutum*, explained as "arranged according to its own style" (!). And lastly, considering the term *organum* as "a composition consisting of a liturgical plainsong to which one or more contrapuntal parts (*duplum, triplum, quadruplum*) are added" (Harvard Dictionary of Music, article *Organum,* p. 626) even the phrase *organa vocibus suaviter* might well be interpreted as singing of polyphonic mu-sic rather than playing an instrument.

Chapter VI

1. *Mandements des Evêques de Québec*, v. 1, p. 134. "... qui sera de première classe avec octave, ainsi qu'il s'est pratiqué depuis plusieurs années."

2. MS. *Hôtel-Dieu*, Quebec, (Armoire 5 -cahier 8).

3. "J'ay recueilly avec plaisir et avec soin ce que j'ay trouvé écrit et ce que j'ay appris de vive voix des personnes qui vivaient dans le temps que la Confrairie de la Ste. Famille a été établie, sur ce qui concerne cette dévotion."

4. *Loc. cit.* "... M. Martin, qui étant habile chantre, composa le chant de la Messe et de l'Office de la Ste. Famille tel qu'il est."

5. "*Eclaircissement Sur l'Institution de la Devotion, Feste et Office de la Saincte Famille establie dans le Pays de la Nouvelle France, présenté à Monseigneur l'Illustrissime et Révérendissime Evesque de Québec, 1689 par l'abbé Charles Glandelet.*" (Archives du Séminaire, 34, no. 149,Québec). "Cet office est composé des Psaumes qui ... sont prises en partie de la Ste. Escriture et en partie des Sts. Peres et de ceux entre autres dont l'Eglise a coutume d'inserer les ouvrages dans les offices ; les Antiennes, les Respons et les Versets sont les mesmes pour la plupart que ceux qui sont adoptez par l'Eglise aux offices particuliers des mysteres et festes de Nostre Seigneur, de la Ste Vierge et de St. Joseph qu'elle celebre durant le Cours de l'année, et s'il s'en trouve d'autres, ils sont tirés de l'Evangile qui rapporte les mysteres de la Ste. Famille ; l'oraison mesme est issue des parolles de la mesme Eglise dans les deux oraisons qu'elle employe, l'une au jour de la Circoncision, et l'autre dans celuy de l'octave de l'Epiphanie. La Messe, pareillement, ne contient que les parolles dont se sert ou l'Ecriture Ste. ou l'Eglise ; il n'y a que les hymnes et la prose qui ont esté faites suyvant l'ordre qu'en avoit donné dez le commencement Mgr l'ancien Evesque de Quebecq

et qui expriment de suite tous les mysteres de la Ste Famille selon l'Evangile qui soient particuliers, de sorte que l'on peut dire que cet office n'est pas nouveau dans sa matiere puisqu'il est tiré des autres offices et mysteres, mais seulement dans sa forme."

6. "... le plus habile poète de notre siècle" — letter, l'abbé Jean-Henri Tremblay, May 3rd, 1698, Séminaire 02, no. 23, pp. 30-31.

7. cf. *Dictionnaire historique* ..., ed. l'abbé F.-X. de Feller, 7th ed., Paris, 1828.

8. *Mémoire sur la dévotion* ..., section 2. "... il corrigea donc et mit dans un stil plus élégant la Prose et les hymnes, et les renvoya à ces messieurs, les remerciant des lumieres qu'ils luy avoient donnez par leurs ouvrages, loüant leurs pensées, et avoüant que s'il y avoit ajouté quelque chose, c'était pour leur obeir, et qu'il avoit été charmé de ce qu'il avoit reçu de leur part ..."

9. Arch. Séminaire de Québec, Séminaire 34, p. 150.

10. The liturgy for a particular devotional purpose is distinguished by the special prayers that are proper for the occasion and used only on the assigned day. The complex structure of the Mass consists therefore of items that vary from day to day *(Proprium Missae)* and those that are invariable in every Mass *(Ordinarium Missae)*, that is, *Kyrie, Gloria, Credo, Sanctus,* etc.

11. "J'ay sollicité deux ou trois fois l'an passé M. l'Abbé de Brisacier d'aller ensemble prier un de ses amis, bon poète, de faire des hymnes de la Ste. Famille. Il ne m'a pas encore pu donner ce temps. Bien plus il me dit vers la fin de l'année qu'il faudrait recomposer tout cet office qui lui paraissait peu estudié. Il faudrait que vous eussiez les offices des nouveaux bréviaires de Cluni, de Paris, d'Orléans & de la Rochelle pour trouver des offices bien composés." (May 3rd, 1698, letter "O" no 23, p. 30).

In a letter to Ernest Gagnon, the noted historian Abbé Amédée E. Gosselin expressed disapproval with M. de Brisacier's rejection of Santeuil's contribution : "I am already quite scandalised to see that M. de Brisacier thought quite mediocre an Office which Santeuil had revised with regard to its form, and in which he had found so much of beauty." (letter, October 17, 1907, Arch. du College Ste. Marie, Montreal). On the other hand, Father Adrian Pouliot, s.j., found

Santeuil's *Sequence* text to *Summae Deus Majestatis* not particularly inspiring. The prose is, as he remarks "... simplement correcte, fruit d'un souci d'orthodoxie doctrinale." In contrast he considers the later *Prose* by Simon Gourdan, *Sacrae Familiae*, the work "... d'un maître ! ... elle est beaucoup plus riche et poétique ...."

12. Jean-Henri Tremblay, letter to Charles Glandelet (May 7, 1700, letter "O" no. 28, p. 6). "... M. Gourdan qui est un Poete aussy recueilly que feu Santeuil estoit dissipé ... eut la bonté de nous faire de fort belles hymnes et une belle prose pour la Ste. Famille. ... Elles sont un peu trop longues."

13. *Ibid.*, "Mais je les ay malheureusement donné a examiner à M. de Brisacier qui les a égarées et n'a pu encore les retrouver. ... Je feray encore mon possible avant le depart des vaisseaux pour les chercher et vous les envoier."

14. Jean-Henri Tremblay, letter to Charles Glandelet (March 31, 1702, letter "N" no. 117, p. 19). "Mais non le chant."

15. *Ibid.*, (May 28, 1702, letter "O" no. 36, p. 39). "... vous aurez enfin cette année l'office de la Ste. Famille ... Je vous en envoie moitié cette année. Je vous envoieray le reste l'année prochaine ... Je n'ay fait faire que l'impression de l'office et de la Messe. Il n'y a rien de Noté ..."

16. "Nous possédons aux archives du Séminaire au moins deux exemplaires de ce qui paraît être l'édition originale de l'office de la Sainte Famille de 1702, petits livrets de 32 pages in-quarto. Comme la fête était de première classe avec octave, l'imprimé comporte des leçons propres pour chaque jour de cette octave. *Par contre, la notation musicale ne s'y trouve pas. L'abbé Tremblay n'avait pas eu le temps d'y voir, comme il le dit lui-même, et il trouvait que l'office coûtait déjà assez cher.* On en resta là, semble-t-il et cela expliquerait la multiplication des copies manuscrites du chant de l'office, qui ont subsisté jusqu'à ce jour, soit en cahiers séparés. soit dans de plus gros livres de chants." (*La Devotion à la Sainte Famille en Canada*, l'Abbé Honorius Provost, Extrait de *La Revue de l'Université Laval*, vol. XVIII, nos 5-6, Jan.-Feb. 1964.

17. Jean-Henri Tremblay, letter to Charles Glandelet (May 28, 1702, letter "O" no. 36, p. 39). "Il ne faut pas que le reste se fasse si tost."

18. Archives du Québec.

19. Henri Dumont (1610-1684), one of the Masters of the Royal Chapel under Louis XIV, and the most prominent exponent of the new style, had in 1669 published the *Cinq Messes en Plainchant,* one of which, the celebrated *Messe Royale,* had been brought to New France and was, according to Gagnon, "still sung in our days (1900) in our Canadian churches as in those of France." (Gagnon, *Jolliet ...,* p. 162). Father Adrien Pouliot, s.j., relates that Dumont's Masses were still sung in 1920, and that he had heard the *Messe Royale* in the Jesuit Chapel of Quebec during an early morning High Mass as recent as 1967.

20. Ernest Gagnon tactfully concerns himself mainly with the Prose, "to speak only of the part of the Office entirely composed by him (Amador Martin)", and which shows, in Gagnon's opinion, great talent and an excellent training. He also considers the music of "... incontestable beauty, written in the first authentic mode of the ancient tonality." *(Jolliet,* p. 141). Helmut Kallmann cites various sources, but believes it doubtful that Martin composed, "anything apart from the 'Prose' section of the office" *(History ...,* p. 23). He had relied at first on the year 1670 as given by Eugene Lapierre in the *Encyclopédie Grolier,* but assumes the year 1674 as the earliest possible date for the composition. However, he reasons correctly that, since Gourdan's text did not become available before 1700, Lapierre's statement is erroneous, and Martin could not have composed the music to *Sacrae Familiae* before 1700.

21. Charles-Amador Martin, the second Canadian-born priest in chronological order, was born at Quebec on March 7, 1648, the son of Abraham Martin, royal pilot and proprietor of the Plaines of Abraham, and of Marguerite Langlois. He studied at Quebec, became ordained in May 1671, was *curé* in various small parishes in the vicinity of Quebec, held the office of Canon of the Cathedral, and died as the first Parish priest at Ste. Foy in 1711. Unfortunately, the omission by his contemporaries to elaborate on or to record Martin's musical activities has stifled any research and prevented more detailed information about the alleged composer of *Sacrae Familiae.*

22. *Graduale Romanum,* Lutetiae Parisiorum, MDCLXVIII.

23. Other early manuscripts of *Sacrae Familiae* are found at the Ursulines, while a large-size *Graduale* in manuscript form by François Borel from the year 1748 contains the *Officium SS Familiae* ad Missam, including the *Prose*, and is preserved at the Archives of the Seminary of Quebec.

24. Mason Wade, *The French Canadian*, p. viii.

Chapter VII

1. *Les Annales de l'Hôtel-Dieu de Québec, 1636-1716,* ed. Dom Albert James, Québec, 1939, p. 6.

2. F. Parkman, *The Old Régime in Canada,* p. 178.

3. *Ibid.,* p. 179.

4. *Loc. cit.*

5. *Le Journal des Jésuites,* February, 1667, p. 353. "Le 4. [Febvrier] le premier bal du Canada s'est fait chez le sieur Chartier. Dieu veille que cela ne tire point en consequence."

6. The final remark in the *Journal* reads : "Il manque icy le reste de l'année 1668, celle de 1668, & 1670 iusque au moys de Novembre." It is also supposed that the *Journal des Jésuites* continued until 1755. Unfortunately, these most valuable volumes have not yet been located. For a description and study of the *Relations* see the excellent article by Father Léon Pouliot in the *Dictionary of Canadian Biography,* p. 455.

7. F. Parkman, *Jesuits in North America,* p. vi.

8. "... jolies, instruites, coquettes, ambitieuses ... elles ont de l'esprit, de la délicatesse, de la voix et beaucoup de disposition à danser. Elles n'ont l'air ni provincial, ni bourgeois, ce sont de vraies femmes du monde, et même des femmes du monde de Paris."

9. Francis Parkman, *Count Frontenac and New France under Louis XIV,* Little, Brown, and Company, Boston, 1890, p. 324.

10. *Ibid.,* p. 325.

11. Ancient French coin, valued at ten francs.

12. F. Parkman, *op. cit.,* p. 334.

13. *Annales ...,* p. 352. "comme il étoit obligeant, il voulut nous faire entendre cette symphonie, et plusieurs fois il envoya ses musiciens

chanter des motets dans nôtre église, ou quelque partie de la Messe, les jours de fête."

14. Ernest Gagnon, *Louis Jolliet*, p. 133. "Nous savons seulement que nulle différence esthétique appréciable ne devait exister entre la musique que l'on faisait à Québec et celle que l'on faisait dans les provinces de l'ouest de la France. C'étaient les mêmes compositions, le même art, et les conditions d'interprétation elles-mêmes étaient à peu près identiques."

15. *Loc. cit.* "Nous avons conservé le chant liturgique grégorien, qui est noté ; nous avons aussi conservé nos cantiques et nos chansons populaires, venus de France ; mais la musique purement instrumentale, la musique de l'unique instrument populaire canadien, le violon, est, de nos jours, exclusivement anglaise, écossaise ou irlandaise ; ce sont des airs de danse : des gigues, des reels, des hornpipes ; rien de tout cela n'est français."

16. *Ibid.*, p. 132. "On peut se faire une idée de la gaîté d'autrefois par les coutumes, les récits anecdotiques, les formulettes, les devinettes, les jeux de société, les chants et les contes populaires qui sont restés de tradition dans les familles canadiennes. En somme, il y avait beaucoup de bon dans cette société du dix-septième siècle."

17. Kallmann, *op. cit.*, p. 21.

18. Andrée Desautels, "The History of Canadian Composition 1610-1967", *Aspects of Music in Canada*, ed. A. Walter, Toronto, 1969, p. 92. In a further attempt to add credence to this supposition the writer cites her own article pertaining to music in Canada in *Larousse de la Musique*, Paris, 1965. Strangely enough, this undocumented assertion regarding the alleged performances of works by the School of Versailles has been incorporated in a mural which decorates a Montreal subway station for the benefit of patriotic-minded and other credulous souls. It would lead beyond the bounds of charity to point to other striking misconceptions by the same writer. Clichés and trite phrases abound, such as "... the brilliance of seventeenth-century France was to leave its mark on this first period of artistic life in Canada", or "... the exceptionally high quality of French-Canadian musical culture during that period can be inferred from a list of works performed in the first basilica of New France", and "... music written during the seventeenth

and early eighteenth centuries was of the ecclesiastic variety and predominantly modal such as the Prose *Sacrae Familiae* by Amador Martin (1684) [sic]." These and other assertions are fallacious and misleading in their implication ! It is indeed regrettable that semi-fictitious accounts have found uncritical acceptance as established facts in a book on Canadian music.

19. See Bukofzer, *Music in the Baroque Era*, p. 163 ; also Champigneuille, *La Musique Française*, p. 83ff.

20. French musical art of the 17th century is represented mainly by church music and the liturgical books extant in the archives of the Ursulines, the *Hôtel-Dieu* and the Seminary of Quebec are evidence of the type of Roman liturgy of Mass and Offices used in the churches of Quebec. Pieces of sacred music by well-known French composers of the 17th century, such as Artus Auxcousteaux, Marc-Antoine Charpentier, have been found in the archives of the religious communities, and the liturgical use of Henri Dumont's *Messe Royale* has already been alluded to. No evidence, however, has been discovered to endorse the claim of performances of church music by J. B. Morin (1677-1745) who, as Mlle. Desautels points out, "... was one of the earliest composers to write French cantates." Unfortunately, neither Mlle Desautels nor her formidable source-reference (*Grand Larousse*, v. VII, p. 520) explain the type of "French cantata" allegedly "heard on the banks of the St. Lawrence." *(Aspects of Music ...*, p. 92).

21. Robert-Lionel Seguin, *La civilisation traditionnelle de "l'Habitant" aux 17e et 18e siècles*, Ottawa, 1967, p. 59. "En Nouvelle-France, habitant et gentilhomme dansent le menuet, signe que l'art ne s'en tient pas aux barrières sociales."

22. *Loc. cit.* "Le quadrille et le menuet se partagent également la faveur de la noblesse, de la bourgeoisie et de la paysannerie."

23. Elizabeth Begon, *Lettres ...*, letter January 29, 1749, p. 73.

24. *Ibid.*, letter December 18, 1749, p. 48.

25. Thomas Chapais, *Le Marquis de Montcalm*, J.-P. Garneau, Québec, 1911, p. 355. "Presque chaque soir, ses salons, magnifiquement illuminés, se remplissaient de dames élégamment parées et d'officiers aux brillants uniformes. On y faisait parfois de la musique, on y dan-

sait souvent, on y jouait toujours, on y soupait ensuite somptueuse-
ment, et ces fêtes se prolongeaient fort avant dans la nuit."

    26. *Ibid.*, p. 356. "L'intendant a rassemblé à l'occasion du con-
cert exécuté par des officiers et des dames, nombreuse compagnie. Il y
a eu d'aussi bonne musique qu'il soit possible d'en exécuter dans un
pays où le goût des arts ne peut avoir gagné."

    27. *Aspects of Music* ..., p. 92.

    28. Kallmann, *op. cit.*, p. 27.

Chapter VIII

1. A number of books, and a fairly large amount of articles in periodicals, encyclopedias and other publications deal adequately with French-Canadian and other folksongs in Canada. It is therefore unnecessary to embark on a specialised study on the subject, but rather to offer merely a few general remarks.

2. Marguerite et Raoul d'Harcourt, *Chansons Folkloriques Françaises au Canada*, Presses Universitaires Laval, Québec et Paris, 1956, p. 6.

3. *Loc. cit.* "... ces mélodies restent, bien entendu, de caractère absolument français."

4. *Ibid.*, p. xii.

5. *Ibid.*, p. 4.

6. *Ibid.*, p. 3. "... le fils de ce même paysan illettré qui avait reçu, au XVIIe siècle, le précieux dépôt de notre trésor populaire."

7. *Ibid.*, p. 185. "Au Canada français, chanter la chanson *À la claire fontaine*, c'est presque hisser le drapeau de l'ancienne France."

8. Maud Karpeles, "La Musique Foklorique, Elément de Rapprochement Social" in *La Musique dans l'Education*, Unesco, Paris, 1955, p. 198. "La musique folklorique est un héritage du passé, mais elle a gardé sa fraîcheur et sa vitalité grâce aux transformations constantes qu'elle a subies au cours de la transmission orale."

9. Loc. cit. "Un chant folklorique se distingue d'un morceau de chant classique non parce qu'il est écrit sans art, mais parce qu'au lieu d'être l'œuvre d'un seul individu il est le produit complexe de plusieurs générations de chanteurs qui, après bien des tâtonnements, ont fini par trouver la forme d'expression qui convenait le mieux au génie de la communauté."

10. *Harvard Dictionary of Music*, p. 275.

11. Karpeles, *op. cit.*, p. 199. "... les meilleures œuvres du folklore sont comparables aux œuvres des grands maîtres."

12. *Loc cit.*

13. d'Harcourt, *op. cit.*, p. 5.

14. *Ibid.*, p. ix.

15. *Ibid.*, p. xi.

16. *Ibid.*, p. 5.

17. cf. George Herzog, "Speech-melody and primitive music", *Musical Quarterly*, XX, 1934, p. 452.

18. Marc Lescarbot, *Histoire de la Nouvelle France*, p. 735. "L'vsage donc de leurs danses est à quatre fins, ou pour aggreer à leurs Dieux (qu'on les appelle diables si l'on veut, il n'importe), ainsi que nous avons remarqué en deux endroits ci-dessus, ou pour faire féte à quelqu'vn, ou pour se rejouïr de quelque victoire, ou pour prevenir les maladies. En toutes ces danses ils chantent, et ne font point des gestes muets."

19. Le Jeune, *Relation ... 1634*, p. 65. "Ie demanday que vouloient dire ces parolles, pas vn ne m'en peut donner l'interpretation : car il est vray que pas vn d'eux n'entend ce qu'il chante, sinon dans leurs airs, qu'ils chantent pour se recréer."

20. Lescarbot, *op. cit.*, p. 736. "Noz Souriquois aussi font des danses et chansons en l'honneur du demon qui leur indique de la chasse, et qu'ils pensent leur faire du bien : de quoy on ne se doit emerveiller, d'autant que nous mémes qui sommes mieux instruits chantons des Pseaumes et Cantiques de loüanges à nôtre Dieu, pour ce qu'il nous donne à diner."

21. Jean de Quen, *Relation ... 1655-56*, p. 93. "... le Sorcier entre auec vne écaille de Tortüe en sa main, à demy pleine de petits cailloux... Il prend place au milieu d'vne douzaine de femmes, qui doiuent l'aider à chasser le mal, le voisinage s'assemble pour voir cette superstition, qui n'est autre, sinon que le Magicien frappant de sa Tortüe sur vne natte, & entonnant quelques chansons, les femmes dancent autour de luy à la cadence de son chant & du bruit qu'il fait avec sa Tortüe."

22. Le Jeune, *Relation ... 1634*, p. 68. "Ils se seruent de ces chants, de ce tambour, & de ces bruits, ou tintamarres en leurs mala-

dies... Parfois cest homme entroit comme en furie, chantant, criant, hurlant, faisant bruire son tambour de toutes ses forces : cependant les autres hurloient comme luy, & faisoient vn tintamarre horrible auec leurs bastons, frappans sur ce qui estoit deuant eux : ils faisoient danser des ieunes enfans, puis des filles, puis des femmes ; il baissoit la teste, souffloit sur son tambour : puis vers le feu, il siffloit comme vn serpent, il ramenoit son tambour soubs son menton, l'agitant & le tournoyant : il en frappoit la terre de toutes ses forces, puis le tournoyoit sur son estomach : il se fermoit la bouche auec vne main renuersée, & de l'autre, vous eussiez dit qu'il vouloit mettre en pieces ce tambour, tant il en frappoit rudement la terre : il s'agitoit, il se tournoit de part & d'autre, faisoit quelques tours à l'entour du feu, sortoit hors la cabane, tousiours hurlant & bruyant : il se mettoit en mille postures ; & tout cela pour se guerir. Voila comme ils traictent les malades."

23. Le Jeune, *Relation ... 1637*, p. 222 (lettre de P.François Le Mercier). "24 personnes furent désignées pour chanter & faire toutes les cérémonies ; mais quel chant et quels tons de voix, pour moi ie croi que si les demons & les damnés chantoient dans l'enfer, ce seroit à peu pres de cette sorte, ie n'oüi iamais rien de plus lugubre & de plus effroiable."

24. Gabriel Sagard-Theodat, *Histoire ...*, p. 287. "Mais ce qui est loüable en eux est, qu'il ne leur arriue iamais de chanter aucune chanson vilaine ou scandaleuse, comme l'on faict icy, aussi lors que quelque François chantoit & qu'ils demandoient l'explication de sa chanson, s'il leur disoit qu'elle estoit d'amour, ou mondaine, ils n'en estoient pas contans, & disoient *Danstan téhongniande*, cela n'est pas bien, & ne le vouloient point escouter."

25. *Ibid.*, p. 293. "Dieu vueille abolir une si damnable & malheureuse ceremonie, auec toutes celles qui sont de mesme aloy, & que les François, qui les fomentent par leurs mauuais exemples, ouurent les yeux de leur esprit, pour voir le compte très-estroict qu'ils en rendront un iour deuant Dieu."

26. Le Jeune, *Relation ... 1634*, p. 49. "Le jongleur ... se mit à siffler d'vne façon sourde, & comme de loin : puis à parler comme dans vne bouteille, à crier comme vn chant-huant de ce pays-cy ... puis à hurler, chanter, variant de ton à tous coups, finissant par ces syllabes

..., & autres semblables contrefaisant sa voix en sorte qu'il me sembloit ouïr ces marionnettes que quelques bateleurs font voir en france ... cependant nostre sorcier qui estoit present prit son tambour, & chantant auec le iongleur qui estoit dans le tabernacle."

27. *Relation ... 1641-42* (report from the mission of La *Conception*, Le Jeune), p. 150. "La conuertion de ce nouueau Ioseph semble d'autant plus considerable, qu'il a trempé vingt ans durant dans l'exercice de l'*Aoutaenhrohi* ou festin & danse de feu, le plus diabolique, & cependant le plus ordinaire remede des maladies qui soit dans le pays."

28. *Loc. cit.* "Au bout de quelques temps il eut vn songe, dans lequel il se vid assister à vne de ces danses ou festins, & manier le feu comme les autres, & entendit en mesme temps vne chanson, laquelle il fut estonné à son resueil de sçauoir en perfection. Au premier festin qui se fit de cette nature, il se mit à chanter sa chanson, & voile petit à petit qu'il se sent entrer en fureur : il prend les braizes & les pieres ardentes auec les mains & les dents du milieu des braziers, il enfonce son bras nud tout au fonds des chaudieres boüillantes, le tout sans lezion ny douleur ; en vn mot le voila maistre passé. Et depuis, l'espace de vingt ans il luy est arrivé quelquefois d'assister à trois & quatre festins ou danses de cette nature en vn iour, pour la guerison des malades."

29. Lescarbot, *Histoire ...*, p. 727. "Ils ont cette charité mutuelle, laquelle a esté ravie d'entre nous depuis que Mien et Tien ont pris naissance."

30. Lescarbot, *op. cit.*, p. 736. "Ils chantent aussi en leurs Tabagies communes les loüanges des braves Capitaines et *Sagamos* qui ont bien tué de leurs ennemis. Ce qui s'est prattiqué en maintes nations anciennement, et se prattique encore aujourd'hui entre nous."

31 Bacqueville de la Potherie, *Histoire de l'Amerique Septentrionale*, Rouen, 1722, 4 vols., v. 2, p. 16.

"Cette danse est donc très celèbre, soit pour affermir la Paix ou se réünir pour quelque grand guerre, soit pour une réjouissance publique, ou pour faire l'honneur à une Nation que l'on invite d'assiter. Ils la font aussi à la reception de quelques personnes considerables, comme s'ils vouloient lui donner le divertissement du Bal."

32. cf. F. R. Burton, *American Primitive Music*, New York, 1909 ; Frances Densmore, *The American Indians and their Music*, New York, 1926 ; Benjamin Gilman, "Hopi Songs, Zuni Melodies" in *Journal of American Ethnology and Archeology*, vols. I. and V.

33. Robert Lachmann, "Die Musik der aussereuropaeischen Natur-und Kulturvoelker" in *Handbuch der Musikwissenschaft*, ed. E. Buecken, Leipzig, 1931.

34. Herzog, "Speech-melody ..." in *Musical Quarterly*, vol. XX, no 4, 1934.

35. Diereville, *Relation* ..., p. 179. "Je les ay plus d'une fois entendu chanter dans l'Eglise du Port Royal à la grande Messe & à Vespres ; les voix des Femmes particulièrement étoient si douces & si touchantes, que je croyais entendre les Anges chanter les loüanges de Dieu."

36. *Relation ... 1647*, p. 218.

37. *Relation* ..., v. LXVIII, p. 273 (letter, Father François Nau). "Il faut necessairement du chant pour nos sauvages qui ne sont pas communement capables d'une grande application d'esprit, c'est pourquoi toutes les prieres se font en chantant, aussi seroit-il grand dommage qu'ils ne chantassent pas, ils y reüissent trop bien. J'ay souvent souhaitté que le R.P. Laudreau qui est si touché du chant de l'eglise lorsqu'il est bien executé put assister à nos grandes messes, il y goûteroit le plus grand plaisir qu'il ait jamais ressenti.

Les hommes qui chantent le premier verset lui representeroient une centaine de Cordeliers dans un chœur, et les femmes qui repondent lui sembleroient être la plus nombreuse communauté de religieuse ; mais que dis-je, ni cordeliers, ni religieuses n'ont jamais si bien chanté que nos Iroquois et nos Iroquoises, ils ont la voix également douce et pleine, et ont l'oreille si fine, qu'ils ne manquent pas une demie note dans tous les airs d'eglise qu'ils savent tous par cœur."

38. Theodor Baker, *Ueber die Musik der Nordamerikanischen Wilden*, Leipzig, 1882, p. 16.

39. La Potherie, *Histore* ..., v. III, p. 24. "la jeunesse est fort libre en paroles, ils raillent sur leurs amours ou sur leurs faits de guerre, ils se divertissent aussi à jouer de la flute."

40. *Les Raretés des Indes,* Codex Canadiensis, Paris, 1930, is a unique album of sketches which are of considerable ethnographical interest in the study of the Canadian Indian. The date of these drawings is not indicated, but has been presumed to be about the end of the 17th century. Its author is supposed to have been Charles Béclard de Granville, born at Quebec in 1675, and died in the same place in 1703.

41. Quoted in P. Scholes, *The Oxford Companion to Music,* Oxford, 1956, 9th ed., p. 1071. Peculiarities of Indian music had also been noted by the early settlers in New England. William Wood, who visited Plymouth and Massachusetts Bay in the early 17th century published an account of his impressions : "to hear one of these Indian unseene, a good eare might easily mistake their untaught voyce for the warbling of a well tuned instrument. Such command have they of their voices." (as quoted in J. T. Howard, *Our American Music,* p. 615).

Many years later, James Adair refers to Indian music, and to a curious instrument which he claimed to have seen and heard : "I chanced to see the Indian playing on one of their old sacred instruments. It pretty much resembled the Negro-banjer [banjo] in shape, but far exceeded it in dimensions ; for it was about five feet long and a foot wide at the head of the board, with eight strings made out of the sinews of a large buffalo. But they were so unskilful in acting the part of the lyrick, that the *Loache,* or prophet, who held the instrument between his feet, and alongside of his chin, took one end of the bow, whilst a lusty fellow held the other ; and by sweating labour they scraped out such harsh jarring sounds, as might have been sufficient to drive out the devil if he lay anywhere hid in the house." *(History of the American Indian,* London, 1775, p. 175). This account must be taken with appropriate caution.

42. Lescarbot, *Histoire ...,* p. 735. "Mais la volupté impudique n'a point gaigné cela sur eux de les faire danser à son sujet, chose qui doit servir de leçon aux Chrétiens."

43. *Ibid.,* p. 281. "... toutes les femmes et filles commencèrent à quitter leurs robes et peaux, et se mirent toute nues montrans leur nature, neantmoins parées de *Matachias,* qui sont pate-nôtres et cordons entre-lassez faits de Porc-épic, qu'ils teindent de diverses couleurs." *Note :* translation by W. L. Grant, Champlain, *Des Sauvages, ou*

Voyage de Samuel Champlain ... *1603,* in the *Works of Samuel de Champlain,* vol. I, Toronto, The Champlain Society, 1922, p. 107.

44. Sagard, *Histoire* ..., p. 292-93. "Dans le païs de nos Hurons, il se faict aussi des assemblées de toutes les filles d'un bourg auprès d'une malade ... on leur demande à toutes, les unes après les autres, celuy qu'elles veulent des ieunes hommes du bourg, pour dormir auec elles la nuict prochaine ; elles en nomment chacune un ... lesquels viennent tous au soir en la presence de la malade, dormir d'un bout de la cabane à l'autre, chacun auec celle qui l'a choisi, & passent ainsi toute la nuict, pendant que deux Capitaines aux deux bouts du logis, chantent & sonnent de leur tortuë du soir au lendemain matin, que la ceremonie cesse ..."

45. Lescarbot, *Histoire* ..., p. 738. "... les danses de noz Sauvages se font sans bouger d'vne place, et neantmoins sont tous en rond (ou à peu prés) et dansent avec vehemence, frappans des piez contre terre, et s'elevans comme en demi-saut."

46. Sagard, *Histoire* ..., p. 288.

47. Paul Ragueneau, *Relation* .... *1647,* p. 106. "Ces danses approchent pour la pluspart des branles de la France : les autres sont en forme de balets, auec des postures & des proportions qui n'ont rien de sauvage, & qui sont dans les regles de l'art : le tout à la cadence & à la mesure du chant de quelques-vns, qui sont les maistres du mestier."

48. Le Mercier, *Relation* ... *1652,* p. 119. "La beauté de leur voix est rare par excellence, particulierement des filles. *On leur a composé des Cantiques Hurons sur l'air des Hymnes de l'Eglise,* elles les chantent a rauir. C'est vne sainte consolation, qui n'a rien de la barbare, que d'entendre les champs et les bois resonner si melodieusement des louanges de Dieu, au milieu d'vn pays, qu'il n'y a pas longtemps qu'on appeloit barbare." In the English edition of the *Relation* this musically interesting remark has been quite wrongly interpreted as it concerns the Huron girls, "... for whom there have been composed, and adapted to the Church hymns, some Huron Melodies." The French text implies without doubt canticles in the *Huron language,* adapted to some melodies of church hymns.

49. *Relation* ..., vol. LXVI, p. 242 (letter of November 1712 by Father Gabriel Marest). "Ces cantiques sont de veritables instructions,

qu'ils retiennent d'autant plus aisément que les paroles sont sur des airs qu'ils savent et qui leur plaisent."

50. *Relation* ..., vol. LV, p. 129 (letter by Father Louys Andre, 1670). "Enfin pour animer de plus en plus leur ferveur ie m'advisay de composer quelques Cantiques Spirituels, que ie n'eus pas si-tost chanté dans la Chapelle, avec une fleute douce (car il se faut faire tout à tous, pour les convertir tous à Jesus-Christ) qu'ils venoient tous en foule & grands & petits."

51. de Quen, *Relation ... 1655,* p. 78. "... on chante quelques motets spirituels. Une petite poche etant jointe et s'accordant bien avec la voix des Sauvages." The *poche (pocket)* was a small, narrow fiddle to be carried in the pocket. Very popular with the dancing masters of the 18th century, it existed in two types : one a diminutive violin, known as *pochette,* the other a descendant of the mediaeval *rebec.*

52. *Relation* ..., vol. LI, p. 205. "... après avoir donné commencement à cette action, par le *Veni Creator,* dont le chant fut entrecoupé du son d'un petit instrument de musique, que ces peuples escoutent avec plaisir et avec admiration."

53. See note by Abbé Richardeau in *Lettres* de Mère Marie de l'Incarnation, p. 131.

"Pour réussir, nous invitâmes tous les sauvages qui étaient proche de nous à un festin solennel, où nous employâmes toute notre industrie et n'épargnâmes ni le son des tambours, ni les instruments de musique.

... Celui qui présidait à la cérémonie joua son jeu avec tant d'adresse que chacun voulait contribuer à la joie publique. C'était à qui jetterait des cris plus perçants. Pour les animer à ce beau jeu, on distribua des présents à ceux qui faisaient le plus de bruit, afin de couvrir celui qu'une quarantaine de nos gens faisaient au dehors dans le transport de tout notre équipage.

... Ils faisait en même temps jouer les flûtes, trompettes, tambours, afin de les faire danser et de charmer l'ennui d'un si long repas.

... Je m'en vais faire jouer d'un doux instrument pour vous faire dormir, mais ne vous levez que demain bien tard ; dormez jusqu'à ce qu'on vienne vous éveiller pour faire les prières. A ces paroles on joua d'une guitare..."

There are some minor discrepancies concerning musical instruments in the accounts of this amazing escape which has been called the "most memorable military retreat in history." In her letter to her son (CXL, October 4, 1658) Mère Marie mentions flutes, trumpets and drums to make noise in order to cover the preparation for the retreat, and the sweet and soft sound of the guitar to lull the satiated Indians to sleep. Father Ragueneau refers only to the "sound of the drum and the musical instruments" while Parkman speaks about the guitar in his account (see Parkman, *Old Régime* ..., p. 35ff).

54. Le Jeune, *Relation ... 1634*, p. 64. "... and even though I told them that I did not understand anything about it, [music] they often invited me to sing some song or prayer."

"... & quoy que ie leur dis que ie n'y entendois rien, ils m'inuitoient souuent à entonner quelque air, ou quelque priere."

55. See p. 51.

56. Sagard, *Histoire* ..., p. 311. "Ayant descrit ce petit eschantillon d'une chanson Huronne, i'ay creu qu'il ne seroit pas mal à propos de descrire encore icy partie d'une autre chanson, qui se disoit un iour en la cabane du grand Sagamo des Souriquois à la loüange du Diable ... ainsi que nous apprend l'escot qui s'en dist tesmoin auriculaire."

57. Archives, Compagnie de Jésus, Chantilly, France ; Fonds Brotier 158.

58. An interesting account of the various arguments, claims and counter-claims may be found in the *Dictionary of Canadian Biography*, v. I, p. 491.

59. La Potherie, *Histoire* ..., v. II, p. 18. "Ils leur donnent un certain tour qu'on ne peut assez bien exprimer par la notte & qui en fait néanmoins toute la garce." Although La Potherie included the *Calumet* song in his work, the song had first appeared some fifty years earlier in Father Marquette's *Recit*.

Chapter IX

1. The first issue of the Quebec *Gazette* appeared on June 21, 1764.

2. Quebec *Gazette*, December 6th, 1764.

3. *Ibid.*, July 1767.

4. *Ibid.*, February 22nd, 1770.

5. *Ibid.*, November 28th, 1771.

6. *Ibid.*, October 24th, 1765.

7. *Ibid.*, December 10th, 1772.

8. Historical Collections of the Essex Institute, Salem, Mass., vol. 1, no. 2.

9. Quebec *Gazette*, January 3rd, 1777. The *Ode* contains the words of Recitative, March, Airs, Ariette, Siciliano, and Grand Chorus ; neither author nor composer are mentioned.

Helmut Kallman has graciously placed at my disposal an interesting reference to the performance of the *Ode*, taken from *Vertrauliche Briefe aus Kanada und Neu-England vom Jahre 1777 und 1778* (Confidential letter from Canada and New England, from the years 1777 and 1778). "Aus Herrn Professor Schloezer's Briefwechsel, Heft XXIII und XXIV : (Goettinger, 1779). In the fourth letter, Professor Schloezer describes the occasion : "31 December [1776] grosses Fest in Quebeck, 1. Jahresfeier der Befreiung als die Rebellen General Montgomery verloren." (31st December, great feast in Quebec, first anniversary of the liberation when the rebels lost Gen. Montgomery). The letter continues : "6 Abends begab sich der Festzug in die grosse englische *Auberge* in einem grossem Saal, wo bereits u[ber] 94 *Dames* und 200 *Chapeaux* sassen. Es liess sich sogleich ein Concert hoeren, bei welchem auch eine englische Ode, die auf diese Feier gemacht war, in

Arien, Arietto's, Recitativen und Choeren abgesungen wurde. Waerend dieser Musik wurden Billets an die Personen beiderlei Geschlechtes ausgeteilt, welche tanzen wollten ..." (6 in the evening the parade went to the great English *Auberge* in the big hall where already more than 94 *dames* and 200 *chapeaux* had been seated. Soon after there was a concert during which an English Ode, which was composed for that festive occasion, in the form of Arias, Ariettos, Recitatives and Choirs, was sung. During that music tickets were handed to those of both sexes who wanted to dance ...). Professor Schloezer also mentions Menuets and English dances, and that after *souper* at midnight, there was continuous dancing until the bright morning of January 1st, 1777.

Odes seem to have been the favourite poetic form to be set to music by amateur composers, such as Mr. Bentley, as it appears from a notice in the *Gazette* of January 1792, which informs us that "... an Ode, selected by a *Gentleman*, was set to music and sung by Mr. Bentley at the Constitutional Meeting on Monday, December 26, 1791."This is the same Mr. Bentley who a few years later in his capacity as organist at the English Church advertised for "... twelve boys of respectable Parents and eight young men of good characters : they will be taught singing by note *gratis* and receive further advantages ..." *(Quebec Gazette,* February 4th, 1802). No further information about Mr. Bentley could be obtained. Whether he also composed the music for the Ode at the above Commemoration Festivities of 1776 could not be determined, but it appears that apart from his duties as Organist and Choir-master he had also been Surveyor of the Roads for the city and district of Quebec.

10. P. G. Roy, *La Famille Glackemeyer,* In *Bulletin des Recherches Historiques,* Lévis, 1916, XXII, p. 195.

11. *Quebec Gazette,* June 24th, 1784.

12. *Ibid.,* June 11th, 1772.

13. *Ibid.,* June 14th, 1781.

14. *The Quebec Mercury,* vol. XXVII, May 26th, 1831.

15. *La Minerve,* Quebec, vol. XIV, September 1844.

16. *Quebec Gazette,* July 13th, 1815.

17. Kallmann, *A History* ... p. 48.

18. Sachs, *The History of Musical Instruments*, p. 368.

19. cf. Dubourg, *The Violin*, R. Cocks, London, 1836, p. 245.

20. *Quebec Gazette*, December 8th, 1791.

21. *Ibid.*, November 12th, 1783.

22. John Lambert, *Travels through Canada and the United States of North America in the years 1806, 1807 & 1808*, 3rd ed., London, 1816, pp. 302 & 328.

Lambert also noted that the Canadians are "... fond of dancing and entertainment at particular seasons and festivals ... no sooner does the clash of the knives and forks cease, than the violin strikes up and the dance commence. Minuets, and a sort of reels or jigs, rudely performed to the discordant scrapings of a couple of vile fiddlers, conclude the festival, or "jour gras" ..." (p. 164).

23. *Quebec Gazette*, October 30th, 1783 :

"Public Night — On Monday next the 3rd of November — THE FAIR PENITENT — Betwixt the Acts — a Solo on the VIOLIN, by SIGNOR GAETANO FRANCESCHINI — Tickets to be had at the Bar of M'PHERSON'S HOTEL at FIVE SHILLINGS each.

24. *Quebec Gazette*, May 13th, 1784.

24. P. Stoeving, *The Story of the Violin*, The Walter Scott Publishing Co. Ltd., New York, 1925, p. 114.

26. *Quebec Gazette*, July 26th, 1787.

27. *Montreal Gazette*, September 3rd, 1789. It should be noted, however, that Kallmann mentions a "Guillaume-Joseph Mechtler (1763-1833), Brussels-born organist of Notre Dame Church [Montreal] from 1792 to 1833, who may be considered the city's leading musician of that time." (Kallmann, *History* ..., p. 84).

28. *Montreal Gazette*, June 18th, 1789.

29. *Quebec Gazette*, August 25th, 1791.

30. *Ibid.*, February 2nd, 1792.

31. David Cox, "English Chamber Music" in *Chamber Music*, ed. Robertson, London, 1957, p. 324.

32. *Quebec Gazette*, December 26th, 1793.

33. *Ibid.*, February 24th, 1794.

34. *Montreal Gazette*, November 1st, 1787.

35. Jean Béraud, *350 Ans de Théâtre au Canada Français*, Ottawa, 1958, p. 14.

36. *Quebec Gazette*, april 8th, 1784.

37. *Ibid.*, March 26th, 1786.

38. Béraud, *op. cit.*, p. 14.

39. *Quebec Gazette*, January 20th, 1791.

40. *Ibid.*, March 10th, 1791.

41. *Montreal Gazette*, November 1st, 1787.

42. *Ibid.*, January 14th, 1790.

43. *Quebec Gazette*, August 1798.

44. *Quebec Herald and Universal Miscellany*, March 1789.

45. *Ibid.*, December 1789.

46. *Ibid.*, December 1789.

47. *Ibid.*, April 1790.

48. *Montreal Gazette*, April 11th, 1796.

49. *Montreal Herald*, January 13th, 1806.

50. *Canadian Courant*, January 1808.

51. Matthew Locke is important in musical history as composer of stage music and as the most eminent predecessor of Purcell. According to some sources the authenticity of the music to *Macbeth* had been questioned and credit for the composition given to Purcell, Eccles and others *(Grove's Dictionary of Music*, ed. Colles, 1935, vol. III, p. 224). Lack of convincing evidence, however, has failed to change the long established tradition which attributes the music to Locke. James Hewitt was born in England in 1770, came to New York in 1792 where he was active as composer, conductor, organist, teacher, etc., and in general as promotor of good music.

52. John Lambert, *Travels through Canada ...*, p. 302ff.

53. *Quebec Gazette*, September and October 1804.

54. *Ibid.*, October 1804 : "Les Messieurs Canadiens prennent la liberté d'avertir le public qu'il ne sera admis que des personnes honnêtes et décentes."

55. A Citizen observes

(1) that some of his compatriots propose to present this winter some theatrical performances ;

(2) that there are amongst them those who propose that only a small number of persons of high birth or noble rank be admitted to the *parterre* [orchestra] :

To this he remarks

(1) that the project is good and that the theatre can do nothing but inspire taste in the new colony ;

(2) that the purpose of the project will not be fulfilled if it is so narrowed ; that it will do nothing but excite hatred and animosity which normally results from such stupid distinctions.

And that is all !

(Montreal Gazette, December 23rd, 1790).

56. A river and the town of Quesnel are named after his son, Jules Maurice, who had taken part in the exploration of the west.

57. F.M. Bibaud, *Dictionnaire Historique ...,* Monteal, 1857.

58. Kallmann, *op. cit.,* p. 49.

59. *Loc. cit.*

60. A few of these volumes, dating from 1824, are in the collection of the author. Among the historically interesting items is Handel's celebrated *Harmonious Blacksmith,* arranged by Edouard Glackemeyer himself for flute, violin, cello and piano, and included in manuscript form in the bound volumes.

61. Kallmann, *op. cit.,* p. 50.

Chapter X

Coda

1. "Noel d'un Tambour — Ville Marie 1665" by Louis-Raoul de Lorimier, as quoted in *La Revue Canadienne,* 1971, p. 437 is an entirely fictitious story, yet had been hailed as "preuve évidente de la culture artistique qu'apportèrent avec eux de France nos ancêtres, colons et soldats." (See "Les Instruments de musique dans les Eglises de la Nouvelle France" in *La Société Canadienne d'Histoire de l'Eglise Catholique,* Rapport 1956/57).

2. A symphony by Calixa Lavallée, supposed to have been performed in Paris in 1874 as mentioned by Eugéne Lapierre in his book, *Calixa Lavallée,* Montreal, 1950, p. 165, has never been located, nor has the alleged performance been corroborated in contemporary concert-programmes.

BIBLIOGRAPHY

Books

Adair, James, *History of the American Indians,* London; Dilly, 1775, reprint of 1930 ed., New York: Argonaut Press, 1966.

Baker, Theodore, *Ueber die Music der Nordamerikanischen Wilden,* Leipzig: Breitkopf und Haertel, 1882.

Bécard de Granville, Charles, *Les Raretés des Indes* (Codex Canadiensis). Paris: Chamonal, 1930.

Begon, Elisabeth, *Lettres au cher fils,* Montreal: Hurtubise, 1972.

Beraud, Jean, *350 ans de théâtre au Canada français,* Ottawa: Cercle du Livre de France, 1958.

Biard, Pierre, *Relation de la Novvelle France de ces Terres Natvrel dv pais & de ses Habitans,* Lyon: 1616.

Bremond, Henri, *Histoire Littéraire du Sentiment Religieux en France,* 11 vols. Paris: Bloud et Gay, 1916-1933.

Bukofzer, Manfred, *Music in the Baroque Era,* New York : W.W. Norton, 1947.

Burton, Frederick R., *American Primitive Music,* New York : Kennikat Press, 1969.

Cartier, Jacques, *Brief Recit & succincte narration de la nauigation faicte es ysles de Canada, Hochelaga & Saguenay & autres,* Paris: Roffet, dict Faucher & Antoine Le Clerc, frères, 1545.

    Discovrs dv Voyage faict par le Capitaine Jacques Cartier, (Rouen: 1598) ed. Tross, Paris: 1865.

Champigneulle, Bernard, *La Musique Française,* Paris: Aubier, 1946.

Champlain, Samuel de, *Works,* transl. & edit., H. P. Biggar, Toronto: Champlain Society, 1922-1936.

Chapais, Thomas, *Le Marquis de Montcalm* (1712-1759) Quebec : J.-P. Garneau, 1911.

Charlevoix, Pierre François Xavier de, *Histoire et description générale de la Nouvelle France,* Paris : 1744.

Daule, Jean-Denis, *Nouveau recueil de cantiques à l'usage du Diocèse de Québec,* Québec: Nouvelle Imprimerie, 1819.

Densmore, Frances, *The American Indian and Their Music,* New York: The Womens Press, 1926.

Dierville, N. *Relation du Voyage du Port Royal de l'Acadie, ou de la Nouvelle France,* Rouen: Besogne, 1708.

Dupont-Ferrier, Gustave, *La vie quotidienne d'un collège parisien.* Paris: Boccard, 1921-25, 3 vols.

Ellinwood, Leonard, *The History of American Church Music,* New York: Morehous-Gorham, 1953.

Gagnon, Ernest, *Chansons populaires du Canada,* Montreal: Beauchemin, 1935, 7th edit.

    Louis Jolliet, Montreal: Beauchemin, 1946, 4th edit.

Garneau, François-Xavier, *Histoire du Canada depuis sa découverte jusqu'à nos jours,* Québec: Aubin, 1845-52, 4 vols.

Gosselin, Auguste Honoré, *Henri de Bernières,* Evreux: Impr. de l'Eure, 1896.

    Le Vénérable François de Montmorency-Laval, Québec: Dussault et Proulx, 1901.

Goyau, Georges, *Les Origines Religieuses du Canada,* Paris: Fides, 1951.

Harcourt, Marguerite et Raoul d', *Chansons folkloriques françaises au Canada,* Québec: Presses Universitaires Laval, 1956.

Howard, John Tasker, *Our American Music,* New York: Thomas Y. Crowell Comp., 1946, 3rd edit.

Kallmann, Helmut, *A History of Music in Canada,* 1534-1914, Toronto : Univ. of Toronto Press, 1960.

La Hontan, Louis Armand, baron de, *Nouveaux voyages de M. le baron de Lahontan dans l'Amérique Septentrionale, 1703-04,* La Haye: Frères Honoré, 1704.

Lambert, John, *Travels through Canada and the United States of North America in the years 1806-07-08*, Edinburgh: Blackwood, 2 vols.

Lafitau, Joseph François, *Les Mœurs des Sauvages Americains*, Paris: 1724.

Lang, Paul Henry, *Music in Western Civilization*, New York: W.W. Norton & Co. 1941.

La Tour, Louis Bertrand de, *Memoires sur la vie de Mgr. de Laval*, Cologne: J.-F. Motiens, 1761.

Le Beau, Charles, *Avantures du Sr. C. Le Beau, ou Voyage curieux et nouveau parmi les sauvages de l'Amérique Septentrionale*, (Amsterdam: Herman Uytwerf, 1738) New York : Johnson Reprint Corp., 1866.

Le Ber, Joseph, *Départ pour le Canada en 1639*, Dieppe, 1939.

Le Clercq, Chrestien, *Premier établissement de la Foy dans la Nouvelle France*, Paris : Amable Auroy, 1691.

Lescarbot, Marc, *Histoire de la Nouvelle-France*, including *Les Muses de la Nouvelle-France*, (Paris : 1609) Paris: Tross, 1866, 3 vols.

   Relation dernière de ce qui s'est passé au voyage du sieur de Poutrincourt en la Nouvelle-France, (Paris: Jean Millot, 1612) Paris: 1832.

   The Theatre of Neptune in New France, transl. by Harriette Taber Richardson, Boston: Houghton, 1927.

Marie de l'Incarnation, *Lettres*, (ed. Richardeau) Tournai: H. Casterman, 1876.

Myrand, Ernest, *Noels anciens de la Nouvelle-France*, Québec : Laflamme & Proulx, 1907.

Parkman, Francis, *The Old Régime in Canada*, Boston : Little, Brown & Company, 1885.

   Pioneers of France in the New World, Boston : Little, Brown & Company, 1891.

   Count Frontenac and New France under Louis XIV, Boston: Little, Brown & Company, 1891.

   The Jesuits in North America in the Seventeenth Century, Boston : Little, Brown & Comp. 1897.

Potherie, Baqueville de la, *Histoire de l'Amérique Septentrionale*, Paris : Nion et Didot, 1722.

Provost, Honorius, *La Dévotion à la Sainte Famille en Canada*, Québec: Presses de l'Université Laval, 1964.

Sagard Theodat, Gabriel, *Histoire du Canada*, (Paris: 1626) Paris: ed. Tross, 1866.

Seguin, Robert-Lionel, *La civilisation traditionnelle de l'habitant aux 17e et 18e siècles*, Montreal: 1967.

Stevenson, Robert, *Music in Mexico*, New York: Crowell, 1952.

Tétu, H. & Gagnon, C-O., *Mandements... des Evèques de Québec*, Québec: A. Coté et Cie, 1887, 2 vols.

Traquair, Ramsay, *The Old Architecture of Quebec*, Toronto : Macmillan, 1947.

Wade, Mason, *The French Canadians, 1760-1945*, Toronto: Macmillan, 1955.

Walsh, H. H., *The Church in the French Era*, Toronto: Ryerson, 1966.

Walter, Arnold, (ed.) *Aspects of Music in Canada*, Toronto: Univ. of Toronto Press, 1969.

Articles, Dictionaries, Documents, and Miscellaneous Reading

Desautels, Andrée, "The history of Canadian composition, 1610-1967" in *Aspects of Music in Canada*, (A. Walter, ed.) Toronto: Univ. of Tor. Press, 1969.

Herzog, George, "Speech-melody and primitive music" in *Musical Quarterly*, XX, 1934.

Lachmann, Robert, "Die Musik der aussereuropaeischen Natur — und Kulturvoelker" in *Handbuch der Musikwissenschaft*, (ed. E. Buecken) Leipzig : 1931.

Lesure, François, "Eléments populaires dans la chanson française" in *Musique et Poésie au XVIe siècle*, Paris: Centre National de la Recherche Scientifique, 1954.

Roy, P.-G., "La famille Glackemeyer" in *Bulletin des Recherches Historiques*, XXII, Lévis, 1916.

Les Annales de l'Hôtel-Dieu de Québec, 1636-1716, Comp. by Jeanne-Fançoise Juchereau de St. Ignace and Marie-Andrée Duplessis de Ste. Hélène, edit. Albert Jamet, Québec : 1939.

Archives of the *Hôtel-Dieu,* Québec armoire 5, cahier 8.

Archives of the *Compagnie de Jésus,* Chantilly, France, fonds Brotier 158,

Archives of the Seminary of Québec.

Archives of the Ursulines of Québec.

Correspondance de Madame Begon, 1748-1753, in Rapport de l'archiviste de la Province de Québec, 1934-35.

Correspondance de M. Tronson aux Messieurs du Séminaire de Montréal, Paris : Biliothèque des Sulpitiens, Tome XIII, 1676.

Dictionary of Canadian Biography, Toronto: Univ. of Toronto Press, 1966.

Grove's Dictionary of Music and Musicians, New York: Macmillan, 5th edit., 1954, 9 vols.

Harvard Dictionary of Music, (ed. Willi Apel) Cambridge, Mass.: Harvard Univ. Press, 2nd. edit., 1969.

Historical Collection of the Essex Institute, Salem, Mass., vol. 1.

Le Journal des PP. Jésuites, (ed. Laverdière et Casgrain) Montréal: J.M. Valois, 2e edit., 1892.

The Jesuit Relation and Allied Documents, ed. Reuben Gold Thwaites, Cleveland: Burrows Bros., 1896-1901 73 vols.

Mémoire sur la dévotion à la Sainte Famille ... etc. (Mère Duplessis de Ste.-Hélène) Ms. Québec: Hôtel-Dieu, Archives, Armoire 5, Cahier 8.

Brief Sketch of the History of the Ursulines of Quebec..., Québec : C. Darveau ed., 1875.

Les Ursulines de Québec..., Québec: C. Darveau, 1878, 2 vols.

Relations du Voyage des Dames Religieuses Ursulines de Rouen à *la Nouvelle-Orléans,* Paris: Gabriel Gravier, 1872.

INDEX